CLASS POLITICS
AND PUBLIC SCHOOLS

Class Politics

New Brunswick, New Jersey

JULIA WRIGLEY

and Public Schools
Chicago 1900–1950

RUTGERS UNIVERSITY PRESS

Library of Congress Cataloging in Publication Data

Wrigley, Julia, 1948–
  Class politics and public schools.
  Bibliography: p.
  Includes index.
  1. Labor and laboring classes—Education—Chicago
(Ill.)   2. Politics and education—Chicago (Ill.)   I. Title.
LC5053.C46W74   370.19'34   81–13932
ISBN 0–8135–0937–8   AACR2

TO MY FATHER,
CHARLES WRIGLEY

CONTENTS

ACKNOWLEDGMENTS

MANY PEOPLE HELPED in the writing of this book. I would like first to thank Philip Wexler, a sociologist of education, for initially sparking my interest in the question of which groups and social classes supported the expansion of the school system and why. Shortly after reading a paper by Wexler on conflicting paradigms in the sociology of education, a conversation with Bernard Elbaum persuaded me that this was a subject that would bear further exploration. It was plain that this issue of the class role of schooling had relevance to a much larger set of political concerns.

I would also like to express my appreciation to the revisionist educational writers, although I criticize their perspective in this book. I admire the boldness of their arguments and their revitalization of debate on the purposes of schooling. Their work, and my own, grew out of a critical analysis of American society and a consideration of the issues raised by the social movements of the 1960s. They have done a great deal to dispel the myths surrounding American public education.

When I moved to Chicago to do the research for this book, I found that I had been lucky in the city I had chosen. Chicago has a fascinating political history, and its school history reflects the interest and vitality of its political life. The city also has a collection of fine libraries, with the University of Chicago Library and the Chicago Historical Society standing out as invaluable repositories of information on the city. The staff of the Department of Special Collections at the University of Chicago Library helped me find correspondence bearing on the schools from the early 1900s, and Archie Motley at the Chicago Historical Society suggested numerous avenues of inquiry among the historical society's manuscript collections. The Oral History Project of Roosevelt University demonstrates the value of this form of data collection, with unique material on the Chicago labor movement. At the Chicago Circle campus of the University of Illinois, the papers of Victor Olander, the long-time secretary-treasurer of the Illinois State Federation of Labor, proved especially useful. The Chicago Public Library, the Newberry Library, and the Northwestern University Library also contain much relevant information and their staffs were helpful in digging it out.

Two people associated with the University of Chicago generously gave me access to unpublished material that they had written or collected. Robert J. Havighurst, professor emeritus in the department of education, allowed me to read interviews collected for a study written by himself, Elizabeth Murray, and Robert McCaul. He also allowed me to read part of the study itself. Paul E. Peterson, in the departments of political science and of education, author of the excellent *School Politics, Chicago Style*, which focuses on the post–World War II period, kindly gave me the drafts of several chapters before the book was published.

The job of anyone researching the Chicago schools is made easier by Mary J. Herrick's fine book, *The Chicago Schools: A Social and Political History*. This book draws upon Herrick's lifetime of involvement in Chicago teachers' unions and reflects her very detailed knowledge of the school system and its history. I would also like to thank this remarkable woman for granting me an interview in 1976, which provided a feel for the Chicago schools unavailable elsewhere.

This book was originally born as a dissertation, and I owe a debt of gratitude to the many students and faculty in the sociology department at the University of Wisconsin who provided both support and detailed criticisms of the work at many stages of its progress. I would particularly like to thank Robert Alford, who stimulated students to undertake research projects in the area of political economy and who created an unusual atmosphere of intellectual community at Madison. I benefited from his insight and his challenging yet tolerant expression of his views. Maurice Zeitlin also made Madison a rewarding place to be through his historical and theoretical knowledge and the example of his own deep investment in his research. Erik Wright read the manuscript with care and offered some exceptionally useful suggestions for improving it. Michael Aiken helped to shepherd the dissertation through the bureaucratic stages necessary for its completion, and Carl Kaestle helped more generally by providing a lively seminar on the history of education. The students associated with the Social Organization Program in the sociology department provided seemingly ruthless but always friendly criticism.

Friends and family also bore with the years of preoccupation necessary for the completion of this book and helped by gathering bibliographic information and offering ideas. Eric Chester stands out in this regard, having offered the kind of advice and encouragement that only someone with his knowledge of history and politics could give. Peter Dreier, Nora Hamilton, Nancy DiTomaso, Catherine Christeller, Judith Lengyel, Marc Renaud, and Louise Roy served as both friends and critics. Charles Wrigley, Margaret Wrigley, James Wrigley, and Laura Hodge all helped to check facts and references. Hartry Field encouraged me to get it done. Willa Speiser, the copy editor for Rutgers University Press, improved the style of the manuscript and served as a model of efficiency. Marlie Wasserman, the senior editor at Rutgers University Press, was helpful through the many stages leading to the production of the book.

While these and other people helped with the book, the interpretation contained in it is solely my own, and I suspect that many of the people named would disown it if they could. Similarly, any remaining errors of fact are my own responsibility.

Lastly, a grant of a Regents' Junior Faculty Fellowship in the summer of 1976 helped me to transform the dissertation into a book. The National Institute of Mental Health had earlier provided partial support during the bulk of the research in Chicago. I would also like to acknowledge the courtesy of Winthrop Publishers for allowing reprinting of some of the general material expressed in brief form in an article, "Class Politics and School Reform in Chicago," in *Classes, Class Conflict and the State,* edited by Maurice Zeitlin (1980).

CLASS POLITICS
AND PUBLIC SCHOOLS

1 INTRODUCTION: IMAGES OF SCHOOLING

IN NINETEEN HUNDRED TWENTY-THREE, the Chicago Federation of Labor denounced attempts to organize the city's public schools on a factory model. The most important issue before the workers of the city, the federation declared editorially, was the attempt to turn the school system into a replica of the Ford automobile plant. The goal of the school board was to pour children into the hopper at one end and grind them out at the other end "as perfect parts of an industrial machine, calculated to work automatically, smoothly and continuously for a short period." When their working lives were over, they could be replaced "by other cheap, simple parts, exactly like them."[1]

The labor federation employed the industrial metaphor as the one calculated to appeal most powerfully to its members. Later generations of school critics have also used metaphors as organizing devices, but they have turned to images of the schools as barricaded outposts in a hostile territory or as urban prisons. As one recent critic charged, the architecture of a Brooklyn school, an "ancient fortress" with "long, narrow slits instead of windows," reflects its purpose of imposing order upon a subordinate and hostile population.[2] Still other critics have depicted the educational system as a gigantic sifting-and-sorting mechanism, providing a meritocratic gloss while slotting people into jobs largely on the basis of their race and class backgrounds.[3]

These bleak images of schooling have coexisted with the dominant optimistic metaphors of the schools as sources of enlightenment and escalators of social mobility. There are many indications of the acceptance of the optimistic images: the United States has built an educational system far more extensive than that existing in any other country, and political leaders often turn to the schools for solutions to social problems. When, in the Cold War atmosphere of the 1950s, the Soviet launching of Sputnik created alarm, Congress hastily passed the National Defense

Education Act to improve science teaching in the secondary schools. President Lyndon Johnson made the popular Head Start the centerpiece of his short-lived War on Poverty. And the civil rights movement has focused on the demand for equal and integrated schools as a central political goal.

Not surprisingly, the diverse conceptions of schooling, the public celebration and the underlying critique, have been reflected in academic writing on the history and sociology of education. These fields have been characterized by deep divisions along ideological and political lines. The standard interpretation that the growth of the public school system represented an example of the democratic transformation of the society was challenged by a host of writers in the 1960s. These revisionist historians contested the previous consensus view that the schools are the products of enlightened social policy and, instead, focused attention on the ideological functions of the school system. The thrust of the revisionists' argument has been that the schools reinforce class inequalities in the society and have been used by the upper class as a means of instilling docility in the working class and in the urban poor.

The most influential of the revisionist writers, Michael Katz, advanced a bold interpretation of the growth of the schools as agencies of social control in his book, *The Irony of Early School Reform* (1968). In this book, which is both imaginative in conception and vivid in style, Katz argued that the conventional interpretation of a labor movement fighting for free public schools is a myth, and that, on the contrary, schooling was imposed on a reluctant and hostile working class. Although the revisionists comprise a very diverse set of writers, other authors expanded on these ideas in a set of studies of the role of the schools in reinforcing the social order.[4]

The revisionist historians have succeeded in shifting the terms of the debate so that more orthodox researchers have been forced to address some of the issues of power and control of the school system that the revisionists have raised. The revisionists have helped make the sociology of education more relevant to political and social realities by giving historial grounding to the critical images of schooling that have long been held by radicals and by some of those exposed to the schools. In many cases, however, they themselves have fallen victim to their image of schooling as social imposition. They have often operated according to a simplified political model and have left many important theoretical and empirical questions unanswered. They have drawn sweeping conclusions on the basis of sketchy historical evidence and have never directly confronted a body of earlier work that suggests the labor movement generally favored the spread of public education.

The issues raised by the revisionist educational writers are relevant far beyond the immediate debate about how and why the schools were established. Sociologists have often argued abstractly about the sources of social power and the role of economic classes in the United States, but the revisionists have posed a set of questions that force the analysis of class relationships in specific terms. If it is true, as the revisionists have contended, that a social elite was able to impose schooling upon a reluctant population, this implies a great deal about the cohesiveness, farsightedness, and power of the elite group. And conversely, it implies the weakness and disorganization of the immigrant and working-class population, which, the revisionists argue, was unable to mount an effective challenge to the imposition of an alien set of cultural values. On a still broader level, the revisionists, by focusing on the class-socializing effects of schooling, have raised the issue of the social role of education but have devoted little attention to the possibility that increased education could lead to heightened criticism of the existing order.

In building a firmer empirical foundation for the development of analyses of class relationships and the schools, we need to move from an abstract to a historically concrete level. We need to know what types of educational issues engaged working-class people, on what occasions business leaders intervened in school matters, how questions of educational structure affected patterns of conflict, and what political means were open to different groups to bring about their educational goals. This book addresses these questions through an analysis of the ebb and flow of conflicts over the expansion and educational content of the Chicago public schools. It is appropriate to examine the dynamics of educational controversies on a metropolitan level, for until after World War II the federal structure of the United States government resulted in education being treated as a matter of local concern. The intent in these pages, however, is to gain insight into the larger pattern of class reactions to the growth and development of the educational system, and, in the final chapter, to consider the implications of this pattern for our understanding of class relations more generally. With these larger goals in mind, the key questions addressed in the book are: in what specific historical circumstances and for what reasons did the public schools become a focus of class controversy?

Education as Imposition:
The Revisionists' Perspective

The revisionist authors, and those historians such as David Tyack and Marvin Lazerson who share at least some of their views, have demonstrated the fruitfulness of examining underlying issues of class and power in explaining even such seemingly bureaucratic matters as why there was a drive to reduce school boards in size in the early 1900s, or why vocational education took the form that it did.[5] They have made it clear that the politics of education have never, in reality, been far divorced from general American politics. As their analysis has provided the impetus for this reexamination of class relations and schooling in Chicago, it is useful to look at the perspective of the revisionist educational writers more closely. There are significant differences among the revisionist authors; some, for example, adopt an explicitly Marxist orientation while others adhere to a more individualistic or vaguely defined elitist model. Their work shares some common assumptions, however, and it is important to analyze these assumptions, because the conclusions they reach, the types of evidence they select, and the very questions they choose to answer must be understood within the framework of their analyses of American society.

The revisionist historians countered, although they did not specifically address, a body of early work in the history of education that stressed the role of the labor movement in fighting for free public schools. In the early 1900s, John R. Commons, the noted labor historian, helped give wide currency to the work of a University of Wisconsin doctoral student, Frank Tracy Carlton, who argued that early workingmen's parties had actively promoted public schools.[6] Commons believed that Carlton's research disproved the earlier "great man" theory of educational reform, and the two succeeded in popularizing what came to be known as the labor education thesis. Many later historians, including Arthur M. Schlesinger, Sr. and Mary Beard, referred to the labor movement's struggles for public schooling, usually citing Commons or Carlton.[7]

These early proponents of the labor education thesis stressed labor's role as an agent of social reform, but after World War II there was an important shift of emphasis in the most influential writings on education. Lawrence Cremin and Bernard Bailyn, who are credited with leading the resurgence of the history of education as a field in the postwar period, differed from Commons and Carlton in that they ascribed no special role to the labor movement and did not view social classes as dynamic elements in history. The labor movement was merely one of many forces, often internally fragmented, that competed in the pluralist arena for the attainment of a particular kind of school system. Lawrence Cremin's well-documented work exemplifies the optimism of the postwar period, the belief that bit by bit, through the working out of an immense variety of competing forces and pressures, the school system was contributing to the growth of a democratic and successful society. Cremin and Bailyn both presented a view of a flexible, variegated educational system that corresponded to the decentralized adaptability of the polity as a whole.[8]

The disillusionment with American society that came in the wake of the urban riots of the 1960s and the Vietnam War found its counterpart in the study of the social role of education. Far from being accepted as the basically beneficent institutions that Cremin and Bailyn portrayed, the schools were characterized by a set of revisionist writers as mainstays of class and racial prejudice. They argued that American popular faith in education was misguided in emphasizing the possibility of individual mobility through increased years of schooling; rather, the schools operated to reinforce class divisions and had been designed to serve a negative and repressive function from the time of their founding. New historical research unearthed explicitly elitist statements made by scores of educators about the goals underlying their promotion of public education. Rather than brushing aside these remarks as historically quaint, the revisionists traced a consistent pattern of attempts to organize the schools to contain politically and socially the growing numbers of working-class children. The schools inculcated the values of upper-class white Protestantism; as part of this critique, the more voluntaristic "melting pot" view of American society gave way to an interpretation that saw the forcible destruction of ethnic communities in favor of a stereotyped, chauvinistic Americanism.[9]

The revisionist authors have generally rejected, implicitly or explicitly, the evidence presented by Carlton and Commons that the working class fought for expanded public schooling. Michael Katz, for instance, writes that his case study of Beverly, Massachusetts, indicates that

> two distinct clusters of antagonists emerge: prominent, prestigious leaders and a working class. But the antagonists' attitudes defined by older historians must be reversed: the Beverly experience reveals that one dynamic of educational controversy was the attempt of social leaders to impose innovation upon a reluctant working class.[10]

Katz's work struck a responsive chord among other authors concerned with explaining the roots of the rigid and repressive school systems they observed. Although few other researchers looked closely at historical data on working-class attitudes toward schooling, many authors writing in the period shortly after Katz published his study broadly accepted his conclusions on the sources of educational expansion. Samuel Bowles, for example, asserted in an early article that "the fact that some working people's movements had demanded free instruction should not obscure the basically coercive nature of the extension of schooling. In many parts of the country, schools were literally imposed upon workers."[11] Martin Carnoy went even further in implying that working people had played no active role in demanding schooling or engaging in disputes over the nature of schooling. Carnoy wrote that, prior to recent times, "there have of course been earlier attacks on the schools. But these—the progressive school movement, for example—came entirely from intellectuals and represented conflicts among educational philosophies that had little to do with today's political and social criticisms."[12] In short, the revisionist authors were sometimes ambiguous about the roles of elite and working-class groups (and few gathered independent information on this), but they generally charged that the schools had been imposed upon a reluctant but passive working class.

It is worth reviewing in more detail Michael Katz's chief piece of evidence supporting his contention that the working class opposed the development of the public school system, for this evidence has significantly influenced many subsequent revisionist writers. In the first section of *The Irony of Early School Reform,* titled "Reform by Imposition," Katz presents a case study of the town of Beverly, Massachusetts, where excellent records were kept of the results of the 1860 referendum to determine whether to maintain a public high school. The vote on retaining the school was negative, and Katz concludes that opposition came primarily from the working class, while the professionals and upper-income residents generally favored the school. There are several caveats to be made about his analysis, however.

The first point is that Katz uses a rather loose definition of the term *working class.* He defines it as "people in the lowest socio-economic categories." In this period, before the massive industrial development of the country, *working class* could not have the meaning it was later to acquire, but Katz's classification of "fishermen, farmers, shoemakers and laborers" as constituting the working class presents major problems.[13] Massachusetts was rapidly becoming dotted with textile factories, and the textile operatives would be counted as working class by any definition, but Beverly contained no factories. Rather, Beverly was a small town characterized by an absence of an industrial working class. This reduces the generalizability of the findings; in addition, there are difficulties in interpreting the vote for the members of the population that Katz does define as working class. Fishermen and farmers engage in the types of isolating work activities that might predispose them against taxes to support community services; there were only 10 laborers in the town, and at the time of the school vote the shoemakers had just begun what turned out to be a prolonged and bitter strike, a circumstance that might have affected their willingness to vote for increased taxes.

There is another more fundamental reason for being wary of drawing any very sweeping conclusions on the basis of the vote totals in Beverly. The logic of Katz's argument suffers from his failure to consider the information on workingmen's political organizations that was provided by Commons and Carlton. This is particularly apparent in the way Katz deals with the issue of compulsory schooling. Katz treats the introduction of compulsory school laws as a particularly glaring example of ruling-class dominance and coercion; he writes: "The reformers have been determined to foist their innovations upon the community, if necessary by force; when permissiveness failed in the 1840s, the state passed compulsory school laws in the 1850s."[14] Commons, however, had cited evidence indicating that working-class political organizations had explicitly demanded compulsory school laws as a means of ending child labor and making schooling a reality. In an era marked by very low wages for adults and the widespread introduction of child labor, parents frequently could not afford to remove their children from the labor market and send them to school. Only if there were a general move, motivated by political pressure, toward compulsory schooling could children be removed from the factories and adults paid sufficient wages to support their families without child labor.

As long as the demands for the abolition of child labor and for compulsory education were not simultaneously achieved, workers might very well resist paying for schools their children could not attend. It is important for this reason not only to look at an individual vote in an individual city but to examine the workingmen's organizations and overall political demands of the period. Without such an overall perspective, the point that it might well be possible for workers to support with complete rationality the general principle of free public schools while rejecting a particular school facility is obscured. Katz fails to provide this overall view, and there is therefore no means, on the basis of his study, of resolving the contradiction between his work and that of the earlier historians who focused on labor's political support for public schools.

In terms of the theoretical underpinnings of their work, the revisionists have presented a class analysis in the sense that they have studied the ways in which education serves the interest of the upper class in maintaining the social order. Many revisionist writers, however, have not considered the working class as a potentially active force capable of disrupting or basically transforming the society. The key concept underlying their work has been that of elite domination. The working class seldom appears in these studies except as an object of socialization by a sophisticated upper class capable of devising and implementing long-range cooptive programs. The domination of the upper class is perceived as being so complete that working-class resistance is described as occurring only through such individualistic actions as simply not sending their children to school or expressing sporadic and undirected opposition to school programs. The revisionists do not generally consider the possibility that there could have been collective counterposing of alternative values or of class-based struggles to transform the nature of the schools. Further, education itself is perceived primarily in terms of how it helps to stabilize the social order. There is little conception that education might potentially foster a critical attitude toward society as well as a passive acceptance of the status quo.

The revisionists' underlying assumption that working people have not played a major role in the shaping of the educational system is reflected in the methodology they have employed. For the most part, they have traced the ideological biases of educators and middle-class school promoters through analyzing their writings, while paying little or no attention to the demands or political programs of the organized labor movement. The Beverly case study is the only section of Katz's book where he attempts in any systematic way to gather evidence on working-class attitudes. The bulk of the book evaluates the views of educators and school promoters. Clearly, they did argue for schools in terms of their contributions to social stability, but neither Katz nor the other revisionist writers explores working-class attitudes and modes of political organization in the kind of depth that is necessary in order to evaluate class responses to schooling.

The Revisionists and the
Theory of Corporate Liberalism

There are larger theoretical issues involved in the debate over the schools in that the revisionist educational historians have stressed the role of the upper class in using social reforms to maintain their dominance. This perspective is similar to that of a group of historians who developed the theory of "corporate liberalism" in the 1960s.* The corporate liberal theorists have emphasized the ability of sophisticated members of the American upper class to use the state with foresight and intelligence to serve their own ends while forestalling dissenters by giving the appearance of offering reforms.[15] Gabriel Kolko's *Triumph of Conservatism* is a classic example of a corporate liberal analysis: the argument is that, in fact, the industrialists in the Progressive era conceded nothing (indeed, they gained from federal regulation, according to Kolko), while reformers were deluded into thinking they had won a victory. "Reforms" could only strengthen capitalism, contrary to the naive beliefs of the radicals and reformers of the period.

This emphasis on the sophistication of the dominant elite is entirely in accord with the main thrust of Katz's work on the

---

*Joel Spring, one of the revisionist writers, explicitly acknowledges the similarity between his perspective and that of the corporate liberal theorists. He writes in the introduction to his book on education in the Progressive era that "more recent interpretations of Progressive politics have stressed the rise of the corporate state. One book with this theme is James Weinstein's *Corporate Ideal in the Liberal State*. While the first chapter of this book was written before the author had knowledge of Weinstein's work, the concepts of the corporate state are strikingly parallel" (Spring, *Education and the Rise of the Corporate State* [Boston: Beacon Press, 1972], p xiv).

schools in Massachusetts. The industrialists and their intellectual spokesmen in Massachusetts in the mid-nineteenth century
were increasingly concerned with the growing restlessness of the
workers in the rapidly expanding factories of New England, and
they were appalled by the "depravity" that met their eyes in the
urban slums. They saw state-provided compulsory schooling as a
means of socializing workers into a proper acceptance of their
lot; thus they "mounted an ideological and noisy campaign to
sell education to an often skeptical, sometimes hostile, and usually uncomprehending working class."[16]

In this interpretation, the creation of a public school system
was simply another attempt to insure the continuance of the
ideological hegemony of the dominant class in the face of the
dwindling ability of religion or of communities to serve as agencies of social control. Reforms and social changes, according to
both the revisionist educational historians and the corporate liberal theorists, are primarily generated by an elite to maintain
their own position and are seldom a response to effective pressure from below. Neither set of historians readily admits the
existence of potentially destabilizing elements in the society.

The parallels between the educational revisionists and the
corporate liberal theorists cut across the differences in the specific institutions they are analyzing. Gabriel Kolko has argued
not that business accommodated itself to federal regulation, a
demand that clearly could be easily absorbed within a capitalist
framework, but that business wanted government regulation.[17]
Similarly, the revisionist historians have argued not that business leaders accommodated themselves to rising educational
demands, but that business leaders promoted increased schooling. In each case, the assumption has been that business control
of the institutions of government and of socialization has been so
assured, so beyond challenge, that business did not hesitate to
strengthen public agencies.

Debates on the autonomy and nature of the state in capitalist
society are highly complex, and even within a class paradigm
there is much divergence of opinion, but the corporate liberal
theorists seldom admit the possibility that public institutions
could become new focal points of class conflict.[18] The hegemony of

the dominant group is reinforced through the development of a range of public and private institutions, from public schools to trade unions, that ultimately serve to incorporate the major elements of the population into the framework of the society. As Gabriel Kolko has written in an unusually strong formulation, "a static class structure . . . might be frozen" into American society, with no effective challenge to the dominant class possible.[19]

This perspective is shared by the revisionist educational writers, who emphasize the social control functions of schooling. As Samuel Bowles and Herbert Gintis have written, the public school system has served "as a method of producing a properly subordinate adult population. . . . [T]he theme of social control pervades educational thought and policy."[20] It should be noted that Bowles and Gintis have increasingly tended to stress the contradictions of the educational system as well as its stabilizing elements. *Schooling in Capitalist America* contains a far more complex account of the development of mass public schooling than that presented earlier by Bowles in "Unequal Education." Their analysis is particularly valuable because of the attempt to systematize a vast amount of material. The emphasis in their work remains primarily on the fit between the educational system and the needs of the economic system, however. In particular, they stress the role of family values, reinforced by the schools, in creating a tractable labor force.

On a theoretical level, the revisionist and corporate liberal historians have posited a social system in which there is no evident mechanism for social change. Their perspective in this crucial respect contrasts with that of class theorists, who emphasize that the development of a social system may itself create conditions that contribute to its eventual alteration. To the revisionist and corporate liberal writers, conflicts between classes are not the dynamic elements in historical change. Rather, in their view, those changes that have occurred have been devised and put into effect by members of the upper class. Class conflicts occur only over relatively trivial issues and have no potential for generating genuine societal changes. The hegemony of the dominant group is reinforced through the development of a range of public and private institutions, from public schools to trade unions, that ultimately serve to incorporate the major elements of the population into the framework of the society.

In their readiness to call attention to the successes of the social elite in dominating and socializing those below, the revisionist historians have given little weight to the social conflicts that have occurred over the creation and shaping of public institutions. On both a theoretical and empirical level, there is, however, reason to look closely at the dynamics of reform struggles and the partial victories that subordinate groups have sometimes gained through them. Trade unions and public schools, for example, may serve at times to incorporate elements of the population into the industrial order, but they may also represent substantial popular victories that in themselves embody contradictions that may subsequently give rise to further conflicts.

Social Reform and the Chicago Schools

In order to explore systematically the political interactions of labor, business, and professional groups around the schools in a major urban center, I analyzed conflicts over the Chicago schools during the period from the turn of the century to the post–World War II era. Chicago was selected as the site of the study because it is a major industrial city that has had a large working-class population and has also been the center of powerful employers' institutions. These characteristics are of critical importance because they allow the examination of the rise of the labor movement and the development of its educational outlook in conjunction with that of the business community.

Clearly, a complex social reality cannot be fully encompassed through an analysis of labor, business, and liberal professional attitudes toward schooling; the schools serve a multitude of functions, and ethnic and religious controversies over the goals of public education have frequently simmered in America's cities. The civil rights drive for equal and integrated schools is only the latest and most intense of a long series of ethnic and racial controversies over the schools. The proposition that there are also class-related interests in schooling has received less attention, however, and this study will focus on exploring the political contexts that give rise to class-related controversies.

Increased schooling can heighten criticisms of the existing order as well as inculcate docility, and this potentially double-edged character can give rise to a complex and shifting set of struggles over the control and direction of public education. In Chicago the response of the labor movement to class-biased instruction varied with the overall ideological position of organized labor within the political context of the city. More specifically, working-class leaders and organizations consistently supported expanded schooling, in contrast to what would have been broadly expected from the revisionists' analysis, but labor organizations in Chicago only engaged in political struggles to change the nature and content of schooling as part of an overall program of social reform. Education has seldom been the main element of labor's political program, but a thrust to democratize the schools can occur in conjunction with a general program to transform social relations during periods of working-class militance. The key issue addressed in this study is the specification of the conditions under which education is treated as a class issue, as opposed to those instances when a more muted labor movement was geared to promoting schooling as a potential means of individual mobility rather than collective good.

Evidence from Chicago suggests that business leaders were not anxious to fund rapid educational development, and that they were somewhat worried by the prospect of an "overeducated" work force. In the early 1900s, working-class children for the first time started attending high school in large numbers, and high school thus lost its former character as a preparation for college for middle- and upper-class children. One consequence was that, increasingly, there were calls for the development of a highly differentiated school curriculum, and the nature and content of schooling began to be more sharply posed as class issues. The business community demonstrated a strong interest in encouraging such goals as "character development" and vocational training, rather than broader intellectual goals.

Business and labor organizations are only two elements of

Chicago's political life. Although the city is famous for its highly developed machine politics, middle-class-based liberal reform groups have long played an active role in seeking an efficient and corruption-free city government. These groups, usually comprised largely of professionals (teachers, professors, social workers, lawyers, and others), have frequently taken an interest in the financing and direction of the public school system. They have played a significant role in influencing the terms of the debate around the schools. Any account of Chicago's school politics would be incomplete if it did not take account of the interconnections of such groups both to the labor movement and to the city's key business organizations. During periods of polarization on educational issues between business and labor groups in Chicago, many influential liberal public figures gave legitimacy and intellectual support to positions broadly identified with the labor movement. On a more long-term basis, however, there were also vital connections between the perceived interests of the middle-class reformers and of business leaders. The goals of the two sets of actors were not necessarily the same, and, in fact, in critical respects were different, with frequent open and bitter disputes between professionally-oriented civic associations and business organizations. Each, however, valued the development of a highly bureaucratized school system removed from politics and run by professional educational administrators. For business leaders, this provided a way of depoliticizing potentially volatile school issues, and the civic reformers placed great stress on the goal of creating corruption-free, efficient, and academically stratified schools.

Political groups are not monolithic, and the labor movement, the business community, and the civic reformers were not infrequently divided among themselves on the best political strategies and ultimate goals. Thus, understanding Chicago's politics requires sensitivity to the differences between, for example, the unions that were affiliated with the Congress of Industrial Organizations (CIO) and those that were affiliated with the American Federation of Labor (AFL) during the 1930s and 1940s, or between the business leaders who were affiliated with the Commerical Club of Chicago, the most elite of the city's business organizations, and those who were primarily identified with the Chicago Association of Commerce.

I examined social conflicts over the schools with the aid of primary and secondary historical materials. I traced business attitudes toward education through the use of documents and records of meetings of such organizations as the Commercial Club, the Civic Federation, and the Chicago Association of Commerce. Although positions adopted in the name of groups and actions taken on a collective basis are more indicative of broad support than are the statements and views of individuals, there are instances where individuals play very influential roles and where their views deserve close examination. The city's reform groups left a large variety of meeting reports, bulletins, and statements by leading members, all of which convey a lively sense of the orientations of these groups.

The most important source materials for studying labor attitudes toward education in Chicago are labor newspapers and pamphlets and special manuscript collections. This study focuses on the attitudes and policies of the organized labor movement of the city rather than on the views of individual working people. The first reason for this is simply that source materials on the attitudes of the latter are not readily available. The second and more fundamental reason is that the organized labor movement represented the political expression of the city's union members. There is often a gulf between leaders and members in organizations, and it is difficult to estimate to what extent this has been the case during different periods of the city's labor history. To the extent that members of the city's unions had a political voice and exerted influence, however, it was through the labor federations that spoke and acted in the name of the Chicago labor movement. As E. J. Hobsbawm has noted, "Working class consciousness . . . implies formal organization," because, unlike employers, who can be politically effective in either organized associations or through informal contacts, members of the working class have no strength except through the power of collective action.[21] Recognizing that there may be a divergence between the goals of members and leaders, however, requires special attention to those occasions when labor pronouncements were not backed up with effective action, as during the social protests that occurred during the Depression over the funding of the schools.

Structure of the Book

Chicago's politics and the nature of the controversies over education changed markedly during the period from the turn of the century to the end of World War II. In order to provide background on the political context of the city and the dynamics of the labor movement during the first decades of the 1900s, chapter 2 explores the rise of the Chicago Federation of Labor within a disordered political system. The most fundamental dispute in Chicago's educational history occurred over the scope of education for working-class children; controversies over the control and organization of the school system were a recurring feature of school and city politics (chapters 3 and 4). These disputes continued when the efficiency movement, the social counterpart of Taylorism in industry, burst upon the educational world with full force in the 1920s (chapter 5). This led to sharp struggles over the differentiation of schooling, the introduction of IQ tests, and the role of teachers in determining school policies. These controversies receded into the background during the Depression as the political context of the city changed markedly. The Democratic party achieved unchallenged supremacy in the city, and this had enormous bearing on the playing out of conflicts around the school system, as disputes were increasingly resolved in closed-door bargaining in the mayor's office (chapter 6). In the post–World War II era, the ideology of "keeping the schools out of politics" has led to a pattern of informal pressures on the school system, while the labor movement has ceased to struggle around broad social reform issues. The history of conflicts around the Chicago schools, however, reveals that the labor movement can and has played strong and highly class-conscious roles in regard to the schools during periods of labor militancy (chapter 7).

2 THE DYNAMICS OF THE CHICAGO LABOR MOVEMENT

THE LABOR MOVEMENT of every city or region develops its own political traditions and identity. In each setting, labor leaders must make adjustments to the city's political system even as the political system is in turn influenced by the extent of organization among the city's work force and the militancy and social consciousness of its members. Further, the dynamics of city politics are often radically changed by forces beyond the control of any sets of individuals or groups within the city's borders. Chicago's distinctive political life, for example, took form at the turn of the century as the city became a magnet for hundreds of thousands of immigrants. Similarly, the marked change in Chicago's racial composition during the 1950s and 1960s, created by the migration of southern blacks to northern cities, had major political ramifications and strongly affected the organized labor movement's political role within the city.

In the first decades of the 1900s, the central labor federation in Chicago adopted positions that placed it on the left wing of the American Federation of Labor (AFL). During this period, the Chicago Federation of Labor (CFL) acquired a national reputation for a commitment to organizing the unskilled and a willingness to defy the cautious leadership of Samuel Gompers. By the mid-1930s, however, the Chicago Federation of Labor was noted for its conservatism and inflexibility within the national labor spectrum.[1] This change in political orientation did not occur because of the development of new leadership; rather, it arose in response to the changing political context of the city as a whole.

In each major phase of the labor movement's development, the dominant ideological perspective in regard to engagement over social issues changed, and the labor movement thus exhibited varying levels of involvement in educational questions. Although Chicago's particular political history is of course unique to it, working-class organizations in other cities are likely to share characteristics of the Chicago labor movement at particular phases of its development. In every city, the breadth of the trade union base, its strength among skilled and unskilled workers, and its relationship to the dominant political powers of the city are likely to affect the labor movement's orientation toward the centrality of promoting broad social goals in addition to narrower economic demands. The variability in the political role of Chicago's trade union movement is thus of particular interest as changes in how unionists approached educational questions enable us to identify more clearly the basic elements in political ideology that might obtain elsewhere in different settings. This in turn allows for an assessment of the conditions under which public education becomes a focus of social conflict.

Chicago's Early Political Culture

Chicago's strategic location as the hub of inland waterways and a national railway network spurred its industrial growth as the nation expanded to the west. After the 1890s, Chicago became a manufacturing center as the steel and iron industries located on the southern shore of Lake Michigan and the printing, needle trades, and electrical-supply industries began operations in the city.[2] Meatpacking became a major enterprise as the city's location at the center of a railway system allowed for rapid meat distribution in the era before refrigerated cars.

Chicago also became the mechandising and financial center for the expanding Midwest. Sears, Roebuck and Company established its headquarters in Chicago, and the city's banks, although not rivaling New York's on the national level, mustered formidable financial resources. Concomitant with the city's industrial and financial development was the formation of a set of power businessmen's clubs and associations, whose political role will be considered in chapter 3.

Chicago's expanding industries required a huge work force, and hundreds of thousands of immigrants poured into the city to meet the demand. The city's population grew at an extraordinary rate: in 1890, the population was slightly over a million; by 1900 it had reached nearly 1.7 million.[3] Growth continued to be extremely rapid, with the population numbering 2.2 million in 1910, 2.7 million in 1920, and close to 3.4 million by 1930.[4] A study of Chicago's population changes from 1900 to 1940 showed that only one-fifth to one-third of the city's growth during that period could be attributed to the excess of births over deaths; the rest was accounted for by immigration.[5]

Chicago's influx of immigrants was so great that as late as 1930, 65 percent of the population was either foreign-born or had foreign-born parents.[6] The ethnic mix was highly varied, as the early German, Scandinavian, French, and Irish immigrants were joined by Poles, Russian Jews, Italians, and Czechs. In smaller numbers came Lithuanians, Danes, Austrians, Hungarians, Greeks, and Yugoslavs. The extreme heterogeneity of Chicago's population resulted from the fact that the city's great period of growth coincided with the last great wave of immigration from Europe. The European immigrants were joined by black migrants from the South who moved to Chicago during World War I to meet the demand for labor caused by the wartime production boom and the simultaneous shutting off of European immigration.[7] By 1930, blacks constituted 6.9 percent of Chicago's total population.[8]

There were deep language, religious, and social barriers among the immigrants, many of whom brought with them from Europe a heritage of ethnic animosity. Immigrants clustered in ethnic enclaves and viewed intrusion by other groups with hostility. Foreign-language newspapers flourished, and the larger groups, such as the Germans, had a collection of native-language newspapers that covered the political spectrum from left to right.

The large immigrant population provided fertile ground for the building of ward fiefdoms by local politicians. Precinct captains and ward bosses performed services for new arrivals, helping them cope with a hostile or indifferent city bureaucracy and controlling access to city jobs. Following the pattern laid out by the railroad tracks, the city was divided into neighborhoods that retained strong feelings of local identity. Each neighborhood usually produced its own political bosses who negotiated and made deals on a bipartisan basis with their counterparts in other wards.⁹ The population's heterogeneity led to the emergence of many local bosses but hindered efforts by any one party or faction to achieve overall dominance. There was very little connection between the national Democratic and Republican parties and their local expression in Chicago in terms of policies, and the political system generally was characterized by corruption, extreme factionalism, and personalistic alliances. Charles Merriam, a close observer of Chicago politics for many years, described the confused nature of the city's politics before the emergence of the Democratic machine in the 1930s:

> These various factions divided federal, state, county, and other patronage, and rose and fell with the currents of political fortune. Their connections and combinations constitute an intricate tangled skein. . . . At times they rallied to the support of their respective parties, and at times they crossed party lines and fought together, especially in local contests, where the national party lines were shot to pieces. Almost any combination of these elements was possible and actual. There was no boss strong enough to control all of these factions even in one party, and as a rule each man fought at the head of his own faction.¹⁰

In spite of the general lack of coherent political differentiation between the parties and their division into competing factions, most ethnic groups gradually came to exhibit an allegiance to one or the other of the two major parties. The two groups with the strongest partisan identification were the city's black residents, who were overwhelmingly Republican, and the Irish, who were the mainstays of the Democratic party. The Germans, who were relatively well off and easily assimilated, tended to be largely Republican, as were the Swedes; while the more recent eastern and southern European immigrants, such as the Czechs and the Poles and, to a lesser extent, the Italians, identified increasingly with the Democratic party.¹¹

Prior to the 1930s, the Republicans were in power almost as often as the Democrats, but party labels were relatively meaningless; both parties were highly factionalized, and city elections revolved less around issues than around flamboyant personalities. There was an almost feudal structure of competing political machines, each built around its ward bosses and pockets of patronage, but in contrast to New York and other eastern cities, no party or faction was strong enough to drive the others into permanent defeat. A study of ethnic voting in the city emphasizes the extent to which voters failed to distinguish politically between the parties:

> Cook County . . . was politically the least stable county in Illinois, partially because of the fluctuating loyalties of its ethnic groups. New immigrants tend to favor the party in power, since it is the organization most able to minister to their needs. The county tended to be more Republican than the rest of the state when Republicans were winning, and more Democratic when the Democrats were winning.[12]

The structure of Chicago's city government increased the problems that parties faced in building cohesive city-wide machines: vast numbers of governmental units claimed jurisdiction over some aspect of city administration. In a 50-mile radius of downtown Chicago, there were approximately 1,600 independent governments with some degree of jurisdiction, and there were eight principal governments with independent taxing power.[13] These eight principal governments included the school board, the sanitary district government, and the park district boards. This chaotic jumble of governmental units meant that even after one party was swept into power holdovers from the losing party could generally manage to retain key positions from which to dispense partronage to their followers. In this situation, as a *Fortune* analysis of Chicago politics in 1936 pointed out, "To capture *all* the patronage is the work of years."[14]

Chicago politics were sufficiently disorganized in the early part of the 1900s that conflicts between competing interests were fought out quite directly rather than being mediated through a powerful and unified political party. Business, labor, and liberal "reform" elements developed strong organizations as they promoted their political programs in the disordered context of the city. These organizations reached the peak of their power and activity during this early period when the Democratic party machine had not yet achieved unchallenged supremacy.

The Chicago Federation of Labor was the largest political and economic organization in the city, and it played an active political role. During the period prior to and around the turn of the century, Chicago's labor movement was characterized by diverse political viewpoints, intense factionalism, and repeated battles between corrupt and honest union officials. During a second major phase of development, marked by John Fitzpatrick's accession to the presidency of the Chicago Federation of Labor in 1902, the CFL adopted a militant and socially conscious stance that led to deep involvement in controversies over the city's schools. This phase lasted until the emergence of the Chicago Democratic machine in the early 1930s. The reasons for the evolution of the Chicago labor movement in this direction deserve closer examination.

The Rise of the Chicago Labor Movement

Chicago's unionists faced the difficult task of building a labor movement in a city where much of the population had only recently arrived in the United States and retained strong feelings of ethnic identity. Language and social divisions hampered efforts at organizing, and the first lasting gains were made in industries or occupations with relatively homogeneous work forces.[15] Skilled workers, who could generally control entry to their craft, provided the nucleus of the early union movement.

Barbara Newell's detailed study of the pattern of metropolitan unionism in Chicago has revealed that the first groups organized were characteristically those who had bargaining strength because they provided services vital to the city.[16] The building service workers, building trades workers, and the teamsters all fell into this category. The mature union movement then built upon this base and expanded into a multiplicity of occupations. By 1924, the Chicago Federation of Labor claimed a membership of 223 affiliated unions with a combined membership of nearly 100,000 unionists.[17] The Chicago Federation of Labor was unusual in that it early tried to move beyond this base to organize mass-production workers. The early efforts ultimately failed, but the CFL's organizing drives produced a cadre of experienced organizers who later aided the CIO.

The CFL's commitment to organizing the unskilled stemmed in large part from a heritage of militancy that arose from the bitterness of early union efforts to gain a foothold in the city. Chicago's history was marked by police and employer repression of the labor movement; union organizing had been punctuated by the bloody repression of strikes and the institution of martial law.[18]

The most famous incident of violence was the Haymarket Riot in 1886, which set off a repressive reaction that dampened union organizing in the city for years afterward. Chicago had been the center of the national eight-hour-day movement, and the riot occurred in the aftermath of intense agitation for the shorter work day.[19] The city became very tense as unionists united to call mass demonstrations throughout the spring; many of the rallies drew more than 25,000 people. Employers responded by arming themselves, and the members of the city's most elite business organization, the Commercial Club, subscribed $2,000 for the purchase of a machine gun for the First Infantry of the Illinois National Guard. On May Day, more than 30,000 workers struck, and many more participated in mass picketing and demonstrations. Three days later, one policeman was killed and 70 more were injured when a bomb was thrown during a rally at Haymarket Square. The police fired into the crowd, killing one person and wounding many more. Seven anarchists were convicted for the bomb throwing and sentenced to death; four were subsequently hanged, despite a scarcity of evidence linking them with the bomb.

The city's labor movement suffered a period of intense repression following the hysteria set off by the bombing. Business leaders debated means of securing the city against future labor uprisings. Three weeks after the Haymarket bombing, the Commercial Club invited Gen. William Tecumseh Sherman to deliver an address on "The Late Civil Disorder: Its Causes and Lessons." The club voted the following month to give the government 632 acres of land along the North Shore of Lake Michigan for construction of a military garrison. As a later member of the Commercial Club expressed it, "The general feeling among business leaders of the time was that troops should be located more closely to Chicago in the event of civil insurrection."[20]

The city's labor movement during this period was further weakened by factional strife. One labor newspaper deplored the factionalism that divided unionist against unionist: "One of the most lamentable phases of the political labor sky in Chicago is the unreliability and divided state of its leaders. An endless number of factions has grown up in the political labor arena here, each led by a man at enmity with all other such leaders. . . . These factions and agitators are hopelessly divided."[21] Chicago had a sizable contingent of anarchists, and as early as 1860 the city was considered to rank second only to New York in the activity of its socialist group.[22] German immigrants were prominent in the union movement, and many of them brought a tradition of Marxism and radical politics from Europe.[23]

By the 1890s, when the labor movement was again beginning a period of resurgence following the repression directed against it, it suffered another crushing setback. Eugene Debs had led the Pullman railroad workers out on strike, and the dispute quickly flared into violence. Over the protest of Gov. John Peter Altgeld, federal troops were used to help break the strike in 1894. The smashing defeat helped set back the goal of industrial unionism in Chicago for another generation.[24] Debs had worked to organize an industrial union instead of narrow, craft-based brotherhoods in the railroads; the defeat was so decisive, however, that the railroads were subsequently organized along rigid craft lines. The railroad brotherhoods could potentially have played an important role in the local labor movement because of their large membership in Chicago. In fact, however, the craft-oriented brotherhoods focused entirely on the national level and never joined the Chicago Federation of Labor.

The defeat of the Pullman strike had wider consequences because several newly established industrial unions, such as the packinghouse workers, who had struck in sympathy with the railroad workers, were driven out of existence. The collapse of many of the more left-leaning industrial unions meant that the balance of power within the Chicago Federation of Labor shifted to the building trades workers.[25] They were able to maintain a high degree of organization because they faced local rather than national employers and were relatively ethnically homogeneous.

The building trades workers' control over the CFL resulted in an intensification of corruption in the union movement. The building trades were rife with racketeering and payoffs; in a locally dominated seasonal market where maintaining a construction schedule was critical, there were many opportunities for corrupt labor officials to enrich themselves by extorting payoffs from employers in exchange for a guarantee of labor peace.[26]

The Chicago Federation of Labor was controlled by corrupt officials until reformers united in 1902 to install a socially progressive, militantly honest leadership. The new president of the CFL, John Fitzpatrick, dominated the Chicago labor movement for the next four decades. He remained as president until his death in 1946, out of office for only one term in 1908. Fitzpatrick and the other members of the new leadership were enormously influential in shaping the direction of the Chicago labor movement. Fitzpatrick's own shifting ideology both reflected and helped produce changes in the Chicago labor movement as a whole over the more than 40-year span of his leadership.

Fitzpatrick, who had emigrated to the United States from Ireland in 1882, was a horseshoer by occupation.[27] This archaic trade proved a handicap in Fitzpatrick's later career as a labor leader. His base of power rested entirely in the Chicago Federation of Labor because he lacked an independent source of strength in a strong union affiliate. Fitzpatrick's authority was not questioned within the Chicago Federation of Labor, but when he challenged Samuel Gompers and the policies espoused by the American Federation of Labor on the national level, his position was weakened by his lifelong affiliation with one of the least powerful of American unions, the Chicago Journeymen Horse Shoers Union.

Fitzpatrick and his close associate Edward Nockels, who was secretary of the CFL until his death in 1937, brought absolute incorruptibility and a commitment to democratic procedures to the Chicago union movement. Fitzpatrick would purchase nothing that was not union made, and his salary remained extremely modest throughout his long tenure as CFL president.* The Chicago Federation of Labor conducted its meetings democratically; its leadership made concentrated efforts to improve communication with the membership and to build general labor consciousness in the city.[28]

Fitzpatrick's orientation was not toward business unionism, with narrowly focused demands and a spirit of accommodation toward employers and political powers. His commitment to the union movement stemmed from an ideological perspective that stressed the role of unions in reforming society. Fitzpatrick was never a socialist, and he clearly differentiated himself from the socialists in the CFL; he believed, however, in the gradual transformation of society through the creation of a strong and independent working-class party similar to the British Labour party.[29]

The CFL's Drive to Organize the Unskilled

The defeat of the Pullman strike had led to the collapse of the early efforts to organize industrial unions in Chicago. The CFL had been dominated for a period by unions with no interest in organizing unskilled workers, but the victory of the reformers in 1902 led to a new orientation. Fitzpatrick was himself from a craft union, but he was impatient with the AFL's indifference to the plight of workers outside the skilled trades. The CFL's earliest differences with the national leadership of the AFL stemmed from the CFL's efforts to encourage a militant new union in the men's clothing trade.

The CFL was sufficiently committed to organizing low-paid immigrant workers to defy the AFL ban on aiding secession movements by providing support for the Amalgamated Clothing Workers of America (ACWA). The ACWA had split off from the

*Fitzpatrick searched for months before he found a union-made wedding ring, which he ordered from New Jersey, and he always brought a bag lunch to eat in his office rather than patronize any of the unorganized Loop restaurants. After his death his widow refused an additional pension, saying that she did not want to take money from the labor organization unless it was earned (Molly Levitas, 1970).

cautious, conservative United Garment Workers in the aftermath of a 1910 strike in Chicago. The CFL had provided aid
during the strike; Jacob Potofsky, later president of the ACWA,
recalled that "the strikers turned to John Fitzpatrick . . . and
Ed Nockels, secretary of the CFL, in whom they found great
friends. They were really concerned with the plight of the immigrant clothing workers."[30]

When the ACWA split off from the United Garment Workers,
the new union was ostracized by the AFL. Frank Rosenblum,
secretary-treasurer of the ACWA, described the difficulty the
ACWA experienced because of its isolation: "All our life . . .
from 1914, when the Amalgamated was formed, until 1933, we
were an independent organization with no affiliation of any
kind. . . . Not only did we have to depend on ourselves, but
very frequently the labor movement officially bucked us, tried to
break our strikes and take over."[31] Secession movements violated
the AFL's most deeply held principles of union organization.
Jurisdictional disputes so bedeviled craft unions that organizational boundaries became sacred, and the ACWA was officially
read out of the labor movement. In this context, Fitzpatrick's
decision to stand by the ACWA members, although they could
no longer be affiliated with the CFL, reflected his commitment
to organizing.

The CFL's support of the ACWA brought pressure from
Samuel Gompers to participate in the excommunication of the
new union. Gompers personally came to Chicago during a long
strike conducted by the ACWA and pressed Fitzpatrick to withdraw aid from the strikers. Lillian Herstein, a member of the
CFL executive board and a leader of the teachers' union, reported later that Fitzpatrick rejected Gompers's urgings. When
Gompers commented to Fitzpatrick that he guessed the strikers,
who had been out for 17 weeks, were having a hard time, Fitzpatrick replied: "'You bet they're having a tough time, and my
place is standing shoulder to shoulder with them on this.' And
here he was, an official of the American Federation of Labor, and
he took a stand with the rebel union. It was the proudest achievement of his life, he often said, really working for the garment
workers."[32]

The working alliance that the ACWA formed with John Fitzpatrick and the CFL lasted throughout Fitzpatrick's leadership of the federation. The ACWA remained outside the AFL until 1933, when it rejoined; it split again three years later with the departure of the CIO. In spite of this long formal separation, however, the ACWA participated enthusiastically in political and union-organizing ventures with Fitzpatrick. The clothing workers' union contributed generously to his attempts to organize the steel industry and supported the effort to organize a labor party in the early 1920s. The ACWA's brand of progressive unionism was very much in accord with Fitzpatrick's, and the important presence of the ACWA in the city (they had organized nearly 100 percent of the industry by 1919) guaranteed a base of support for CFL programs.[33]

The CFL's most sustained effort to organize the mass-production industries occurred in the aftermath of World War I. The central labor federation coordinated organizing drives involving thousands of workers in both steel and meatpacking. The CFL's attempt to organize the steel industry was the largest-scale unionizing drive in American labor history.[34] The ultimate failure of the two campaigns stemmed principally from the lack of a national organization capable of bolstering the unionizing drives as the CIO did 15 years later.

Fitzpatrick first directed the resources of the CFL toward aiding the packinghouse workers. The meatpacking industry had an extremely ethnically diverse work force. The work in the packinghouses was so unpleasant and, for the most part, required so little skill, that turnover was high and new immigrants frequently found their first jobs in the packing industry.[35] Employers played upon ethnic divisions as a means of increasing their control. They imported black workers as strikebreakers in 1894, and other workers' bitterness toward blacks remained long after the strike collapsed.

The Chicago Federation of Labor established an organizing committee in the stockyards and met with considerable initial success. The Amalgamated Meat Cutters had lost a major strike in 1904, when blacks and immigrants were imported as strikebreakers, and the union had subsequently directed most of its attention to organizing the city's retail butchers. John Fitzpatrick and the CFL's chief organizer, William Z. Foster (later head of the American Communist party), persuaded the retail butchers to help organize the packing workers. The organizing drive proceeded so well that in 1918 President Wilson appointed a national arbitrator to avert a nation-wide strike.[36] The arbitrator's settlement brought the eight-hour day to the industry and introduced overtime rates, guaranteed lunch breaks, and equal pay for equal work.

This settlement rated as a significant victory for the hard-pressed immigrant workers, but when the pact expired three years later the employers refused to extend the agreement and instead cut wages. Forty-five thousand packinghouse workers went out on strike in December 1921, when the employers refused to take the matter to arbitration. In spite of widespread initial response to the strike, however, it ultimately failed, due to tensions generated by factional disputes, company unions, and craft jurisdictional jealousies. These problems continued to bedevil organizing attempts over the next decade and a half, and meatpacking was not organized with long-term success until the CIO entered the industry in the 1930s. The initial unionizing effort by the CFL produced a core of experienced organizers, however, and helped lay the groundwork for the later emergence of the Packinghouse Workers Union.

Before the employers' 1921 refusal to extend the arbitration agreement, the CFL's venture into organizing in a mass-production industry appeared to have been highly successful. This achievement helped provide the impetus for an attempt by the Chicago Federation of Labor to organize the steel industry.[37] This industry posed some of the same types of organizing problems as the meatpacking industry: skilled craftsmen made up only a small minority of the work force after World War I, and the Chicago-area steel plants in particular hired large numbers of unskilled immigrants and migrants from the American South. The Chicago mills had a more ethnically diverse labor force than any of the other major steel plants in the United States.

In spite of a record of unsuccessful strikes in the steel industry (led by the AFL-affiliated Amalgamated Association of Iron,

Steel, and Tin Workers of North America), Fitzpatrick and Foster felt that the steel industry could be organized if there were a concerted national drive. Accordingly, they requested and received unanimous Chicago Federation of Labor support to urge the AFL to hold a national conference to spur intensive organizing in steel. Gompers came to Chicago to preside officially over the meeting, but Fitzpatrick and Foster were the real forces behind the drive. They obtained resources from the participating unions to hire 100 to 150 organizers.[38]

The organizing drive ran into immediate problems, however. The craft-oriented Amalgamated Association of Iron, Steel, and Tin Workers was disturbed by the scope of the unionizing effort and feared its organization would be swamped. It therefore did little to aid the organizing committee. Its reluctance affected other AFL affiliates, many of whom had not been noted in any case for their eagerness to organize unskilled immigrant workers. The 24 craft unions represented on the steelworkers' committee contributed a pathetic $100 apiece to the unionizing drive. Fitzpatrick recognized that he could not count on the jurisdictionally jealous and uneager craft unions and turned instead to the needle trades unions for support. The Amalgamated Clothing Workers gave $100,000 to organize the steelworkers, and the International Ladies' Garment Workers Union, itself not fully organized at the time, gave $60,000.[39]

In spite of the aid from the garment workers, the resources for a truly nation-wide drive did not materialize. In September 1919, the organizing committee called a nation-wide strike. The strike had solid support in Chicago, but in most other parts of the country the steel mills continued operating. By January 1920, it was apparent that the strike was lost, and the workers returned to the mills.

This major defeat marked the Chicago Federation of Labor's last large-scale attempt at industrial organizing. The CFL's militant tradition, combined with Fitzpatrick's ideological orientation, had led to an unusual commitment to organize industrial workers. Fitzpatrick combined strong feelings of loyalty to the American Federation of Labor as an institution with a profound conviction that the AFL would have to broaden its base if it were not ultimately to be left behind by the mass of workers. The national labor federation responded only minimally to the organizing challenge, and the C F L bore the brunt of the attack on the huge steel corporations. When steel was ultimately organized in the 1930s, the United Mine Workers, under John L. Lewis, poured money and organizers into the battle under the umbrella of the C I O. These resources were not available to the C F L as a city central labor body, however, and the early organizing drives proved to be premature as they foundered amid craft union indifference.

The failure to organize the mass-production industries was due in large part to lack of support from craft unions and lack of an alternative national power base. It also became apparent in the years after World War I that the American labor movement was facing a period of severe retrenchment and repression. The booming war years had led to hopes that the unions would make rapid gains after the war, but, in fact, the government aided employers in crushing unionizing efforts as part of an overall postwar campaign against radicalism and political dissent. The national membership figures of the A F L reflected the overall curve of brief growth and then sudden membership losses. In 1915, the A F L claimed 1,946,347 members, a figure that grew to 4,078,740 in 1920. By 1926, the national membership had plummeted to 2,803,966.[40] The conditions for the C F L's venture into mass-production organizing were not propitious in the normalization era of the 1920s.

Organizing Chicago's Teachers

In spite of the C F L's failure in mass-production organizing, during the early 1900s it had scored a breakthrough in securing the affiliation of another group of workers who were often ignored by the trade unions of the period, public school teachers. Chicago's teachers, confronted with low pay, little job security, and no voice in decision making, formed the Chicago Teachers' Federation (CTF) in 1897.[41] The organization was almost entirely made up of the least powerful, most badly paid members of the teaching force—women elementary school teachers. Two of these teachers, Margaret Haley and Catharine Goggin, rose to leadership in the CTF after a short initial struggle over the control of the fledgling organization. Their partnership was to remain unbroken until Goggin's death in a street accident in 1916; under their leadership, the CTF became a political force to be reckoned with in Chicago, even though its women members lacked the vote.

The CTF gained political power in Chicago by approaching issues imaginatively and actively seeking political allies, focusing primarily on the labor movement. It won its first major victory in the early 1900s when, in response to board of education claims that there was no money to pay for promised salary increases, it initiated a tax suit to force the major corporations to pay their authorized share of taxes. In 1897, more than 3,500 teachers had signed a petition to the board of education asking for increased salaries; at that point, teachers' salaries had remained almost stationary for nearly 20 years.[42] The board of education raised salaries by a small amount, then rescinded the increases for the academic year of 1900, claiming that no money was available.[43] Margaret Haley investigated and found that Chicago corporations had managed to avoid paying taxes on land valued at more than $100 million. She persuaded the CTF to initiate a court suit to try to force certain of the corporations to pay their taxes; in 1902 the courts ruled that the corporations owed $597,000. The board of education, which gained an additional $250,000 from its share of this suit, refused to use the money to pay the teachers their originally approved salaries.[44] The CTF again went to court, and in 1904 it won a ruling from Judge Edward Dunne that the board of education had to uphold its contract with the teachers and pay them their full salaries. The battle was not yet over, because the school board voted to appeal the decision. In response, the CTF backed Judge Dunne for mayor in 1905; he won and promptly appointed a new school board that disbursed the additional tax monies to the teachers in the form of salary increments.

In a city renowned for the corruption of its tax-collection mechanism, the CTF had won a victory that quickly gained it the political respect of reformers and the labor movement and the undying hostility of major businessmen.[45] This hostility was cemented when the CTF challenged the school board's policy of granting long-term, fixed rate leases on valuable Loop land owned by the district. The powerful *Chicago Tribune* held one of the 99-year leases, and it lost no occasion to lash out at the CTF, which persistently publicized the *Tribune's* extraordinary business relationship with the school board.[46] The Chicago Teachers' Federation had entered the political arena with a vengeance, but its leaders felt the need for more strength than they could obtain on their own. On November 7, 1902, the Chicago Federation of Labor invited the CTF to join the labor federation. John Fitzpatrick sent the CTF a letter expressing admiration for "the splendid fight the Teachers' Federation, alone and unaided by any other organization, is making in behalf of the schools against the tax-dodging corporations." Fitzpatrick continued, "The time has come for the workingmen of Chicago to take a stand for their children's sake, and demand justice for the teachers and the children so that both may not be crushed by the power of corporate greed." He concluded by asking "the Chicago Teachers' Federation to give to the 200,000 affiliated workingmen and voters of Chicago, the right to take up the cause of the teachers and children in the only way that it can be done promptly and effectively,—that is, by affiliating and sending representatives to the Chicago Federation of Labor, with the power to act for your body, and present your wrongs and those of the children."[47]

Many teachers expressed hesitation about the idea of affiliating with the CFL.[48] It was an unusual and bold step to take at the time, but the leaders of the teachers' federation carried the day with their arguments that the working people were more deeply interested in the schools than were any other group in the city. The Chicago Federation of Labor, declared the CTF's leaders, represented the largest body of voters interested in the public schools through their children and not through their pockets. Margaret Haley later wrote that Catharine Goggin, who had always been a suffragist, "brought home to the teachers in her unique, forceful way the revelation of their disadvantage as nonvoters. I remember the effect it had on the audience of teachers when she said, 'Why shouldn't the City Council give our money to the firemen and policemen? Haven't they got votes?' There was no doubt but that this incident converted many a teacher to the cause of woman's suffrage."[49] The labor federation also had the political strength to aid the teachers in their battles both with the board of education and with the corporations of the city. On November 7, 1902, the CTF formally joined the labor federation.

The strange thing, the teachers' federation later commented, was not that the teachers had joined with the labor federation, but that it had taken so long for the teachers and the labor unions to unite in their mutual interest.[50] The identification with the labor movement sprang from a shared political perspective as well as from a belief that the teachers' power would be increased by the affiliation. Catharine Goggin later repeatedly told members of the CTF that classroom teachers, the hardest-worked and poorest-paid school board employees, had much in common with the laboring population and that their strength, too, lay in numbers and in organization. There were so many classroom teachers that they could not hope to obtain special privileges through behind-the-scenes politicking; their only recourse was to use the strength their numbers gave them to seek overall reforms, just as the labor movement had to do.[51]

The teachers' action in affiliating with the labor federation seemed to have been rewarded when, two months later, the board of education voted the 5,000 elementary teachers in the system a raise of $50 a year.[52] As a later commentator put it, "The Federation of Labor represented *votes*!"[53] The affiliation with the CFL was to have more long-range consequences, however, as it brought the Chicago Federation of Labor into close connection with the teachers. This partnership in turn highlighted the mutual interest in educational questions, with the teachers bringing the labor movement direct knowledge of the school system and the labor movement bringing the teachers political support and a broader social context in which to place their struggles. The partnership occurred not fortuitously but as a result of the active orientation of the CFL in seeking out new members and in helping to organize groups often left on the margins of the labor movement.

Labor's Role in City and National Politics

The Chicago Federation of Labor did not achieve its goal of expanding into the mass-production industries in the early 1920s, but it stood out as a significant political force in the city. As George S. Counts wrote of the labor federation in 1928, when mobilized, it could prove a "decisive factor in Chicago politics."[54] Throughout the first decades of the 1900s, the CFL pursued an independent political policy, challenging both Gompers with the AFL and the city's major political parties within the municipal arena.

The Chicago Federation of Labor pursued political programs within the city that were at variance with relatively conservative national AFL policies. Fitzpatrick had early stated his belief that the CFL had the right to determine its own political positions. If such independent stands results in a break with the American Federation of Labor, Fitzpatrick seemed to accept that as a possibility that had to be contemplated. In 1914, Fitzpatrick expressed his belief that the CFL could operate independently:

> In July, 1914, the counsel for the Commission on Industrial Relations asked John Fitzpatrick what control the American Federation of Labor had over the Chicago Federation of Labor. Previously, John Walker, president of the Illinois State Federation of Labor, had told the Commission that the AFL had "absolute" power over the state central organization. Fitzpatrick, however, answered that the national federation issued the charter of the city central and that in the case of the Chicago Federation of Labor's violation of AFL policy the latter could do "nothing more than to withdraw the charter." He was unwilling to concede absolute power to the AFL, and he felt that even if the charter were withdrawn . . . the organization would still function.[55]

The CFL pushed ahead with its support for left-wing or progressive causes even over strong opposition from Gompers. Fitzpatrick, for example, throughout his career threw the weight of the CFL behind trade unionists who had been accused of violence. He believed that such charges often resulted from reactionary collusion between employers, the press, and judges. The Chicago labor press gave great publicity to Sacco and Vanzetti, and the CFL organized to raise money for their defense. Similarly, the CFL waged a long campaign to free Tom Mooney from prison; Mooney, an AFL official in San Francisco, had been convicted of throwing a bomb into a war-preparedness parade in 1916, in spite of strong evidence that he was over a mile from the parade at the time of the attack. Fitzpatrick and Edward Nockels made the campaign a national issue. On January 14, 1919, William Z. Foster, then an organizer for the CFL, chaired a meeting attended by Bill Haywood from the International Workers of the World (IWW), Alexander Berkman, the anarchist, Jim Larkin, the Irish nationalist, and a crowd of radicals and unionists that called for Mooney's immediate release. The Chicago Federation of Labor threatened to call a general strike if Mooney were not released; nothing came of the threat, but Gompers reacted strongly. Gompers denounced the CFL for associating with radicals, and the executive council of the AFL specifically reminded Edward Nockels that the city centrals were not empowered to call strikes on any issue.[56] (The CFL refused to drop the issue, however. In 1930, it invited Mooney's partner, Warren K. Billings, recently released from prison, to address the CFL's Labor Day rally. William Green, then president of the AFL, declared that he thought it "scarcely possible that such action was taken.")

The CFL also differed more fundamentally with national AFL policy. The CFL early hailed the Russian Revolution as an enormous step forward for the working class; the leaders of the Chicago federation were later to become bitterly disillusioned with the Soviet government, but in the years immediately after the revolution, they argued that it was the duty of the American labor movement to defend the Soviet Union, and they were fearful that the Allied powers would invade and crush the new government. In 1920, Poland and Russia went to war, with the Allied governments backing Poland, and the CFL feared that this was the opening step in an Allied campaign to destroy the Soviet Union. The CFL passed a resolution that called for massive labor action if the United States tried to engage in a direct war with Russia. Gompers and the national AFL leadership were already extremely hostile to the Soviet government, and Gompers denounced the CFL for passing the resolution. Edward Nockels replied to Gompers that

> the CFL was asking for "united opposition by American labor to an imperialistic war," calling for "a general conference of labor organizations to devise a way of making American Labor's power felt," and demanding that "the Russian people be let alone to work out their own problems." Nevertheless, Gompers again criticized the CFL as an irresponsible advocate of the general strike, unworthy of power within the American labor movement.[57]

The issue that drove the deepest wedge between the Chicago Federation of Labor and the AFL was the CFL's support for an independent labor party. The AFL adhered, during these years, to an officially nonpartisan policy, although in practice it increasingly favored Democratic candidates.[58] The Chicago federation defied this AFL tradition by initiating a labor party movement in the aftermath of World War I.

There was a general upsurge of labor interest in independent politics in the years immediately after World War I, and the CFL both reflected and reinforced labor party sentiment by founding the Cook County Labor party in November 1918 as a first step in the effort to create a national labor party. The founding of the Cook County party helped spur the establishment of local labor parties in Massachusetts, Connecticut, New York, West Virginia, Ohio, Kentucky, and Wyoming.[59] The Chicago party was founded on the basis of a 14-point program, presented by Fitzpatrick and Nockels, that was first approved by the CFL's executive board and then unanimously endorsed by the delegates to the labor assembly.[60]

Labor's 14 Points reflected a nonsocialist but outspokenly radical labor philosophy. The points ranged from labor's right to organize and engage in collective bargaining, the eight-hour day, and the minimum wage, to nationalization of all public utilities under worker management. Inheritances over $100,000 were to be confiscated, unemployment was to be ended through stabilization of industry and public works, and women were to have equal rights with men. The seventh point was the abolition of "Kaiserism in Education." The plank called for the "democratization of education in public schools and universities through the participation of labor and the organized teachers in the determination of methods, policies, and programs in this fundamental field."[61] The final plank called for workers' internationalism, with "a league of the workers of all nations pledged and organized to enforce the destruction of autocracy, militarism, and economic imperialism throughout the world."

The Chicago party was a constituent unit of a national Labor party that was founded in November 1919. The national party was modeled on the British Labour party which, at that time, was achieving its first successes in England. John Fitzpatrick was the "outstanding leader and central figure of the labor party movement."[62] He delivered the keynote addresses at both the 1919 and 1920 conventions of the newly organized party. His presence as a leading AFL official helped give legitimacy to a party that, from the beginning, had to struggle against strong national AFL opposition. The party was organized by local unions and rank-and-file members, with a sprinkling of city central federations (such as the CFL) providing support. The delegates to the founding convention came from a wide variety of unions across the country; in spite of AFL opposition, there were delegates present from over half of the AFL's affiliated unions.[63] The preamble to the program of the new party summarized the central tenet of the Labor party:

> The Labor Party was organized to assemble into a new majority the men and women who work, but who have been scattered as helpless minorities in the old parties under the leadership of the confidence men of big business.
> . . . [T]hroughout the world the workers have reached the determination to reverse this condition and take control of their own lives and their own government.[64]

The organizers of the new party were careful not to antagonize the AFL leadership unnecessarily. Robert M. Buck, the editor of the CFL's newspaper, *The New Majority,* and a close friend and associate of Fitzpatrick and Nockels, declared that the party would not interfere with any of the union prerogatives so carefully guarded by the AFL. "The party scrupulously refrains from trying to dictate to the unions as to how they should run themselves. The Farmer-Labor Party has no theories for the conduct of the labor movement, nor any criticisms to make of the conduct of unions or union personnel. It is concerned only with the politics of labor."[65]

This cautiousness did not reassure Gompers, however. In 1920, Gompers acknowledged that the CFL was determined to pursue an independent political policy, but he added grimly that "it is to be hoped that we shall live at least until after the close of the coming campaign when we, too, may be in a position to compare notes as to who will have the excuses and the regrets to feel and express."[66] Fitzpatrick responded only that "the AFL is trying to scare everyone to death who dares to rise up and oppose its political ideas."[67]

The CFL set about mustering support for the new party within the state of Illinois. Federation leaders brought labor's 14 Points to the floor of the annual convention of the Illinois State Federation of Labor (ISFL) in December 1918. The president of the ISFL, John Walker, a leader of the miners' union, had long been a labor party supporter. He declared at the founding convention of the Labor party the next year that "it is almost fourteen years since I introduced a resolution in the . . . convention of the Illinois State Federation of Labor submitting the question of forming a labor party to the membership of the labor movement. I have never changed my views of it. I have always felt that the ordinary men who work every day have to be brought together before we can make progress."[68]

Support from Walker and others helped insure the passage of labor's 14 Points by the state labor federation. The convention also voted to hold a state-wide referendum on the question of forming a labor party based on the 14-point program. The results of the referendum were tabulated in March 1919, and they indicated overwhelming support for the new party. Two hundred forty-five affiliated unions voted for the formation of the Labor party, and only 25 unions opposed the new party. Of the voting unions that were not affiliated with the Illinois State Federation of Labor, 100 out of 112 favored the Labor party.[69] The miners' union in downstate Illinois provided particularly strong support for the new party.

Buoyed by these results, the Cook County Labor party entered the municipal elections in the spring of 1919, with Fitzpatrick running as the party's candidate for mayor of Chicago. Margaret Haley of the Chicago Teachers' Federation played an active role in the new party, serving on the Labor Party Executive Committee and helping to organize a Women's Campaign Committee.[70] Fitzpatrick and the other labor candidates spoke at union meetings across the city; on one occasion, Fitzpatrick addressed a mass meeting of over 5,000 needle trades workers on the need for independent political action.[71] Frequently, however, the Labor party candidates suffered rebuffs at the hands of union locals. The unions often had conservative leaderships that supported the AFL's nonpartisan policy and placed obstacles in the way of Labor party speakers when they appeared at local meetings.[72]

The results of the election were disappointing to the Labor party advocates. Fitzpatrick polled 54,467 votes, roughly 8 percent of the total cast, in the mayoralty election.[73] The Labor party made a better showing in the smaller towns and cities of downstate Illinois, where the coal-mining districts elected several Labor party candidates.[74]

The leaders of the Labor party declared that they intended to persevere and build their party in spite of the failure to make significant inroads against the candidates of the established parties. At the 1920 convention, the party changed its name to the Farmer-Labor party to try to attract some of the Populist voters who had previously been organized through the Non-Partisan League.*

The party's leaders decided in 1923 to try to expand the party's

---

*According to Robert Buck, editor of the CFL newspaper and a strong Labor party supporter, the original CFL founders of the party were not enthusiastic about the change. He wrote that "neither Fitzpatrick nor any of the rest of us were for a *Farmer*-Labor Party in 1918. We started a Labor Party" (Keiser, "John Fitzpatrick," p. 154).

membership base by once again making the kind of appeal to
the rank and file that had given the party its start. They sent
convention invitations to a large number of local unions, political groups, farmers' organizations, and local political parties.
They adopted this expedient in the hope of managing an end run
around the conservative AFL officials who had helped block the
party's success. The tactic proved disastrous, however, as it resulted in the attendance of a large number of determined representatives of the newly formed Workers' party, the American
branch of the Communist party, who ultimately split the convention into warring factions.

Fitzpatrick and Nockels at first welcomed the Workers' party
delegates because they were led by William Z. Foster, Fitzpatrick's close associate in the campaigns to organize the meatpacking and steel industries. Foster had won the respect of most
of the key figures in the Chicago labor movement for his unquestioned organizing ability. Fitzpatrick had gone to Foster's aid
earlier in 1923 when Foster had been arrested in Bridgeman,
Michigan, in a roundup of participants at a Communist party
convention. Gompers sent word to Fitzpatrick to have nothing to
do with Foster, but Fitzpatrick disregarded Gompers's warnings
and attended the trial in Michigan every day to indicate his
support.[75]

Even before the 1923 convention of the Farmer-Labor party
officially opened, however, Fitzpatrick and Nockels had begun to
have doubts about the participation of the Communists. These
doubts were increased when the Communists insisted on creden-
tialing and seating numerous delegates from such questionable
groups as the Workmen's Gymnastic Association, the Joint Conference of Lithuanian Societies, and various obscure "Workers'
Circles."[76] Too late, the Farmer-Labor representatives tried to regain control of their conference by moving that only representatives of the Farmer-Labor party itself and of trade unions and
city central bodies should be credentialed. This motion was defeated by the Workers' party forces, and from then on the Communists were in charge of the convention.[77]

The takeover by the Workers' party delegates caused a complete break in relations between them and the original Farmer-

Labor party supporters. Fitzpatrick denounced the Workers' party delegates on the floor of the convention, declaring that "the head of the Communist Party has no responsibility; I have responsibility for 500,000 working people."[78] Over the objections of the original Farmer-Labor party members, the Communists insisted on the immediate founding of a new party, the Federated Farmer-Labor party. Fitzpatrick declared that the Communists had taken control of the convention by "ruthless force" and said that Labor party advocates should not join in a party with any organization that was affiliated with the Third International or that "advocated other than lawful means to bring about political changes."[79]

The Workers' party takeover of the Farmer-Labor party resulted in the death of the labor party movement in a spirit of great bitterness and factionalism. Fitzpatrick viewed the takeover as an act of aggression that revealed the Communists' disdain for democratic procedures and political honesty. The Communists had been invited with the expectation that they would operate in accordance with the general guidelines laid down by the founders of the Farmer-Labor party, but they had instead proved that they were not "folks other folks could work with."[80] In later years, Fitzpatrick responded to any suggestion of association with groups that might contain Communists with the statement, "I was burned once."[81] He became lastingly bitter and far less eager to engage in innovative political programs as a result of his experience with the 1923 Farmer-Labor party convention.

The 1923 convention helped create a schism in the American labor movement that had long-term political consequences. From being considered legitimate left-wing adherents of the same cause by union leaders such as Fitzpatrick, the Communists came to be considered bitter enemies of established unionism.* The Chicago Federation of Labor had defied Gompers to

*The Communists gained little even in the short run, for the Federated Farmer-Labor party had no legitimacy in the eyes of the old supporters of the Labor party. So many of the original Farmer-Labor party members left immediately that a St. Louis labor paper ran the sarcastic headline, "Workers' Party Captures Itself and Adopts a New Name" (*St. Louis Labor*, quoted in Weinstein, *Decline of Socialism*, p. 285). The Federated Farmer-Labor party died a natural and unnoticed death a few years later.

pursue an independent political policy, only to have that policy fail in political factionalism and hostility.

The vulnerability of the CFL's position as a city central in opposition to the national AFL leadership now became more obvious. The CFL was in a particularly difficult position because the power of the city central federations was being gradually eroded within the American Federation of Labor at the very time that the CFL had moved into its period of most explicit opposition to Gompers. Gompers brought increasing pressure to bear to force the CFL into line with the AFL's avowedly non-partisan policy of rewarding its friends and punishing its enemies. Other city centrals had already capitulated under the weight of Gompers's displeasure; they were more vulnerable than dissenting national unions because their charters could be revoked at any time by the AFL's executive council. This particular vulnerability was reflected in the pattern of participation by city centrals in the Farmer-Labor party. A significant number of city centrals had participated in the party's founding convention in 1919, but their numbers had dropped sharply by the time of the 1920 convention.[82] The decline in the participation of the city centrals was much greater than that of the national or local union organizations. (Some city centrals, however, in addition to Chicago, braved Gompers's displeasure and remained active in the Farmer-Labor party until the Workers' party takeover in 1923; they included those from Detroit, Buffalo, Manhattan, and the Bronx.[83])

Fitzpatrick, although deeply disillusioned, did not immediately abandon his membership in the party. He paid dues until December 1923, and his wife paid dues until March 1924. But for all practical purposes, his experiment with third-party politics ended after the Workers' party takeover in July 1923.[84] Fitzpatrick came under increasing pressure from within both the Illinois State Federation of Labor and the Chicago Federation of Labor to sever all his links with the party in order to reinstate himself in the good graces of the AFL officialdom. This changed sentiment was reflected in the debate on independent electoral action at the 1923 convention of the Illinois State Federation of Labor. CFL representatives introduced a motion in support of independent political action, and John Walker, the former long-time supporter of a labor party, was joined by the relatively conservative secretary-treasurer of the state federation, Victor Olander, in opposing the motion.[85] William Z. Foster spoke as the main defender of the resolution, which did little to widen the base of support. The motion was defeated, and Fitzpatrick felt that few options remained to him other than acceptance of the AFL's political policies.

Fitzpatrick's move toward the AFL's "nonpartisan" stance was encouraged by his closest associates in the CFL. Robert M. Buck, a former city alderman and later the editor of the CFL newspaper, joined with other CFL leaders in a two-day conference with Fitzpatrick to persuade him that the risks of continuing to buck the AFL leadership were too great. The time was not propitious for a labor party movement, and the CFL could not sustain an independent party, given the decline in the union membership in the mid-1920s and the factionalism dividing the labor party adherents.[86] As Buck had been one of the most enthusiastic and committed labor party supporters, his switch to an opposition stance had a telling effect.

In 1924, Fitzpatrick reluctantly abandoned his efforts to create an independent party to voice labor's interests. Ironically, 1924 was the only year in which the AFL itself supported a third-party presidential candidate, Robert M. LaFollette. The LaFollette candidacy united the Socialists, the railway brotherhoods (who had been antagonized by federal policy toward them in the aftermath of the war), the Populists, and the supporters of the Conference for Progressive Political Action.[87] There are indications that the AFL's support reflected not a real shift in its nonpartisan policy but a desire to finally destroy the Farmer-Labor party, which LaFollette, in a complicated series of events, had repudiated.[88] The CFL leaders mustered no enthusiasm for LaFollette's campaign, which they felt to be a sorry shadow of a genuine labor party effort. Fitzpatrick gave only token support to the campaign, and Robert Buck wrote to him in September 1924 that "the only existing political movement that I believe in is the one that has been more or less gently put to sleep."[89]

The LaFollette candidacy won nearly 5,000,000 votes in spite of the AFL's withdrawal of all but symbolic support after he was nominated, but, as Fitzpatrick and Buck had predicted, the campaign did nothing to aid in the formation of a labor party. It marked, rather, the end of the era in which third-party politics had seemed to left-oriented labor leaders to be a viable alternative to the acquiescent "attack your enemies, reward your friends" politics of the AFL.[90]

Fitzpatrick was unwilling to contemplate leaving the AFL, but he found it difficult to make a partial capitulation to the official leadership. There was increasing pressure to conform in many areas besides the key one of which political party labor should support. The CFL's well-edited, lively, and iconoclastic newspaper, *The New Majority,* was taken over by a conservative editor under the name *The Federation News.* The new editor proclaimed that "such a labor publication would give poor service if it allowed use of its columns for matters of controversial nature instead of bringing members of various local unions into closer contact."[91] The newspaper was, of course, unable to avoid all issues "of a controversial nature," but it did focus on relatively routine events.

The trend toward suppression of dissident opinions within the AFL intensified when the Illinois State Federation of Labor issued a report in 1925 declaring that all union papers would have to follow the political line of the federation if they wanted official approval.[92] Top-down control over the expression of opinions, which later became a regular feature of union politics, was becoming institutionalized during the period of crackdown after the failure of the labor party movement. As part of the crackdown, the Federated Press, a national labor news service organized by CFL figures, underwent increasing political censorship and repression.

The final symbol of the AFL officialdom's supremacy over the progressive politics of the CFL came when Fitzpatrick was forced to resign from his position as a member of the labor coordinating committee of Brookwood Labor College in 1928. The AFL executive council had decided that Brookwood encouraged radical politics and dissident movements within unions, and on August 7, 1928, the AFL directed all affiliates to withdraw support from the labor college. Fitzpatrick resigned, although he told AFL president William Green that he was "deeply grieved on account of the way in which this matter was handled."[93]

Conclusions

The Chicago Federation of Labor had achieved organizational stability by the first decade of the 1900s. The city's labor movement had faced intense employer resistance, and attempts at union organizing had been punctuated by violence and repression. The strong opposition had helped create a labor movement with a militant tradition and a commitment to mass organizing. The CFL's attempt to build a labor party in the city foundered, however, and the labor federation, under strong pressure from the national AFL, returned to a policy of intermittent support for the established parties.

Chicago's social and political environment before the entrenchment of the Democratic party machine in the 1930s encouraged the creation of strong organizations to fight for group political interests. The lack of centralized control meant there was no central mediating agency to resolve conflicts between contending groups. The educational system became a particular focus of conflict in this setting. Conflicts over the schools were not routinized, nor did they occur behind the scenes. Instead, as the city struggled to create an educational infrastructure for the rapidly expanding population, basic questions of the control and direction of the schools remained unresolved and created bitter controversies that in themselves had lasting impacts on the way each of the participants viewed educational matters. It is now time to consider the nature of the educational controversies that galvanized labor and business involvement in the years before World War I.

3 | CONFLICTS OVER THE CONTENT OF SCHOOLING

In nineteen hundred two, the Chicago Federation of Labor, in its earliest full statement on educational questions, challenged the idea that the children of working people should receive a different education from the children of the wealthy. While conservative newspapers and businessmen mounted a campaign to remove "fads and frills" from the public schools, the Chicago Federation of Labor charged that the rich, in fact, highly valued the very subjects that they denounced as fads when introduced into the public schools. A CFL report claimed that "the wealthy delight in teaching their children music, art and languages; they send them abroad that they may peep into those art galleries where repose the masterpieces of the world." The students were then "put under the tuition of the musical masters of Europe" and when they returned to the United States, "their parents and the public press acclaimed their varied accomplishments."[1] Working-class students, meanwhile, found that classes in music, art, and foreign languages evoked hostility from businessmen when taught as a basic part of the public school curriculum. The CFL announced its regret that studies such as drawing and music, "which are looked upon as desirable accomplishments in any person, should be denounced as fads for no other apparent reason than that they are taught your children in our public schools."[2]

This early controversy prefigured an extended political battle between the labor movement and the major employers' groups in Chicago over the scope of education for working-class children. Many other conflicts flowed from this dispute, such as those in the 1920s over the use of IQ tests, the introduction of junior high schools, and the development of tracking systems. In the years when the Chicago Federation of Labor stood as a progressive labor organization, it consistently and repeatedly argued that the children of workers should receive a broad liberal education.

Equally consistently, the employers' organizations pressed programs that were intended to provide training in the three R's and specific skills. The conflict began in the late 1800s, gained momentum during the first decade of the 1900s, and became one of the critical issues of Chicago politics in the years from 1913 to the mid-1920s. The leading educational advocates from both the labor movement and the employers' groups developed considerable sophistication on educational issues after years of debate, and the controversy thus took on a generality and a marked class character that otherwise might not have appeared so overtly.

The initial debate began in the 1890s in the period when Chicago was beginning its extraordinarily rapid growth as an industrial and merchandising center. The school system grew very rapidly, even though in the early years many immigrant children attended school only sporadically and for brief periods. This growth led to efforts to change the basic character of public education. In the early history of the city, the schools above the elementary level had been designed for the children of the well-to-do and the middle classes. The curriculum at the high school levels retained a classical flavor (although Greek had been dropped as a required course), and high schools were geared toward students who planned to enter college. As the school system grew to more than 200,000 pupils in 1896, however, demands increased for the creation of a curriculum suited to the needs of those who were not college bound.[3]

There was general acknowledgment that the school system would have to change as its role shifted from that of an elite training center to that of mass agent of education for hundreds of thousands of children, many of whom spoke little or no English. But the direction of change was unclear, and there were those who spoke in defense of the notion of the high school as the preserve of the college-bound academic elite. The response of most business organizations in Chicago to the influx of working-class students was to stress the need for increased manual training. College preparatory programs, they reasoned, would be worthless for the vast majority of working-class children, while manual training would prepare students for useful occupations.

A generally unspoken but simultaneous belief was that training students in industrial skills would help undercut the power of craft unions to determine occupational entry. The leading Chicago businessmen were not alone in their view that manual training would provide the answer to the changing needs of the school system. A nation-wide move toward manual training programs began after 1870. Taking Germany as their inspiration, educators acclaimed the worker satisfaction and social efficiency that followed from properly directed manual training programs in the schools.

The initial attempts to establish manual training schools in Chicago were privately financed by businessmen. Civic activists among Chicago's business leaders had long regretted the fact that Marshall Field, the department-store owner and one of the richest and most powerful men in the city, was rarely outspoken in support of new projects. In the case of manual training, however, Field took the initiative in proposing and financing a technical school. In 1882 he was bestirred to give a rare speech at the Commercial Club, of which he was a founding member, in support of the establishment of the Chicago Manual Training School. Field started the subscription list with $20,000, and other club members raised $110,000.[4] The club's later president, John B. Drake, was particularly active in encouraging the proposal. Marshall Field, Richard Crane, and John Crerar, all among the key business leaders of the city, each served on the board of the new school.[5] In 1896, the school was turned over to the University of Chicago to operate, and in 1904 it became part of the university high school.[6]

The Commercial Club pursued several other ventures in direct sponsorship of manual training schools in the years around the turn of the century. Club members established a $100,000 fund for the Illinois Manual Training School at Glenwood, $50,000 of it in cash and $50,000 in a trust fund. The club also donated $100,000 to buy a site for the St. Charles School for Boys, designed to rehabilitate young delinquents and fit them for a useful role in society.[7]

Marshall Field had the fixed idea that education should not be excessively intellectual because it would detract from the young's ability to work with concentration and dedication. He deplored the quality of the workers turned out by the city's public schools, maintaining that it was difficult for his firm to find qualified employees.[8] Unlike some other business leaders, however, his belief that intellectual education only encouraged dilatoriness applied to the children of the well-to-do as well as to the children of the working class. He represented the generation of aggressive entrepreneurs who had risen to the top by their own efforts, and he had little use for highly trained college graduates who did not possess what he believed to be the necessary drive and single-minded business focus.

> In later years [Field] never regretted that he missed a college education, for he suspected that such advantages spoiled young men for business. "The truth is," he declared, "that for most young men a college education means that just at the time when they should be having business principles instilled into them, and be getting themselves energetically pulled together for their life's work, they are sent to college. Then intervenes what many a young man looks upon as the jolliest time of his life. . . . Often when he comes out of college the young man is unfitted by this good time to buckle down to hard work, and the result is a failure to grasp opportunities that would have opened the way for a successful career."[9]

Other business leaders, however, stated their belief that humanity could be divided into two divisions—those who could profit by general academic studies and those who were suited to engage in practical work. The Merchants' Club of Chicago, an organization of major business leaders that was founded in 1896 and merged with the Commercial Club in 1907, sponsored a discussion on commercial high schools in February 1901. The speakers at this meeting primarily addressed the issue of why manual training should be introduced into the city's schools with the maximum speed. Professor Jeremiah W. Jencks of Cornell University was brought to Chicago for the occasion because the club's executive committee felt that it "lacked experience and wisdom which we would have to seek from the outside."[10] Professor Jencks set out to answer the question, "What can the public schools, as a whole, lower grades as well as higher, do to prepare the boys and girls for the duties of citizenship? Particularly, how can the schools aid them to earn an honest living?"[11]

Jencks answered this question by asserting that the schools would have to begin playing a different role in American society. Jencks explained that workingmen often suffered from unemployment because they lacked the adaptable skills required to switch jobs as economic conditions changed. With machinery occupying an increasingly important place in industry, workingmen would have the potential opportunity to rise if they were not ignorant. The schools were defaulting on their responsibilities by not training children in manual skills and not supplying the necessary character reinforcement to encourage workers to give their best to each job. He commented regretfully that working-class parents often seemed uninterested in the proper development of character: "My impression is, so far as the parents of children in the public schools are concerned, that their ideals are often limited by their environment, and that lofty conceptions of noble character play little part."[12]

Even abandoning the idea of elevated character training, however, the schools could still do much more to train children to fill occupations in the real world. Jencks detailed the failings of the schools in this regard:

> What, as a matter of fact, along all these lines do our schools accomplish? Do they give skill to the workingman so that he can do his work better? Of the hand training, they give practically nothing. For the work done by clerks in our stores they do very little. . . . Speaking generally, our public schools, with the exception of some few in our cities, do almost nothing in the way of developing the skill the workingman needs.[13]

Jencks's answer to the problem posed by the role of the school in industrial society was that instead of having manual training tacked on to academic subjects, "you would start with manual training, and the other subjects would fall into place as necessary parts of it."[14] Only in this way could the schools genuinely aid the industrial development of the country and simultaneously benefit the future working people by providing them with the skills they would need to earn their living.

Jencks concluded his lecture with a cautionary note. He had suggested that individual workingmen might be able to rise if they were educated in the right manner, but he did not want to imply that this would be possible for the bulk of humanity. The sad fact was that intelligence was unequally distributed:

> We ought not to expect too much from our public schools.
> We ought to realize the fact that while all people can be im-
> proved, still not many people can make a great industrial
> success. The schools cannot furnish brains, and a very large
> proportion—I will not put it in that way—and a great
> many people in the community have not the ability, and can
> never get the ability to be very successful in business
> life.[15]

This perception of the unequal distribution of intelligence was reinforced by the next speaker, the superintendent of the Chicago public schools, Edwin G. Cooley. Cooley played a critical role in conflicts over public education in Chicago, and, in fact, the vocational training bill that excited years of controversy bore his name. His views will be elaborated at more length later, but here it is important to note that he shared the general view of education held by Professor Jencks. The development of society required a shift from academic subjects to manual training in the schools; students should not be trained in specific skills, however, because these could become rapidly obsolete. Rather, the schools should teach "the fundamental elements of all trades." All students must be reached because "the individuals who are not educated to grow in the direction along which society is moving will soon be left behind, and will join the great class of misfits who burden society at the present time."[16]

Cooley noted approvingly the shift from abstract, academic subjects in the high schools to subjects with a practical application. The process had not gone far enough yet, however, and manual training and business subjects had not reached far enough down in the elementary school. The schools, by their failure to truly develop these subjects, were unfairly discriminating against children with a practical turn of mind. These students made up the vast majority of the student body and came disproportionately from the working classes. The interest of working-class students in practical matters should not be surprising "when we remember that 90 per cent of the human race are men and women engaged in manual labor." For these children, "heredity would seem to make it certain that a large proportion . . . go to school with impulses and interests mainly of a practical nature." It was the task of the educator to capitalize on the "special type of mentality" of such children by developing a form of education that combined motor activities with special training in citizenship.[17]

Cooley explained that the reason so many of these children had "motor classes of mind" was that "intelligence was a variation in the life history of animals selected on account of its special fitness to aid in the struggle for existence." People engaged in manual activity had no reason to need an abstract form of intelligence, and thus this faculty had never been fully developed in the great bulk of humanity. By sheer genetics principles alone, then, it seemed clear that the schools would have to shift their focus from academic to practical subjects.[18]

The president of the Merchants' Club had introduced Cooley with the remark that his views carried great weight. "Our superintendent has of himself what you might call the commendatory power; and his recommendations made to this Club, if they appeal to our good sense, impose upon us a responsibility that we, as businessmen, must recognize."[19] The businessmen of Chicago ultimately did accept Cooley's recommendations, and this led to years of controversy in the next decade.

In the meantime, however, the intensive battle over vocational education had not yet begun; instead, labor and conservative interests were involved in a conflict over "fads and frills" in the schools that was a small-scale forerunner of the later vocational education controversy. In 1893, the conservative newspapers of the city had mounted an attack on the "fads and frills" of the public school curriculum.[20] For nearly half a year, the issue was a source of controversy in the press, in civic associations, and in public meetings. The *Chicago Tribune* was the most vituperative; in one year it published 30 editorials critical of the waste of public money on frivolous subjects.[21] During the 1893 mayoralty election, the *Tribune* interjected the fads as a political issue, criticizing the Democrats and their candidate.

The conservative outcry against the fads stemmed from a number of roots. On the one hand, the opponents of the fads branded the teaching of all foreign languages as frivolous and unwarranted. This was a way of striking against the power of the Germans in the city. In 1865 German had been introduced into the six upper grades as a means of trying to encourage German-speaking residents to keep their children in the public schools.[22] Throughout the early 1890s the newspapers intermittently criticized the teaching of German.[23] The school board responded to this pressure in April 1893 when it abolished German in the elementary grades but continued it in the upper grades.[24]

The campaign against "fads" was not limited to attacks on foreign-language teaching. The *Tribune* was equally vituperative in denouncing singing, drawing, nature study, clay modeling, and physical education. Arguing that the schools were already too expensive, the *Tribune* demanded the narrowing of the curriculum to the three R's. One Chicago newspaper, the *Record,* estimated the cost of the curricular "fads" as a million dollars a year.[25]

The Trades and Labor Assembly, the forerunner of the Chicago Federation of Labor, defended all the special subjects and said that if they were taught in schools for the children of the rich, they should be taught in the public schools.[26] One self-described "ardent faddist," Tom Morgan, spoke to Chicago Socialists in appealing for labor support. He said that the children of workingmen were just as much "entitled to study music, Delsartes, physical culture . . . as the children of Phil Armour, Allerton, and countless others." The *Tribune* responded to arguments that the narrowing of the curriculum would be unfair to working-class children with the comment that such theories would compel "sending to college all the children of working men" who wanted to go.[27]

During the late 1890s public controversy over a broadened curriculum diminished, although the issue occasioned debate into the early 1900s. At the Merchants' Club meeting in 1901 where Jencks and Cooley spoke, the third speaker was John G. Shedd, the first president of the Chicago Association of Commerce. Shedd declared that the issue of teaching fads and frills in the public schools had been somewhat misconceived. He explained: "I don't think that fads are objected to, so long as they do not interfere with the ordinary education of the masses. But when we come to apply fads, we try to apply them to ninety-five per cent of those who are neither prepared for them nor desire them. Then, I think, we are making a mistake in letting the fads occupy the principal part of the curriculum of our public schools."[28]

In 1893, the school board compromised on the teaching of the special subjects. Drawing would be dropped from the first grade and reduced in the second and third grades; there would be less singing; and clay modeling would be allowed only in kindergarten and for deaf mutes. Physical education would still be taught, but by regular and not by specially trained teachers.[29]

The labor organizations of the city resented the attack on the "fads and frills," claiming that the calls for economy and the slashing of the curriculum had stemmed from a desire to educate the children of the workers as cheaply as possible. The conflict moved from the issue of what would be taught to how it would be taught. The old style of pedagogy had relied heavily on the memorization of facts. Partly under the influence of educational reformer Col. Francis Parker, the schools had begun to introduce methods of teaching that called more upon the children's overall understanding. When the new teaching methods came under attack, the newly formed Chicago Federation of Labor requested its legislative committee to report on the teaching practices in the city's public schools.

In 1902, after several weeks of "earnest investigation," the committee produced its report, *A Report on Public School Fads*. When the report was presented to the federation, it was unanimously endorsed by the 350 delegates present, and 10,000 copies were printed and distributed throughout the city.

The report is written in the style of working people who themselves have not had extensive education. The committee visited numerous classrooms throughout the city where it had "been represented that fads detrimental to the best interests of society flourished in our schools."[30] The committee members observed the practices in each classroom they visited, and they were generally very favorably impressed with the teaching methods and the responses of the pupils. They found that the children acted in a relaxed, natural, and intelligent fashion and were encouraged to draw upon their own experiences. In a first-grade class

> a pupil was told to carry out instructions given by the teacher, and other pupils were asked to describe the act, giving details. This was done very cleverly; the pupils describing the color of the eyes and the clothing of the subject of the description. Many other examples of the experience of the children were related by themselves, which indicated that the pupils have as clear a grasp of the English language as is seldom met with among children of the tender ages of six and eight years.[31]

The committee noted the fact that a third-grade teacher, Miss May Solke, wrote "Wheat belongs to a family of grasses" on the board and then asked the students to write their ideas on wheat. They "did so fairly well. One young fellow gave as his view that 'some wheat belongs to the farmers.'"[32]

The committee looked briefly into a German class, but, "your committee not being able to speak German," passed on to another room. They thoroughly approved of the manner in which drawing was taught. At the Medill school, "the drawing department disclosed remarkable opportunities for developing the tastes for mechanical and artistic drawing. It gives the pupil, the teacher and parents an opportunity to readily discover any special ability that a given scholar may have in those directions, without which many a splendid chance now in the grasp of the children of the masses would be forever lost." The students showed "pleasure, knowledge and interest" in the drawing classes. The committee members had some doubts about the actual drawings created by the students; they remarked dubiously that "some children [were] apparently partial to glaring colors, others color blind," but hastened to add that "the standard of drawing should not be measured by the work of the beginners" and that the children's enjoyment resulting from this study "compensates for the work."[33]

Leaving the art field, the committee paid special attention to the visualization method of teaching, which had been criticized as a faddish innovation. In the visualization method, instead of having students memorize sections of books, pupils were asked to carry out simple specific actions when requests were written on the board. There was also a concentration on developing powers of oral description and mental arithmetic. The committee found the method effective and desirable and said it was particularly appropriate in classes where there were pupils who could not speak English, as the teacher could more easily "compose and supply appropriate selections" than could a book compiler. In fact, the committee concluded, the visualization method "reflects great credit upon those who first perceived the advantages to be derived."[34]

In its general conclusions, the committee rejected the claims that the public schools were being weakened and destroyed by faddish teaching methods and concentration on frivolous subjects. Rather, "there was remarkable quickness in seeing and doing." Students in the new classrooms were not overtaxed, yet

> in written expression of thought the pupils showed great power and gave evidence that the work was not mechanical but mental, the outgrowth of thinking. Reading, writing and spelling are taught simultaneously, so that the child writes every word it reads, and, of course, in writing spells the word. This is the method we saw employed, and when contrasted with the old medieval system its superiority is beyond successful dispute.

The committee pointed out that "we do not name the letters to an infant learning spoken language; we boldly permit it to hear the expression of thoughts." Surely, the committee suggested, it is not incredible "that a similar process might result to advantage in learning written and printed language, or reading." But even if the new teaching methods had not been demonstrably superior, the report went on, "its spirit and aim would still have deserved commendation."[35] The committee was impressed by the children's pleasure in activity, their mutual helpfulness, their courtesy, and their persistence in working out problems. The methods were in harmony with the children's natural interests, and, above all, the children were being taught to think instead of merely to recite.[36]

Why, then, the committee inquired, had the new methods aroused such a storm of controversy, since the children were both learning well and enjoying their schooling? The committee answered its own question by observing that "no reform was ever effected without the cry that it was visionary, expensive, impracticable and delusive."[37] The rich felt free to denounce "fads" in the public schools because their own children were safely enrolled in exclusive private schools. "The rich may place their children where they will and thus secure immunity from the effects of Gradgrind methods." The opinion of the rich, reinforced by the "frothings of prejudiced critics," should be ignored. Persons who sent their children to private schools "should not for a moment be permitted to put the weight of a straw in the way of the public school and its enlightened methods." The labor movement had to be organized to resist the influence of the privileged minority on the school board.[38]

The public schools were not perfect, and the school board wasted large sums of money on the payment of political obligations, but working people should support the extension of public education, the report concluded. The real disgrace of the public schools was that so many children were required to leave school to go to work; the report estimated that 50 percent of all children between the ages of 10 and 12 left school to enter the factory or workshop.[39] This was "the saddest of all commentaries that can be made upon our industrial system."[40] The state "should forever destroy the institution of child labor by passing and enforcing such laws as will keep in school every child until he has graduated from the highest grade." The schools, furthermore, should be organized in such a way that expenses to hard-pressed parents were minimized. "Writing can be taught without putting parents to the expense of buying several copy books in nearly every grade. Sheets of plain white paper are better and much cheaper." Similarly, spelling books were an unnecessary expense because "words should appear in their proper relation in sentences"; they could be taken from newspapers and written on the board. And drawing books were both costly and harmful because children should draw from their own observation rather than copying pictures. But, although wary of unnecessary expenses and acknowledging that the school system wasted money in bribes and kickbacks, working-class parents would not object to increased educational taxation "if honestly applied to the purposes for which it [had] been obtained. Taxes levied for education are the most righteous and best investment the public is called upon to make."[41]

This report contains the earliest full statement of the Chicago labor movement on public education. The positions it outlined were to be more fully developed in subsequent years, but the general principles remained the same. The organized labor groups in Chicago consistently supported increased taxation for the public schools, the shift to more child-centered teaching methods, and the teaching of a wide range of subjects. The extent of labor's commitment to these principles was put to the test in the second decade of the 1900s when several business groups in Chicago combined to present a vocational education bill that would indeed have stripped those schools attended by working-class children of all "fads and frills."

The Vocational Education Controversy

Organized labor, both nationally and locally, generally supported the idea of vocational education but was uneasy about the form such education might take. There were two main sources of concern: the first was that the vocational training might be intended to produce skilled workers who would then undercut the apprentice programs of the craft unions. The public schools would become "scab hatcheries" by producing a ready reserve of skilled labor with no union ties. The second source of concern was that the vocational program would squeeze out academic studies and working-class children would receive a narrow training for specific occupations. In Chicago, both fears were intensified because the main business organizations of the city proposed a vocational education plan that would have created a dual school system under completely separate direction from the academic public schools. The battle over the vocational education plan became one of the most bitter in Chicago politics, and it left the labor movement with a greatly heightened sensitivity to what it perceived as businessmen's attempts to manipulate the public schools to their advantage.

Business organizations presented the Cooley vocational education plan to the state legislature in 1913, 1915, and 1917, and each year the legislature defeated it. The business groups finally decided not to reintroduce it after the 1917 defeat, both because the federal government had passed a different vocational education program (the Smith-Hughes Act) and because the emotions aroused in Chicago by the plan had become so intense that the businessmen ultimately decided it would be wisest to let the issue drop. In the four years of controversy, the issue had become "a sharp focus of class antagonism."[42]

Chicago trade unionists had long supported the introduction of vocational education into the schools, but only in a limited and controlled manner. The 1902 *Report on Public School Fads* had advocated manual training as an addition to the school program.[43] Such studies were to be introduced in conjunction with the overall academic courses. In the fall of 1908, the Chicago Federation of Labor approached the board of education and offered to form an advisory committee to aid in the establishment of an industrial and commercial education program. The offer was rejected, but in January 1909 the CFL joined the Association of Commerce and the Industrial Club of Chicago in establishing a vocational education committee to advise the board.[44] The Chicago school system had grown so large that private business experiments in founding manual training schools could only reach a tiny fraction of the students, and business had shifted its efforts to persuading the school system as a whole to adopt vocational education programs. Labor and business cooperation did not seem intrinsically impossible: both sides had expressed an interest in supporting vocational education.

In the next few years, however, it became apparent that labor and business organizations had very different intentions regarding the establishment of vocational education as part of the public school system. Business groups developed a clear and specific conception of the type of vocational education they had in mind, and labor organizations were appalled by the business proposals.

The key figure in crystallizing Chicago business leaders' conceptions of vocational education was Edwin G. Cooley, who was superintendent of Chicago's schools from 1900 to 1909. Cooley originally came from a small town in eastern Iowa, Strawberry Point, and he was largely self-educated. He worked his way up to being a principal at LaGrange, Indiana, and then decided to try to get a degree at the University of Chicago. Although Cooley had had no formal college education, he was granted three years' credit for what he had taught himself.[45] While completing his degree at the University of Chicago, Cooley became known to Chicago educators as an energetic and efficient administrator and, in a surprise move, was offered the city school superintendency when his predecessor resigned after having antagonized the board of education.

Cooley attempted to restructure the Chicago school system according to principles of business efficiency. (The particular reorganization policies he adopted and the reaction of the teaching staff and labor movement will be considered in chapter 4.) Although he had close ties to business organizations, Cooley believed that he was above political considerations and that the school system could be administered in an entirely efficient and neutral manner. In October 1901 he wrote to William Rainey Harper, president of the University of Chicago and a powerful figure in the city's educational circles, that he was astonished and shocked that a Mr. Melton should have accused him of bowing to politics. He wrote that he was sure that Mr. Melton was "as you say, a man of no weight. Some of the charges he makes, however, touch me to the quick, especially when he accuses me of 'playing politics.' I am ready to admit that I have made mistakes. I am ready to admit almost anything, in fact, except that charge."[46]

Cooley left the superintendency in 1909 after a series of conflicts with the school system's unionized teaching staff and with the board of education. He accepted employment with a school textbook company and remained in that position for two years until the Commercial Club of Chicago hired him as its educational advisor in 1911. Business groups in Chicago had often expressed their respect for Cooley's work as superintendent.[47] Cooley was so highly regarded by the Commercial Club that in 1912 one of its leading members, Theodore W. Robinson, who was also the head of the club's education committee, stated that Cooley had full authorization to speak for the club on all educational matters: "Please let it be understood that Mr. Cooley in his educational efforts is The Commercial Club, and when he goes out to speak and when he writes on matters concerning our problem, it is The Commercial Club that is speaking or writing."[48]

The Commercial Club did more than simply provide Mr. Cooley with a forum; it provided the organizational support to try to bring about full implementation of his programs. The Commercial Club was the most powerful and most selective of Chicago's business organizations. The criterion for membership was "conspicuous success in one's private business," and membership was limited to the 60 or so most important financiers, merchants, and industrialists in the city. The Merchants' Club of Chicago merged with the Commercial Club in 1907, and the merged club took the leading role among the city's business institutions.[49] The Commercial Club's two chief projects during its most active years (the period from about 1910 to the 1920s) were the passage of its vocational education bill and the formulation and implementation of a plan to drastically restructure the city's downtown business district. The club often invited key business figures to speak at its forums, and the records of its closed meetings provide insights into the views of some of the nation's major business figures on such issues as government regulation of trusts, the effect of wartime controls on companies' ability to resist unionization, and business influence on government policy makers.

The Commercial Club became the chief promoter of a plan to reorganize the public schools to make them more vocational, but other business groups had also indicated their interest in developing a vocational education system. In 1909, the Chicago Association of Commerce had published a report on *Industrial and Commercial Education in Relation to Conditions in the City of Chicago*. The Association of Commerce, formed in 1904, was by far the largest of the city's business organizations, but it was less influential than the Commercial Club because its membership was not limited to the city's industrial and financial giants.[50]

The Association of Commerce report stressed that liberal education was no longer adequate to meet the needs of an industrial society. Vocational training was necessary to provide a skilled work force, as there was "no doubt that the type of 'liberal education' in vogue for a century is inadequate to meet the just demands of society for an education that trains for 'social efficiency.'"[51] This theme of "social efficiency" was to become increasingly prominent in the writings of businessmen and educators in the next decade. The report opened by stressing that a key aspect of education was equipping the individual to get the most out of life, but some of the specific occupational suggestions it offered were not likely to strike the average worker as being particularly fulfilling. The report emphasized that vocational education should cover girls as well as boys, and suggested that girls be trained for "high-grade domestic service."

> Many believe that in the last named branch of education
> lies the reasonable hope of material social betterment,
> in raising domestic service more nearly to the rank of a
> profession, and in the training to the arts of home making
> not only those who must maintain themselves but those
> who will become the wives of wage earners. The very fact of
> placing Domestic Science in the course of study gives it
> dignity.[52]

The purpose of education, the report declared, was not only to equip the individual to get the most out of life and to achieve maximum social efficiency, but also to train children in the proper civic duties. The school would have to teach future wage earners that they could satisfy the "rightful demands of the state" by being "intelligent, moral, and patriotic." The students would have to be taught the necessity for "a dominant class of men and women in whose hands the state will be safe."[53]

Part of the impetus for the spate of vocational education plans generated during this period may have been the shortage of skilled labor in the city. The City Club, with its usual fondness for gathering data, surveyed 181 Chicago employers with 111,606 employees in 1912 to ascertain whether they had trouble hiring skilled workers. The club found that three-fourths of the employers, 74.7 percent, reported difficulty in hiring sufficient numbers of these employees.[54] It was expensive and difficult for employers to bear training costs by themselves, and the shortage of skilled workers also rendered the employers vulnerable to pressures from craft unions. If the schools could take on the training of skilled workers, or at least lay the basis for later refinement of industrial skills, this socialization of part of labor costs would be a major benefit to employers. Reorienting the schools toward vocational education could also insure that those who entered manual work, whether skilled or unskilled, would not be exposed to a type of education that would make them skeptical of industrial labor or of management control of the work process.

The Commercial Club was the organization in Chicago most capable of devising and implementing long-range programs. Its plan for remodeling the city's downtown area was accepted by the City Council and implemented at a cost of millions of dollars and years of labor. The club was self-consciously aware of its role as the initiator of long-range business programs. Its meetings were noteworthy for the range of subjects discussed and the breadth of focus of the participants. While the Association of Commerce made only fitful efforts to carry through vocational education programs, the Commercial Club determined to reorganize the Chicago public school system fundamentally and devoted years to achieving this goal. Its eventual failure was due to the intensity of opposition that the sweeping plan aroused from labor and, ultimately, from middle-class civic organizations.

The Commercial Club engaged Edwin Cooley to tour Europe and prepare a comprehensive report on European systems of vocational education. Cooley spent months visiting schools in

Austria, Switzerland, England, Scotland, and, most particularly, Germany.[55] The club had expected that Cooley would return with concrete suggestions for reforming Chicago education based upon his European observations. Cooley did not disappoint them. The schools of Germany had particularly impressed him, and he returned with several fixed principles of school organization in mind. The key point, in his view, was that vocational schools would have to be administered separately from academic schools. Vocational schools would have to be closely connected with industry if they were to serve their purpose, and therefore such schools should be governed by boards composed of "practical men."[56] Cooley did not consider educators practical men.

Cooley's belief that the schools would have to develop practical, business-oriented curricula was not a product of his European tour, however; it was a conviction he had already expressed during his superintendency of the Chicago public schools. In September 1906 he gave a speech on "Public School Education in Morals" that prefigured his later enthusiasm for vocational education, although at the time he did not offer a concrete plan for the development of manual training.[57] The speech lamented the decline in moral standards in the business and political worlds, as well as in society at large. The schools would have to play an important role in the revitalization of moral standards. This could only be done, however, if the schools had a vocational thrust, because working-class students were not interested in academic subjects. Cooley stressed that the real goals of education should not be intellectual but moral: "We must realize from the start in our educational efforts that the moral reformation of the child is of more importance than the sharpening of his intellect." But it was "clear to all thoughtful men of to-day that we must broader our notion of education if we expect the school to be really effective in preventing wrong-doing."[58] The "old-fashioned curriculum of the three R's" would not enable the school to fulfill its function as a moral instrument, and it should therefore be altered to include vocational subjects.[59]

Cooley's notion of moral virtues was highly practical. The prime virtue to be inculcated was industry. In dealing with children as well as with savages, industry had to be the basis of all other virtues.

Industry is the one fundamental virtue that the wise reformer has always insisted upon in his efforts at raising the
savage to a higher plane. In dealing with the moral, intellectual, and social conditions of the inferior races, the
statesman of to-day tries to approach them from a practical
point of view and to induce them or to compel them to
form habits of industry. Slavery was wrong, but whatever
else it did or did not do, it compelled the acquisition of
habits of industry in the slave and marked a step in advance
over the previous condition of savagery.[60]

The labor movement was not likely to find this analogy encouraging.

The other two virtues that Cooley stressed were punctuality
and obedience. These, in combination with industry, "form the
basis of good moral character," although Cooley acknowledged
that "these virtues are not placed very high in the hierarchy
of the moralist."[61] Punctuality was worth more to the child than
spelling, and "the school by insisting on this virtue is doing
much to suppress a certain kind of selfishness and waste that
seems to be inseparable from the man or woman who refuses to
conform to time regulations."[62] Obedience, Cooley noted, seemed
to be "somewhat in disfavor" in American democracy where "we
spend so much energy shouting for liberty," but it nonetheless
formed the basis of civilization. The savage reappears as an example of the consequences of the lack of this virtue, as savages
follow "mere lawless impulse." Cooley recommended that the
schools "be given the right to use such coercive influences as are
absolutely necessary to secure obedience."[63]

The virtues cited by Cooley correspond to those valued by
businessmen to a remarkable degree. It is not surprising that
the Commercial Club should have sought Cooley's advice on how
to reorganize the school system to encourage more fully the development of these traits in the students.

The specific vocational education plan developed by Cooley
and adopted by the Commercial Club called for regular common
schooling for all children up to the age of 14. At 14, children
would either go to work or continue in an academic program.
Children who worked would be required to attend "continuation
schools," which would be entirely vocational in orientation. The

children would hold regular jobs but would be released for a certain number of hours each week to attend the continuation schools. The Commercial Club defined vocational education as "all forms of specialized education, the controlling purposes of which are to fit for useful occupations, whether in agriculture, commerce, industry or the household arts."[64] The vocational schools would be administered by a specially constituted State Board of Vocational Education to be composed of two employers, two skilled employees, two farmers, one person "who has made a special study of women's work," and one educator. The state superintendent of public instruction would be an *ex officio* member of the board. The Commercial Club stressed that it was essential for the vocational schools to be administered separately from the regular public schools.

> An efficient system of vocational education requires different methods of administration, different courses of study, different qualifications of teachers, different equipment, different ways of meeting the needs of pupils and much greater flexibility in adapting means to ends than is possible under the ordinary system of public school administration. For these reasons these schools should be under a separate board of control . . . so that they may be free to realize their dominant purpose of fitting for useful employment.[65]

In its promotional pamphlets and in private club discussions, the Commercial Club primarily stressed the gains in individual and social efficiency that would accrue from the schools. Cooley's elaborate justifications of vocational education as a means of promoting moral worthiness did not meet with disfavor from Commercial Club members—on the contrary—but in their own writings, social efficiency was more frequently presented as a rationale. They or their invited guests frequently argued that although the United States had won economic preeminence through use of its abundant resources the nations of Europe were catching up through the more efficient utilization of their labor force. The days when the United States could afford to be wasteful had passed, and if the country were to maintain its economic position, it would have to have state help in training skilled workers.

Theodore W. Robinson, first vice president of the Illinois Steel Company, attended the 1910 annual convention of the National Education Association (NEA) as the Commercial Club's representative, and at the order of the club's executive committee, his speech at the NEA meeting was printed in pamphlet form for distribution among the club members. Robinson declared: "This country has been sleeping a self-complacent sleep of confidence, born of stupendous resources. Meanwhile, old nations, like Germany, are rapidly becoming new by industrial education, while our new world will become old unless we awake."[66] If the earning power of each individual could be raised by only ten cents a day—a reasonable goal, Robinson thought—the gain in social efficiency would save the country nearly a billion dollars a year, sufficient to pay off the national debt. The educational system should be geared to producing "the highest type of manhood and womanhood," but to accomplish this purpose, "reasonable individual efficiency, as determined by reasonable individual earning power, must be attained."[67]

In another speech delivered three years later to the American Steel Institute, Robinson was still more explicit about the international competition faced by the United States. He declared:

> There is perhaps no greater object lesson of the possibilities of vocational training than the phenomenal industrial advance of Germany during the last generation. . . . This has been accomplished primarily because forty years ago German statesmen were sufficiently farsighted and progressive to inaugurate the comprehensive system of vocational education by which the German youth acquire a better training for their life's work than the youth of any other nation.[68]

In contrast, the United States had lagged far behind in the development of an educational system that could contribute to industrial efficiency. "The United States, of all great nations, is the most deficient in caring for the vocational education of its people."[69] The need was so pressing that Robinson believed that "vocational education is not a passing social expedient, but one of our most far-reaching national questions."[70]

The Commercial Club continued its exploration of the issues surrounding vocational education by inviting George L. Vincent, president of the University of Minnesota, to address the club on the subject of "Education for National Efficiency." Vincent explained that, with the closing of the frontier, the new social watchword had to be efficient use of resources. Labor power was a prime resource that had to be fully developed and appropriately used. The nation would have to learn to "put value on expert knowledge and specialized skill. We must train our children for places in a well-organized and highly efficient national mechanism."[71] The days had passed when "America spelled Opportunity in capital letters." Instead, it was "Efficiency" that was "being put in italics, if not capitals."[72] Individual workingmen no longer had much prospect of advancing Horatio Alger-style; rather, the nation would have to concentrate on increasing the efficiency of each of its constituent units—the factories, the railways, the city governments, and the nation itself as a competing unit in the world system. In this way, individual workers would receive their just reward for increased efficiency through the preeminent place gained by the group as a whole.

Even Cooley altered the stress of his rationale for vocational education in a pamphlet that he wrote for publication by the Commercial Club. In 1914, the Commercial Club published Cooley's *Need for Vocational Schools in the United States*, in which the author argued that the nation needed a new system of vocational schools because workers were not being adequately trained for their jobs. At the same time that the old system of on-the-job training was becoming less effective, increasing demands were being placed on workers because of more sophisticated industrial processes. Master workmen no longer had time to instruct younger employees in the intricacies of their jobs, leaving them instead "to the tender mercies of . . . [their] associates for . . . trade instruction."[73] Cooley again brought up the contrasting example of Germany, which had so successfully solved its manual training problem: "The abundant resources and superb efficiency of Germany are facts that should make Americans eager to inquire into the source of her power." This power Cooley attributed to the fact that "she has endeavored to conserve all her resources, both natural and human, by her systems of education."[74] The industrial school ended inefficiency due to imperfect training and helped insure that waste would not result from the evolution of modern systems of production. Cooley was unable to avoid all mention of the moral advantages to be derived from continuation schools: if not properly trained to a particular job, he said, the boy "soon regards his work as mere drudgery and thus become an easy learner of the lesson of the street."[75]

Cooley's moralizing was held in check in his 1914 pamphlet, but his fundamental outlook was expressed in his promotion of Dr. Georg Kerchensteiner of Germany as an international educational spokesman. Kerchensteiner had directed the vocational schools of Munich since 1896, and Cooley had been extremely impressed by Munich's vocational system when he visited the city on his European tour. On Cooley's return to the United States, he had extolled Kerchensteiner to the Commercial Club.[76] In 1900, Kerchensteiner had won a national prize for having written the best essay on the subject "How are [Germany's] young men, from the time of leaving the elementary school (age 14 years) until the time of entering military service (age 20 years) to be educated for citizenship?" Cooley persuaded the Commercial Club to secure the English translation of Kerchensteiner's essay and then publish it in the United States. The Commercial Club asserted that Dr. Kerchensteiner's book-length essay was a "substantial and valuable contribution to educational literature" and that it should for the first time have been made available "to English readers through the Commercial Club" was a "matter of gratification."[77] In 1910, Kerchensteiner came to the United States to deliver a series of lectures under the auspices of the National Society for the Promotion of Industrial Education. His Chicago lecture was sponsored by the Commercial Club, and the club later printed it and two other lectures in pamphlet form. The club distributed 3,000 copies of the pamphlet and, in addition, arranged for the Chicago lecture to be printed in *The School Review,* a journal published by the University of Chicago.[78]

In the prize essay, published as *Education for Citizenship* under the Commercial Club's auspices, Kerchensteiner primarily emphasized the necessity of training workers to be industrially efficient. Even moral education had to take second place to the development of industrial skills. As a practical matter, it was difficult to teach moral principles: "For several reasons civic education must be limited to the modest aim of explaining, clearly and convincingly, the dependence of the special economic and social needs of the pupil on the interests of his fellow-citizens and of his native land."[79] This theme of social interdependence was a frequent one in the writings of vocational education proponents; Theodore Robinson also suggested that it should be relatively easy to explain to future workers that all wealth derived from cooperation, the "joint effort of capital and labor." It would not take a "mature mind" to comprehend this, thought Robinson, and it could readily be explained in an elementary way that "there will always be differences in individual character and ability, and that no social plan can be maintained which goes contrary to these basic truths."[80]

The difficulty came in going beyond these "basic truths." Kerchensteiner pointed out some of the problems standing in the way of full-fledged moral education: of necessity, such training would have to be brief because of the "immature state of the pupils' minds, which cannot be disregarded" and "the short time available under modern conditions for an extensive intellectual training." The key stumbling block was the "absolute necessity of providing for an all-round professional efficiency, without which civic usefulness would be greatly impaired."[81] The moral education would have to be sufficiently restricted to avoid encroaching upon the time needed for teaching the requisite industrial skills.

This practical limitation did not prevent Kerchensteiner from expounding at length on the moral benefits to be derived from vocational education. Conveniently, true moral enlightenment could best be achieved through hard work. "Character is not to be gained by the reading of books or the hearing of sermons, but by continuous and steadily applied work."[82] This solution allowed Kerchensteiner to maintain that moral education was of the utmost importance and value, yet insure that the Munich vocational students kept their attention firmly fixed on learning specific technical skills. Working-class people generally had to labor long hours in the industrial conditions of pre–World War I Europe and America, and declaring that inestimable moral values followed from the students' early introduction to work provided convenient justification for a German educational system that did not even attempt to introduce working-class students to academic subjects. Kerchensteiner, in fact, was insistent that working-class children destined for industrial jobs should not be unduly exposed to intellectual ideas. In the vocational schools, "every theory which goes beyond the intellectual capacity of the pupils must be excluded from the curriculum."[83]

The profound anti-intellectualism of Kerchensteiner's program of working-class education echoes that of Edwin G. Cooley. In both cases, the high goal of "moral education" is counterposed to that of intellectual education, but the actual content of the education proposed consisted of simple hard work at industrial jobs. While Cooley had written in 1906 that "we must realize from the start in our educational efforts that the moral reformation of the child is of more importance than the sharpening of his intellect," Kerchensteiner wrote in his prize essay that the continuation school would become valuable only when it was "permeated with the thought that moral education is more important than intellectual [education]."[84] Kerchensteiner later expressed this even more bluntly, telling an interviewer "that nowadays brains were being overeducated to a point rendering thousands of young men useless for practical work."[85] The goal of achieving the child's moral enlightenment was exalted, but the labor movement, more cynically, viewed this "moral education" as consisting largely of putting the child out to work at age 14 (rather than, as the labor movement demanded, providing for compulsory education to age 16), then providing several hours a week of education oriented to industrial training.*

*John Dewey, who joined the Chicago Federation of Labor in attacking the Cooley Bill, poured scorn on the businessmen's use of "eulogistic question-begging epithets" that obscured the real purposes of the vocational education bill. He observed that, "examined in the light of the details of the Illinois bill and of the arguments in its favor put forward by its representatives, vocational

The Commercial Club was heartened to observe that in near-by Wisconsin a system of vocational continuation schools was successfully put into operation. The Commercial Club distributed 3,000 copies of a pamphlet on the vocational education system in Wisconsin.[86] Children who went to work at 14 were required to attend the continuation schools for five hours a week until they reached 16. H. E. Miles, president of the Wisconsin State Board of Industrial Education and the chairman of the committee of industrial education of the National Association of Manufacturers, published several articles explaining the benefits of continuation schools to businessmen. One such article, titled "What I am Trying to Do," answered its own question in a capitalized subheading: "TO GIVE TWO MILLION CHILDREN A CHANCE IN VOCATIONAL CONTINUATION SCHOOLS—THE BUSINESS MAN'S SOLUTION OF THE SCHOOL PROBLEM—TO ORGANIZE EDUCATION SO THAT GOOD VOCATIONAL TEACHING COSTS ONLY $10 PER YEAR PER CHILD."[87] Miles emphasized the extraordinary cheapness of this form of education, and it will be readily acknowledged that even in 1913, $10 a year per child qualified as cheap education. Miles explained that, in some localities, the average annual cost per child was reduced still further to $7, and that overall, the continuation schools were operated at a yearly cost less than half that of the common schools.

The children in the continuation schools received the customary dose of moral education, in this case taking the form of courses in "elementary personal and social hygiene, and in citizenship," but in the allotted five hours per week "the main stress is laid on the relation of the school work to the work the child is actually doing in the shop or store." Textbooks, of course, were not required in most instances, and the continuation schools were able to effect a great saving because, since the children

---

education is nothing but technical trade-training dignified with a high-sounding title" (Dewey, "Splitting up the School System," *New Republic* 2 [April 17, 1915]: 284). For a debate between David Snedden, a major proponent of the efficiency movement in education, and John Dewey on the meaning and purposes of vocational education, with particular reference to the Chicago situation, see "Vocational Education" by Snedden, *New Republic* 2 (May 15, 1915): 40–42; and Dewey, "Education vs. Trade-Training—Dr. Dewey's Reply," *New Republic* 2 (May 15, 1915): 42–43.

were already at work, the very factories and stores where they were already employed contained the necessary equipment. Thus the continuation schools did "not have to spend any public money for expensive buildings and equipment."[88]

Miles was one with Cooley and Kerchensteiner in asserting that these schools perfectly suited the intellects of the great mass of working-class children. As Kerchensteiner had stressed, "All men cannot be educated to the same extent," and Cooley had argued that the principles of heredity, in most cases, precluded those employed in manual labor from producing offspring able to grapple with abstract topics, Miles argued that the continuation schools provided for the "concrete-minded child."

> The main trouble with our common schools is that they are
> designed essentially for the abstract-minded children.
> . . . These . . . constitute certainly not more than half of
> all the children that attend the public schools. I should
> judge the proportion to be considerably less than 50 percent.
> And the public schools . . . make no provision whatever
> for the other half, the concrete-minded child, who can, only
> with extreme difficulty and then imperfectly, learn from
> the printed page. I call these "hand-minded" children.[89]

These "hand-minded" children, Miles argued, would be much better off in the world of work than in the classrooms of the common schools. The education they received should concentrate on the immediate, practical goal of better fitting them for their employment. As Miles declared in a speech at the fifth annual convention of the National Society for the Promotion of Industrial Education, those interested in industrial education should demand that it be extremely practical. "They want it to bear upon its face the grime of the factory and the stress of the store and the counting room. It must be free from any slightest touch of sentimentality. Work is real; work is hard."[90]

The Commercial Club responded to these sentiments and solicited the aid of the other important Chicago business organizations in promoting the Cooley plan. The Chicago Association of Commerce and the Illinois Manufacturers Association, "with their usual public spirit and clear insight into the true interests of the community," joined the Commercial Club in its lobbying efforts.[91] The Hamilton Club, an organization of younger business-men, and the Bankers' Club also "asked that they be permitted to cooperate with [the Commercial Club] in a movement which they understand is both far-reaching and of increasing moment."[92] The Commercial Club developed an exalted view of the impor-tance of its educational undertaking; at a closed meeting in 1915, club members congratulated themselves on being able to record that "Chicago is regarded as the center of this forward educational movement. Reports and pamphlets issued under the auspices of the Club are in constant demand throughout the United States and there is recognition of its work in foreign countries."[93]

What led the Commercial Club to throw its energies behind the reorganization of the public school system, and why was it able to persuade other business organizations to join in the ef-fort? No complete answer is possible, but it is apparent that the system of continuation schools proposed by the Commercial Club offered businessmen several advantages. First, continuation schools were far cheaper than regular common schools. The Chi-cago public school system was so underfinanced that class sizes were very large and many schools operated on double shifts. If the compulsory school age were raised to 16, additional massive funding of the schools would be needed to accommodate the in-creased numbers, without even dealing with the original prob-lem of overcrowding. Under the Commercial Club's plan, stu-dents from the ages of 14 to 16 would attend special continuation schools for a limited number of hours per week; unlike the pro-gram developed by Miles in Wisconsin, the Commercial Club did envision that the continuation schools would have separate buildings, but clearly the cost would be far less than if the stu-dents were in regular schools full time. Chicago businessmen never stated that they supported the continuation schools be-cause they were cheaper than regular schools, but on previous occasions, businessmen had demonstrated reluctance to increase school funding. Cooley remarked that advanced thinkers in ed-ucation believed that children should receive public schooling up to the age of 18, but he entirely dismissed the prospect of this occurring and suggested as an alternative that a supplementary system of vocational schools be developed to allow children to hold jobs while attending school.[94] The businessmen regarded the idea of prohibiting child labor until age 16 as visionary, and they proposed having 14-year-olds both work and attend school for a few hours as an alternative to the extension of public schooling for all children until the age of 16.

Second, the vocational schools would help solve the problem of the shortage of skilled labor. Beginning in the late 1800s, Marshall Field had bemoaned the lack of qualified employees. The initial business-sponsored attempts to found manual training schools had been intended to deal with this problem. The situation had become more critical by the time of the City Club report of 1912, which indicated that three-quarters of the businesses surveyed had trouble finding skilled workers. Furthermore, the craft unions had become stronger by the second decade of the 1900s, as the Chicago labor movement gained its first lasting organizational successes. Many workers in the construction trades were unionized, and these workers—carpenters, electricians, and others—possessed skills that were taught under the auspices of the unions. If union control over apprenticeship programs could be broken, then union control over entry into the occupation would be ended or greatly weakened. This, in turn, would greatly strengthen the employers. A ready supply of skilled laborers would undoubtedly have helped lower wage rates and weaken organizing drives and union ability to mount successful strikes. Thus, the development of an extensive vocational school program would be of lasting benefit to Chicago business firms.

Third, the continuation schools would be able to inculcate the morality of hard work without the students suffering from the distraction of studying general academic subjects. The students would, in fact, already have received an object lesson in the importance and necessity of work from having begun their employment at 14. These students were "hand-minded" and could not be expected to profit from an abstract education. Both Cooley and Kerchensteiner made it clear that a training in ideas was the last thing these students should ever be exposed to; rather, the schools would train them in punctuality, obedience, and industry by the simple expedient of combining their education with their work. The high-flown "moral education" that businessmen wrote about reduced itself to a few simple principles that Miles summed up concisely, if bluntly: "Work is real; work is hard. A love of work must be developed replacing a present love of ease."[95] When businessmen wrote of more extensive moral education, they generally referred to the necessity of instructing students in the interdependence of society and the clear and simple truth that labor and capital would have to cooperate for the mutual benefit of both. These ideas, businessmen felt, would be well received if properly explained.

Fourth, the continuation schools would be separately administered from the academic schools and would be under the control of "practical men." Businessmen would not have to negotiate with other interests and adopt indirect means of making their influence felt; rather, the very purpose of the schools would be to bring industry and education into close connection, and business intervention and direct control would be natural and legitimate. Many businessmen felt that previous experiments in vocational education had failed both because they were not far-reaching enough and because they were under the control of educators, who allowed the schools to lapse back into an academic direction. This principle of separate administration was so important to the Commercial Club that it refused to modify the original Cooley plan even after middle-class civic groups joined the labor movement in a storm of denunciation of the proposed "dual system."

The Labor Response: The Battle Begins

When the Cooley Bill was first introduced in the state legislature in 1913, the Chicago Federation of Labor reacted with bitter opposition. This opposition intensified when the plan was reintroduced in two subsequent sessions of the legislature, and the tensions generated by the bill affected political disputes over the schools in Chicago for more than a decade to follow. The Illinois State Federation of Labor joined the Chicago Federation in denouncing the Cooley Bill, and the issue assumed a statewide importance.

From the time of the earliest discussion of the dual school plan in 1912, organized labor responded that the bill was intended to turn the public schools into a supply house for docile workers.[96] The labor movement attacked the bill as being clearly designed to serve the interests of the employers. The unionists argued that the "dual system" would create class distinctions in the public schools and that working-class children would be shunted into the vocational program while middle-class students remained in the academic division. The working-class students would be taught narrow industrial skills designed to fit them for employment, instead of receiving a liberal education. The provision for a separate vocational board of education, composed of "practical men and women," struck the labor federations as an obvious attempt at employer control.

The Illinois State Federation of Labor reacted angrily to the claim that the vocational schools would cater to the real needs of working-class youth who left the schools because of disillusionment with academic subjects. At the 1914 annual convention of the state federation, a comprehensive report on vocational education was presented. The report argued:

> It is idle to intimate that children act as free agents and
> voluntarily leave school when they reach the age of fourteen
> years because of dissatisfaction with the prevailing cur-
> riculum. Economic conditions largely determine the school
> life of the children. Parents do not take their children
> from the school and place them in the workshop because of
> lack of interest in the school or because they desire to
> press into economic service the labor of their children, but
> conditions are such as make it difficult to support them
> and keep them in the schools.[97]

The report commented skeptically that it was strange to see the employers in the role of catering to the "alleged fancy of the school children," and suggested that, in reality, they were not "actuated in the purpose of giving the children a broad and general education, but seek rather to substitute industrial training for general education."[98] The report argued the necessity of raising the school-leaving age to 16. Rather than encouraging children to leave regular schooling at age 14, "it is our firm belief that the industrial and commercial life of the children should not begin until they have reached at least the age of sixteen years."[99]

The Illinois State Federation of Labor rejected the example of the German educational system, which had been unceasingly presented by business interests over the previous few years. "We hear much of the European system of vocational education and industrial training," but such education was not applicable to the United States unless the labor movement was willing to accept a form of education in which the fostering of mechanical skills was the prime objective, and students were directed into different educational programs on the basis of their social class. The state federation cited no less an authority than Dr. Kerchensteiner himself on the fact that the German system separated the students into two distinct groups after the first four years of schooling.[100] The German trade unionists, the report said, were continually protesting the very system that American business interests were holding up as a model.

The report attempted to probe underlying problems of vocational education more deeply by exploring the effects of intensifying industrial specialization. Braverman, Noble, Aronowitz, and other authors have examined the ways in which the development of capitalism led to the routinization of industrial tasks and the increasing shift of decision making from the shop floor to the higher reaches of management.[101] The report prepared by the ISFL demonstrates that the labor movement was sensitive to this process; the report stated that workers were losing the opportunity to practice skilled trades and that the endless process of subdivision of vocations had led to a degree of specialization that confined workers to monotonous and automatic tasks. Work itself was no longer educative. Whereas previously the very practice of their jobs had provided workers with opportunities for more "than mere sustenance of physical existence," now specialization forced workers to do jobs that were neither mentally nor physically stimulating. Vocational education could only be a farce if the students were to be trained to become cogs in a machine. "What good will come from giving vocational training in the public schools if we continue to permit our children to be chained to machines which require but the repetition of a few muscular motions?"[102] The solution to the problem of monotonous industrial labor would not readily be found, the report conceded, but any system of production that reduced human beings to the level of machines ought to be opposed. At least the discussion of vocational education might have the effect of focusing public attention on "the terrible conditions prevailing in many industries."[103]

This theme of the connection between the nature of education and the nature of work was further developed by the Chicago Federation of Labor. In later years, the CFL frequently argued that business wanted to make education monotonous and dreary in order to accustom students to monotonous and dreary work. The employers did not want the students to experience an interesting, challenging curriculum that would involve their minds because there would be no place for active intelligence in the jobs they would later occupy. Rather than expose students to general subjects, which would at least have the potential to exercise their imagination, business wanted students to be taught the basic literacy skills, then to follow a vocational course that would prepare them for industry. Even if one goal of the vocational education program were the training of skilled workers, there was, in fact, a proportionally diminishing need for such workers as specialization increased in factories. The bulk of the students would not even be taught a trade in the vocational schools; rather than getting an education of any kind, they would be inculcated with "moral values" as an alternative to real education. The much-vaunted "moral education" that Cooley and others spoke of, in fact, reduced itself to a justification for the absence of education. Business wanted to keep education a "hurried, machine-like process" because they wanted students turned out, not with critical minds, but as "meek little manikins" trained to "take whatever slaps and jabs the boss is pleased to inflict in the form of low wages, long hours and other bad working conditions, without having sense enough and courage enough to fight."[104] The CFL newspaper commented that it would be difficult to change the mechanical processes of factory work in this generation, but that "neither will we be able to change it in succeeding generations, unless we make a determined stand against permitting the factory atmosphere to be introduced into our children's classrooms."[105] The employers did not want children taught to think; instead, they wanted them to have an early introduction to the "nerve-destroying pacemaking of industry."

This issue of the connection between the nature of the education provided and the future work situation will be discussed further in the context of conflicts over the "efficiency movement" in public education and the attempted introduction of platoon schools in Chicago, but it was in the years when the Cooley Bill was a bitterly fought issue in Illinois that labor first developed the critique that the increasing routinization of industry had led employers to promote the increasing routinization of education.

The aspect of the Cooley plan that excited perhaps the most suspicion and hostility was the proposal for a separate school board for the vocational schools. There was general labor support for some form of vocational education, but the provision for a separate school board at once invited the idea that under the particular plan proposed the schools would serve the needs of industry. The Illinois State Federation of Labor declared that the "Dual System of Administration is a Menace" and proposed as a condition for all vocational education programs that they be administered by, and form a part of, the general academic school systems.[106] The president of the ISFL, John Walker, said in 1915 that the Cooley Bill was "positively the most vicious thing that was introduced" in the last session of the state legislature, and he cited as one of its most dangerous aspects the provision for a dual system of administration.[107] In the vocabulary of organized labor, the very phrase *dual system* invited hostility, due to the long tradition of opposition to dual unionism. Walker said that the real purpose of the "dual schools" would be to place the education of workers' children "under the complete control of corporations."[108] If employers directly controlled the school system, they would use the schools "as a training place for turning out a plentiful supply of the most highly skilled industrial workers with the least possible amount of other knowledge," who would have had their minds "trained and developed in such a manner as to make of them willing scabs."

Reform Groups Oppose the Cooley Bill

The issue of separate control of vocational schools led Chicago's leading middle-class civic organizations, such as the City Club, to oppose the Cooley Bill. The City Club was made up largely of men drawn from the "newer as well as the classic professions, from public administration, from political and reform organizations," from the fields of literature and art, as well as from the ranks of the city's smaller businessmen.[109] The City Club took educational issues seriously and characteristically intervened in public debates through the medium of well-prepared reports, often replete with statistics and comparisons of practices in Chicago with those in other cities. In 1912 the City Club issued such a report on vocational education; it was a 315-page book written by a committee chaired by Professor George H. Mead of the philosophy department of the University of Chicago.[110] The report emphasized the need for practical vocational training, but it rejected the idea of creating a separate school system for vocational education. The City Club advocated raising the school-leaving age to 16, in line with the proposal of the state and local labor federations.

The City Club issued its report in February, a few weeks before the Commercial Club issued its own document on vocational education.[111] The City Club's education committee tried to mediate the differences between its vocational education proposal and that of the Commercial Club.[112] The City Club prepared its own vocational education bill for discussion and possible submission to the state legislature, but it emphasized that it was advancing the bill with the thought of ultimate compromise.[113] These efforts at compromise failed, as the Commercial Club remained immovable on the principle of a separate school system and the City Club held firmly to the idea of a unitary system. Declaring that it wished to avoid the two extremes of completely separate vocational programs or of vocational training that largely overlapped with the academic curriculum, the City Club emphasized that a dual school system would place the stamp of class bias upon the public schools.[114] Parents would hesitate to enroll their children in vocational schools, even if the children had little academic aptitude. They would fear that their children would be entering a school that was organized "merely to teach children *how to work*."[115] If the industrial schools were under the control of a separate board of education, they would carry the stigma of being schools for the laboring classes. The Commercial Club's plan would destroy one of the greatest assets of the American public school system; the City Club's education committee believed that "the public school system is good in proportion as it holds the respect and interest of all classes of people."[116]

The City Club lobbied for its own vocational education bill in the state legislature in opposition to the Cooley Bill. Leading educational figures, such as Charles H. Judd of the University of Chicago, also declared their opposition to the Commercial Club's plan for a dual school system.[117] The middle-class women's clubs disapproved of the Commercial Club's plan because of the rigid boundaries it would set up between academic and vocational education.[118] John Dewey entered the fray with several articles critical of the Cooley Bill, which were extensively quoted by the labor groups. Dewey asserted that, if passed, the Cooley Bill would lead to segregation of the schools along class lines.[119] Cooley wrote an article, in reply to Dewey, saying that the only segregation in the schools would be of the sort that segregated art students from music students, or civic engineers from electrical engineers, "purely for the sake of special study and increased efficiency."[120]

The business groups, led by the Commercial Club, had so framed the issue that they isolated themselves even from sectors of opinion that occasionally supported them. The intensity of the labor protest had galvanized a far wider response to the dangers of the proposed bill. The Commercial Club could not hold even those groups, such as the City Club, which emphasized the need for expanded vocational training. Even in the face of mounting opposition, however, the Commercial Club would not modify the bill to remove the provision for separate control of the vocational schools. At an April 1914 meeting of the Commercial Club, note was made of the labor opposition, with the report that "it cannot be said that the representatives of organized labor, which appeared before the committees of the Legislature, favored any of the bills presented." The labor representatives held strongly to their own view of the proper organization of education, with the Commercial Club noting that while the labor representatives "expressed belief in vocational instruction and advocated employment of teachers with practical experience, they seemed to feel that, unless they had control of the influences surrounding the children in vocational schools, such schools would be detrimental to their cause."[121]

In spite of the labor opposition, the Commercial Club was reinforced in its belief that separate administration of vocational and academic schools was necessary. Deliberation on the subject during the year had confirmed the conviction that "separate administration is required for practical vocational teaching." This was due to the fact that "only under separate boards of control equal in importance, and both subject to the State, can the public school pupil receive the all-around education required to meet the demands of modern civilization."[122] The Commercial Club spokesmen did not make it clear how the provision of entirely separate boards of control would lead to the provision of "all-around education," but they did make it clear that they would not abandon the principle of separate vocational and academic school systems.

After the bill failed in the 1913 session of the state legislature, the Commercial Club, in coalition with other Chicago business organizations, reintroduced it in the 1915 session. The club once again noted with surprise the intensity of labor's opposition. At a closed meeting of the club on April 10, 1915, Clayton Mark, vice president of the National Malleable Castings Company and a former school board member, attributed labor's opposition to blind class prejudice: "Organized labor expresses suspicion because this legislation originates in the Commercial Club. It cannot comprehend that a group of 'rich men' so called can be interested in any movement for the vocational training of children which does not have the ultimate aim of exploitation for personal gain."[123]

The president of the club, Bernard E. Sunny, head of the Chicago Telephone Company, urged club members to go to Springfield to support the bill before the state legislature. He declared that the vocational education bill was the main business before the club, and he suggested that Commercial Club members use their personal influence with the legislators:

> I believe that we should go down to Springfield in a suf-
> ficiently large number, twenty-five or thirty of us, and
> circulate among the members of the general assembly and
> show them that we are interested in this measure, that
> we believe it to be a good thing, that it represents the best
> judgment of the men who have devoted themselves to
> an inquiry of the subject, and then I believe there will be a
> very fair chance of this bill going through.[124]

He persuasively noted that club members would not have to endure any discomfort on the trip:

> We will have our special accommodations, comfortable
> accommodations, on the Illinois Central, and at the hotel in
> Springfield. Springfield is an interesting place to visit.
> The representatives in the general assembly and senate are
> a fine lot of fellows and you will be glad to meet them.[125]

In spite of the best efforts of the Commercial Club, the bill was again defeated. The Chicago Federation of Labor, the Illinois State Teachers Association, and the Illinois State Federation of Labor once again registered their bitter opposition to the bill, and when it was defeated, they claimed full credit.[126] The newspaper of the state federation reported grimly on the bill's failure to get out of committee, declaring that "the House Committee on Education took action on May 5 to report out the *notorious* Cooley Industrial Training bill and all other so-called vocational training bills . . . with a recommendation that they do not pass." In strong language, the article went on: "It is hoped that this will put a stop to the vicious attempt which has been made to destroy the democracy of the public schools, and that commercial interests and others who are trying to split the schools, create class distinctions and prevent proper education of children of working people will realize schools are held too sacred by working people to prevent misuse."[127]

The Commercial Club persisted and, for the third and last

time, reintroduced the bill at the 1917 session of the legislature. The bill once again failed and the Commercial Club at last accepted its defeat. After nearly five years of conflict over the Cooley Bill, the Commercial Club finally recognized that the hostility aroused by its attempt to restructure the school system might have overshadowed the benefits of the bill itself, even had it passed. Sewell Avery, the chairman of the club's educational committee, told the club, "I think it would be difficult for the members here to appreciate how widespread throughout the State is the sentiment against the dual system as recommended by Mr. Cooley." Avery went on, with rueful perplexity, to say that "in some way the opponents attribute the plan to The Commercial Club and quite openly charge the most sinister motives. The idea that we are laboring in an altruistic spirit for the general welfare is not accepted at all."[128]

Conclusions

Far from the labor movement accepting that the Commercial Club had been working in an altruistic spirit for the general welfare, few other issues in Chicago history have caused such widespread distrust of business motives. The labor federations, with the particularly active aid of the CFL-affiliated Chicago Teachers' Federation, had successfully organized a five-year protest movement against the bill. The labor groups had also succeeded in winning the support of middle-class civic organizations, such as the City Club of Chicago, who on other issues had not infrequently adopted stands more akin to those of business leaders than to those of the labor movement.

The Commercial Club, with its open sponsorship and advocacy of the bill, had made the educational system the focus of sharp class antagonism. Local and state labor federations charged the business organizations with deliberately working to restrict the education of working-class children in order to suit them better for later factory life. The moral principles that businessmen sought to introduce to working-class students were derided as obvious attempts to justify cheap, authoritarian, mass-produced education for the children of working people, while middle-class children attended academic schools. The earlier antagonism over "fads and frills" in the schools had broadened into a general dispute over the control and extent of education for working-class children. As Victor Olander of the state labor federation reminded a meeting of the Chicago Teachers' Federation in 1924, the fight over the Cooley Bill had served to politicize school affairs for years to follow.[129]

The Commercial Club realized belatedly that its venture into open educational policy making had been damaging. Sewell Avery, who had warned club members of the hostility generated by the attempts to press the Cooley Bill, suggested that the club would be well advised to lie low on educational issues for a time.[130] As the focus of much of the hostility, the club had brought the business community in general an unwelcome amount of publicity and obloquy. Business motives were viewed with suspicion, and it would take a considerable time to repair the damage.

Avery hastened to assure the Commercial Club's members that, in any case, dropping the Cooley Bill would not represent defeat because the federally sponsored Smith-Hughes Act provided for the establishment of vocational education in each state that passed enabling legislation. Avery was not entirely sure of the provisions of the bill, but thought that they would meet with the approval of the Club:

> . . . the big problem with which the Club has been laboring
> for the past several years may have been answered in
> the passage of the Smith-Hughes Bill just referred to. I do
> not know as much of its actual working as I should like
> to in speaking on the subject. . . . The principles that are
> guiding the Federal Board are, generally, those for which
> the Commercial Club has stood, and this is the great ac-
> complishment.[131]

The Smith-Hughes Act, signed by President Wilson on February 28, 1917, provided federal support for vocational education, but it did not establish a dual system of education of the kind that the Commercial Club had promoted in the Cooley Bill.[132] The Commercial Club's goal of a dual educational system was never realized, and in this respect, the labor movement had won a clear victory.

The Commercial Club's unintended heightening of conflict around educational issues had not served its purpose, and in the future, business groups took a fundamentally different tack in approaching school issues; they very rarely took aggressive public stands as the Commercial Club had done. The Commercial Club had gone so far as to have its own members, the leading businessmen of the nation's second largest city, travel to Springfield to lobby personally for the passage of the vocational education bill. In later years, even when businessmen did in fact play aggressive policy roles, they tended not to operate in their own name, but rather exerted power through the mayor and the Chicago political machine. "Citizens' committees" of leading businessmen replaced the Commercial Club as the instigators of business programs for the schools.

Even before the focus of business policy making shifted from the clubs and associations that dominated the earlier era to liaisons with the mayor, Chicago business organizations had already reviewed their approach on educational issues. Instead of provoking direct conflicts, business groups in most cases attempted to work with reform-oriented civic associations to secure revisions of the school system's structure. The goal of "efficient" school administration was common to both (at least in certain eras) and provided justification for many changes that met with business approval. In the 1930s business groups once again deeply antagonized the middle-class civic organizations, but they were able to do so with impunity because the labor movement was politically immobilized and business had formed a powerful alliance with the mayor. Business organizations did not again have to confront the aroused forces of both labor and reform groups simultaneously, as they had during the battle over the Cooley Bill.

Direct clashes over the content of schooling were only the most overt of the controversies that engaged the city's municipal organizations during the first decades of the 1900s. On a less dramatic level, Chicago's major political groups attempted to influence the structure of the Chicago school system in ways that would maximize their indirect control and their ability to achieve their educational goals. In the politically contentious atmosphere of the city, even the most seemingly technical and mundane adjustments in the organizational structure of its schools were scrutinized for any bearing on the larger political question of who would control the schools and for what purposes. It is to an examination of these controversies over the administrative structure of the schools that we now turn.

4 | CENTRALIZATION VERSUS DEMOCRACY IN THE SCHOOLS

THE TURN OF THE CENTURY was an era of enormous growth and development for American industry. Mass-production methods transformed factory work, and firms reached unprecedented size through mergers and consolidation. The principles of "scientific management" were introduced as a means of rationalizing the work process while forcing the maximum output from each worker. Hailed as the prophets of a new scientific gospel, teams of efficiency engineers studied factory processes to subdivide tasks into units and find the "one best way" to achieve maximum production. The enthusiasm for industrial efficiency helped spawn a social counterpart in drives to transform public institutions to conform with efficiency principles.[1] With their single-minded adherents and specialized jargon, both the social and industrial efficiency movements had the characteristics of national fads. The efficiency mania subsided by the 1920s, but in a deeper sense, the movement ended only because the principles it espoused were incorporated into private industry and public institutions.

The key goals of the social efficiency movement arose before the development of the system of factory engineering that bore the name of Frederick Taylor, but the drive for social efficiency received increased impetus from the national focus on restructuring industry to improve output. The main principles of the social efficiency adherents were an emphasis on the need for direction by scientific experts, a desire for centralized control, and an impulse to standardize and test the methods and products of social institutions. In the educational sphere, business leaders and progressive reformers sought ways of restructuring public school systems in the name of these goals. In particular, business groups made repeated efforts to increase the power of the superintendent and to reduce the strength of the organized teachers. The labor movement viewed these actions as reinforcing business influence over the schools, and in Chicago this led to many skirmishes over school-reorganization proposals.

The structure of the Chicago public school system was still fluid in the early 1900s. The fact that few firm organizational principles had yet been widely accepted increased the intensity with which labor and business promoted their own educational plans. During the decades when fundamental issues of power and authority in the school system remained unresolved, underlying class perspectives on schooling emerged with particular clarity.

The Rationalization of the School System

In the closing years of the nineteenth century, the Chicago public schools clearly needed reorientation and guidance on how to cope with the vastly increased numbers of students and the building of an effective administrative system. In 1898 Mayor Carter Harrison appointed an educational commission of 11 members to report to the city on a plan for administrative reorganization. The mayor named William Rainey Harper, president of the University of Chicago, as the chairman of the commission.[2]

William Harper played an active role in Chicago school politics throughout his tenure as first president of the university, which had been founded in 1892 by John D. Rockefeller. The enormous financial resources of the university enabled its officials to speak with authority to the city's business and political leaders. The Civic Federation recommended Harper's appointment to the school board in 1894, and he was actually appointed in 1896. He retained the chairmanship of the Civic Federation's education committee while he served on the school board because, he said, it gave him "a chance to work both from the outside and from the inside."[3] In 1898 Harper was instrumental in having his close friend, E. Benjamin Andrews, appointed superintendent of the school system.

The Harper Commission drew upon the advice of 50 prominent educational experts in other cities.[4] The commission's report, produced one year after its members had been appointed, reflected the general national elite consensus on the direction that school districts should take. For decades to come, the Harper Commission's wide-ranging recommendations laid the basis for efforts to reorganize the school system. The report began by acknowledging that it was not surprising that "the school machinery of Chicago is largely defective."[5] The city had grown rapidly but had retained an administrative structure suitable for a much smaller school system. This administrative structure required radical improvement in several directions: the commission recommended that the power of the superintendent be greatly increased and that the school board be made much smaller.[6] The commission emphasized above all the need to shift toward more centralized, expert direction of the school system.

The commission argued that the Chicago school system could not be significantly improved until a "high class of men and women" was ready to serve on the board, and that this could not be accomplished unless the board were made smaller and raised in the public estimation.[7] The board should be reduced from 21 to 11 members to allow each member to play an active role in molding school policy without having the board take on the management of petty details. The commission opposed the election of board members, arguing that more able members could be obtained through mayoral appointment than through the rough and tumble of elections. This emphasis on a small, selective, appointed school board was in accord with a national trend toward smaller school boards.[8] Tyack cites figures demonstrating that in 1893 there were an average of 21.5 school board members per city in the 28 largest cities of the country.[9] By 1913, the average number had fallen to 10.2 board members per city.

Similarly, the commission's emphasis on strengthening the superintendent's powers reflected a national move toward governance of the schools by "experts." The commission cited an authority who declared that the superintendent is "employed as an expert, just as a physician is, and in the range of work in which he is so employed he is independent of dictation."[10] This medical analogy was pleasing to the rising corps of school administrators who maintained that they were engaged in a profession based on scientific principles. The superintendent would be protected from political buffeting by a six-year term of office, and the commission urged that a high salary be offered to attract qualified administrators. The stress on the neutral, scientific nature of school governance encouraged the development of top-down, centralized direction of the schools, comparable to the movement for the "non-political" control of the nation's cities.[11] In both cases, the ideology of expert control justified the attempted or actual restructuring of school and city governments to limit popular participation.

The commission also stressed the need to adopt business principles in running the schools, arguing that "the established laws of business cannot be violated with impunity in the management of the professional details of our schools." The commission recommended that the school system's business affairs be handled by a business manager who would enjoy a freedom "similar to that of the executive head in any well-conducted business enterprise."[12] This would assure the dispatch of school business with economy and efficiency.

Reducing the size of the school board and increasing the power of the superintendent would help remove the schools from public controversy, but the superintendent would still have to cope with the system's militant and highly politicized teaching force. Several of the smaller teachers' organizations, such as the Ella Flagg Young Club, criticized the recommendations of the Educational Commission, citing particularly the provision for a smaller school board and increased power in the hands of the superintendent.[13] More significantly, the Chicago Teachers' Federation, which at the time ranked as the largest such teacher organization in the country (with 2,500 members) came out in full opposition to the commission proposals.[14] Catharine Goggin, elected to the presidency of the Chicago Teachers' Federation the year that the commission presented its report, commented caustically on the absence of women members or of teachers from the commission. While the commission had actively sought the opinions of educational experts from around the country, it had not bothered to solicit the opinions of the largely female teaching staff.

"To be sure," Goggin wrote, "teachers were *permitted* to send to the Commission letters touching upon the Commission's work," if, in the principals' opinion, there were "any in the school whose opinion or experience would be of value."[15] Even the complicated wording of the commission's proposals could not conceal the fact that the superintendent, with increased authority to hire and fire teachers, would have greatly increased power.

The Chicago Teachers' Federation established a formal committee to evaluate the Harper Commission recommendations. The committee formulated a list of specific objections to the commission proposals; the CTF unanimously endorsed the committee report and began a political campaign against implementation of the recommendations. The CTF believed that its suspicions about the all-male, elitist Harper Commission had been justified when the Commission recommended that teachers be fired or retained on the basis of their teaching efficiency, with the principal being the initial arbiter of each teacher's efficiency. The superintendent would have the power to fire teachers if they were three times judged inefficient by their school principal and the assistant superintendent; in fact, the superintendent was then required to fire the teacher unless overriden by a majority vote of the board.[16] The Chicago Teachers' Federation had been agitating for tenure for the city's teachers to stop arbitrary firings, but the report's recommendations moved in the opposite direction.

More fundamentally, the CTF objected to the increase in the superintendent's power and the diminution in the size of the school board. The teachers' federation declared its opposition to "the centralization of power in the superintendent, in the matter of hiring his assistant principals, supervisors, teachers and other officials, and the selecting of text-books." The CTF condemned this centralization as undemocratic and argued that it reduced the ability of either teachers or parents in a heterogeneous city to influence school policy.[17]

The teachers' antagonism was fueled by the commission's assertion that many teachers were overpaid and that a system of merit pay should be instituted. The report declared that "a spirit of enthusiasm and of progress can be best engendered among the teachers by proper recognition of successful effort" and therefore urged that the pay of each teacher be based on "proved efficiency."[18] The teachers had long believed that merit pay only encouraged favoritism and discrimination in a school system already riddled by patronage; they also argued that it served as a means of reducing payroll costs by keeping most teachers at the low end of the salary scale. The commission advocated yet another policy that would have increased divisions among the teaching force—the payment of higher salaries to male teachers. This won the opposition of a district superintendent, Ella Flagg Young, an administrator with close ties to the Chicago Teachers' Federation who later became superintendent of the Chicago schools. Young received an ovation from a teachers' meeting when she attacked the proposal to differentiate salaries along sex lines, a proposal that was anathema to the organized teachers.[19] The commission had inserted the recommendation because it believed that male teachers were more adequate authority figures than were female teachers, with greater stamina and influence over boys.[20]

The report did call for the establishment of teachers' councils, but only in an advisory role. The councils would focus the "experience and thought of five thousand Chicago teachers" and would therefore prove of benefit to the school system.[21] The Chicago Teachers' Federation was not placated by this call for strictly advisory councils, as it believed that in reality the rights of teachers would be greatly reduced and no advisory council could cover that fact.

The commission's major recommendations involved the administrative reorganization of the school system, but it also ventured into other areas. The report said that kindergartens should be established in the densely populated areas of the city, that more playgrounds should be provided, and that the city should establish one central commercial high school and two new manual training schools. The commission's final recommendations concerned the need for improved citizenship training. In the future, the commission urged, all candidates for teaching positions in the elementary schools should be required to show proof of ability in citizenship training. The goal of the training would be to "awaken an enlightened sense of patriotism" and to "emphasize the duties as well as the rights of American citizenship."[22] The report said that not enough was currently being done in this direction in the Chicago schools and cited Albion Small, professor of sociology at the University of Chicago, on the necessity for more intensive training. Small minced no words in his statement that schools that did not inculcate respect for authority were a "serious social menace." These schools encouraged self-expression over social control and thereby turned education into a "screaming burlesque."[23] "If you force the self-expression idea beyond a certain point you make it unsocial, non-cooperative, disintegrating, demoralizing, anarchistic." The schools would create "social monstrosities out of the pupils" if they did not repress self-assertion in favor of respect for society as a whole. Small concluded: "It is, therefore, not a disadvantage, but an indispensable advantage, to retain in school some strong features of authoritative discipline which the pupils must observe with military promptness and precision. Straight-out obedience, not merely sugar-coated willfulness, is a needful part of every child's education for citizenship."[24]

The Harper Commission Report in total contained virtually the full range of "efficiency" provisions for the schools. The report's recommendations were incorporated in the form of a bill presented to the state legislature in 1899. The Chicago Teachers' Federation galvanized labor opposition to the bill and mounted a vigorous campaign against it. The Chicago Federation of Labor and the Chicago Woman's Club joined the CTF in lobbying against the bill in Springfield, and the CTF presented petitions containing 50,000 signatures calling on the legislature not to pass the bill.[25] Margaret Haley, the head of the CTF, told legislators that if the bill were passed, the superintendent would have "autocratic powers unknown to the Csar of Russia."[26] Haley had earlier gained CFL support in opposing the bill by declaring in a speech at a labor federation meeting that Harper was the tool of Rockefeller, who in turn was the greatest example of "one-man power in American business." The Harper Bill represented nothing more than an attempt to introduce this same system into the public school system. Haley's approach to the CFL on this issue led to the first sustained contacts between the teachers and the organized labor movement.[27]

The linking of Harper with Rockefeller led to widespread distrust of his influence in the city school system. The letters between Harper and two Chicago school superintendents, E. Benjamin Andrews and Edwin Cooley, indicate that all three men thought it wise, for public relations purposes, to minimize the connection between Harper and the city's public school superintendents.[28] The Socialist press in the city seized upon the connection to build opposition to school reorganization attempts. In the early years of the University of Chicago, there had been little sensitivity to public reaction to the idea of Rockefeller funding, and the university's official stationery bore the name "University of Chicago" followed by the imprint "Founded by John D. Rockefeller." Years later, the Chicago newspaper *American Socialist* declared that the Harper Bill "was the first great cause of a universally expressed discontent at the close connection between Rockefeller's University of Chicago and the Chicago board of education."[29]

The combined forces of the Chicago Federation of Labor, the Chicago Teachers' Federation, and the Chicago Woman's Club were sufficient to defeat the Harper Bill at the 1899 session of the state legislature. Even Mayor Carter Harrison, who had appointed the Harper Commission, had kept his distance from the actual recommendations; the teachers had created a climate in which public officials had to consider their reactions.[30]

Andrews, who had been president of Brown University, was appointed to the Chicago school superintendency after the previous superintendent, Albert G. Lane, was not reappointed. Lane was not rehired as superintendent (he was instead appointed as assistant superintendent) both because Mayor Carter Harrison, a Democrat, disapproved of his Republican politics and because Harper had expressed objections to Lane's lack of a college education.[31] Harper wrote to Andrews on June 16, 1898, enthusiastically urging him to accept the Chicago superintendency:

> I need not assure you that it will be one of the most delight-
> ful things in the world for all of us at the University if
> you can be persuaded to come to Chicago as the superin-
> tendent of schools. . . . The time is ripe. With the mayor
> back of us we can introduce a great number of reforms. Of
> course this can be done more easily in connection with
> a new superintendent than with the old staff.[32]

Andrews arrived hoping to implement some of the reforms
indicated in the Harper Report through administrative means,
but he soon found his plans stymied by the resistance and antagonism of the city's teachers and, ultimately, of the board
of education.[33] The teachers were immediately suspicious of
Andrews because of his close connection with Harper, and his
first public pronouncements did nothing to quiet their fears. His
first public address to the system's assembled teachers and principals, on October 8, 1898, was a masterpiece of paternalism. He
directed the teachers and principals to

> be heedful of your character and influence as man or
> woman, gentleman or lady. . . . Pay your bills promptly. If
> possible, avoid being in debt over a month.

He also instructed them to remain always healthy:

> You cannot attain the ideal I have described, or any other
> worthy ideal, without a good degree of health. . . . I there-
> fore emphasize the duty resting upon teachers, especially
> upon those charged with administrative responsibility,
> to have good health. Resolve and plan to be always well.

He impressed upon them the sacredness of their calling and the
futility of expecting monetary remuneration equal to the spiri-
tual satisfaction that the teachers and principals would receive
through uplifting society.

> Our profession is noble: let us do our part to keep it so.
> Its history is a history of sacrifice, or self-denial, or unre-
> quited toil. Faithful teaching, such as most of you are
> doing, never has been, it never will be, nay it never can be,
> adequately remunerated with money. It and filthy lucre
> are not comparable quantities, any more than holiness and
> muck.

The teachers were enjoined to carry out their noble mission through attention to cultivation and morality, to manners, to etiquette, to proper dress, "and to every social, political and moral obligation." If this were not already a weighty enough task, Andrews concluded his advice with the injunction to "never remit effort. . . . Criticize others keenly; criticize yourself severely, even savagely."[34]

Few teachers and principals could have listened to this address without a sinking heart. Andrews made clear that they would be tightly supervised and that he would expect the utmost effort from them without providing them with genuine professional responsibility or adequate pay. He indicated his willingness to interfere in the pettiest details of school administration: he encouraged teachers to decorate the schools with high-quality art to raise the esthetic standards of the pupils, but then told them that "if in doubt about any art piece, do not install it without due counsel, which will at any time be made available to you on application at my office."[35] Teachers quickly came to resent what they viewed as Andrews's petty tyranny, and they nicknamed him "Bulletin Ben" in response to the stream of memos that poured from his office.[36]

School board members displayed little more enthusiasm for Andrews's attempts at bureaucratic innovation than did the teachers.[37] They disliked his authoritarian attitude and felt that he rode roughshod over their prerogatives as board members. They occasionally went so far as to hold committee meetings without informing the superintendent, and Andrews found that he could not expect to receive the degree of deference that had been accorded him as a university president.[38] His autocratic actions also alienated his administrative subordinates, including Mrs. Ella Flagg Young, his highly popular district superintendent, who resigned in 1899 in protest of his centralizing tendencies. Her resignation led the editor of a local educational journal to speculate openly whether Andrews was worth the trouble that he brought: "It will not take long for the teachers, or even the board of education, to choose between old and well tried servants and a new and reckless one, whose mistakes are so frequent and annoying that even his acknowledged abilities cannot longer atone for them."[39]

Andrews's belief in the uplifting mission of the public schools rested upon a fundamental contempt for the culture of the immigrant population the schools served. He did not hesitate to express his opinion that the poor people of the cities lived as they did because "they [had] no arousing wish for any better fare."[40] He believed that it was the task of the public school system to awaken the slumbering humanity of the poor, and to this end he extolled the methods of the kindergarten, which produced results that were "more than gratifying." If the schools could reach even one child per family, the effects might be incalculable:

> Not only do most of the little ones [in kindergarten] themselves acquire a beautiful unselfishness and sweetness of temper, but each becomes in its own home a missionary force. Cases are not rare where a single child three or four years old trained in the kindergarten has reformed the house habits of an entire family; the mother first, then the elder sisters, then the rude big brother, and last the coarse, grimy, dull father, coming to be personally cleaner, tidier about the house, less piggish at table, less animal and more human, cultivated and moral every way.[41]

Andrews found that his talk about turning kindergartens into missionaries fell upon increasingly deaf ears as he antagonized nearly all elements of the school staff. He also realized that his friendship with Harper was viewed as a liability by many members of the community who were suspicious of Harper's Rockefeller connection and disliked the Harper Commission's plan for reorganizing the schools. Harper recognized this also, having written to Andrews, "I am inclined to think that it will be just as good for you and me if we are not seen too much together." In another letter, he commended Andrews for holding his own against the board of education and urged, "If at any time I can serve you in a quiet way, please command me."[42] Andrews had confided similar doubts about their being publicly linked; in December 1898 he wrote to Harper, "Many times I shall send you counsel. At present, for reasons which I fully understand, we must work apart."[43] As Andrews's popularity plummeted, however, he forgot his own scruples and sent Harper a desperate scrawled note requesting immediate aid in forestalling his ouster by the board of education.

> Latest advice makes it certain that the plot is on to oust me . . . and to administer [the schools] absolutely in the interest of City Hall politics. If I am displaced the next Superintendent . . . will be absolutely subservient . . . to political interests. . . .
>
> Personally I care nothing about the result, but if the plot succeeds it will set back the Cause of the Schools fifty years. It will mean the permanent repression—for our time—of all that the [Harper] Commission sought.[44]

Andrews told Harper in the same letter that "the only help" lay in the possibility of Harper approaching key figures at the Chicago newspapers and explaining the true situation to them. He assured Harper, "If any doubt as to the meaning of the firing movement still figures in your thought I should be glad to talk with you on the subject." Harper's response is unknown as no copy of his reply survives, but he either could not or would not forestall Andrews's dismissal. Andrews, who had proved a political failure on every count, returned to the quieter world of university administration, taking up the presidency of the University of Nebraska after his departure from the Chicago school system in 1900.

The first attempt to implement some of the goals of the Harper Commission through administrative means had failed, but business and civic organizations continued to press for legislative enactment of the commission's recommendations. Bills embodying the commission's recommendations were presented to the state legislature in Springfield in 1901, 1903, and 1905.[45] The Civic Federation of Chicago, an organization that claimed to represent both business and labor, but, in fact, in Chicago was made up almost exclusively of businessmen, called a conference of leading citizens to prepare a new bill after the original Harper Bill failed in the legislature.[46] Andrew Draper, president of the

University of Illinois, presented an address to the Education Commission of One Hundred of the Civic Federation, in which he urged that citizens should work actively for reform of the school system along the lines indicated in the Harper Commission Report. Draper, who was formerly the New York commissioner of education, was one of a rising breed of educational administrators.[47] He insisted that the board of education should be small and that its members "should be representative of the business and property interests, as well as of the intelligence and genuine unselfishness of the city."[48]* The Civic Federation indicated its agreement by drawing up its own bill to present to the 1903 session of the state legislature. The bill called for increased powers for the superintendent, who would control appointment, promotion, and firing of teachers, and would determine the course of study. The superintendent would be given a five-year contract in order to insulate him from political pressures. The school board would be reduced to 9 members from the original 21.[49]

Clayton Mark, a businessman who had served a term on the school board and later became head of the Commercial Club's education committee, joined with newly appointed Superintendent Edwin Cooley in writing yet another school reform bill for presentation to the 1903 session of the legislature. The Mark–Cooley Bill resembled the Civic Federation's bill except that it did not call for a reduction in size of the school board.[50]

---

*Draper's speech ended on a note of Anglo-Saxon chauvinism and exaltation seldom found even in the frequently explicitly elitist writings of the period. He concluded his address with the peroration:

> Doubt not the final outcome. We will go forward in the spirit of the Saxon race. That race has abundantly shown its ability to govern. It is both forceful and tolerant. It can command order. It leads to better things. It wages hard battle: and it mends, and heals, and helps. When Kitchener proposed to set up a Gordon Memorial College at Khartoum he represented the power, and he expressed the purpose, of English-speaking peoples throughout the world. In Kipling's virile verse,
>
> *They terribly carpet the earth with dead, and before their cannon cool,*
> *They walk unarmed by twos and threes, to call the living to school.*

A strangely bloody vision of public schooling! (Draper, 1900)

Both bills failed in the state legislature, due in large part to opposition by the Chicago Teachers' Federation, which succeeded once again in mobilizing the labor movement against the school centralization measures.[51] The CTF also won the support of such middle-class civic organizations as the Chicago Woman's Club and of reform leaders such as Louis F. Post. Post, later a member of the school board and still later President Wilson's assistant secretary of labor, wrote that "taken all in all, the Civic Federation school bill is about as vicious a piece of school legislation as could well be devised at this stage of municipal progress."[52] Post directed most of his fire at the provisions of the bill that increased the power of the superintendent, charging that teachers would be deprived of voice in an autocratic system. He dismissed complaints that the teachers had abdicated their professional status by joining the CFL, observing that such complaints came with "ill grace." In his view, the members of a liberal profession who were "deemed fit only to obey orders abjectly without consultation, [did not need] be especially vain about the liberal character of their profession."[53]

The Chicago Teachers' Federation felt in a strong enough position after the defeat of the school reorganization bills to promote its own school reform measure, a move for the direct election of school board members rather than their appointment by the mayor. The Chicago Federation of Labor had long supported the election of board members, and it threw its weight behind the teachers' drive to win an elected board.[54] With help from their allies, the teachers organized a petition drive to call a city-wide referendum on the question of an elected versus an appointed school board. The referendum was held in April 1904, and the elected board won by a better than two-to-one margin.[55] The state legislature subsequently killed the plan for an elected board, however, and the mayor retained the power of appointment.

The Charter Fight

Conflicts over school reform bills were becoming regular features of Illinois legislative sessions, but in 1907 a larger political dispute occurred that bore upon the schools. Chicago as a city lacked the power of home rule; beginning in 1903 local officials and businessmen tried to secure piecemeal reform legislation giving Chicago increased powers, but they soon decided that Chicago's progress would be hindered as long as it remained largely dependent on the state legislature for approval of local measures.[56] The City Council responded to the pressure by mandating the establishment of a charter convention in December 1905. The charter convention was assigned the task of drawing up the new charter that would be required if Chicago achieved home rule; it had 74 members who were appointed by the political powers of the city. Reformers such as Charles Merriam, a University of Chicago political science professor who later served as alderman and ran for mayor as a progressive Republican, viewed the charter convention as an unprecedented opportunity to reorder the city's administration along rational lines and to introduce the principles of sound city government. Initially, the project won support from most elements of the city, as there was general agreement that the interests of Chicago would be best served if it were not tied to a state legislature dominated by downstate rural representatives.

The members of the charter convention quickly found themselves facing difficult political decisions. Controversies developed over the drawing of ward boundaries and over the redesigning of the city's taxing authority.[57] The charter convention finished its work, however, and the completed document was given to the state legislature for its approval. The legislature substantially altered the charter, removing provisions such as that calling for direct primary elections, and the charter was then submitted to Chicago's voters for final approval.

The charter immediately met with strong opposition. The Chicago Federation of Labor and the Chicago Teachers' Federation campaigned for a "no" vote on the grounds that the charter contained autocratic provisions. The middle-class reform community split on the question of whether to support the charter, with some adopting the view of the labor organizations that it deserved to go down to defeat and others arguing that, while flawed, it would represent a step forward for Chicago. The business community was also internally divided on the charter question; fierce opposition came from ethnic groups who argued that the charter would result in a ban on Sunday drinking.

The educational provisions of the charter typified the aspects of the charter that led the labor movement to oppose it. The Merchants' Club of Chicago, which merged with the Commercial Club a short time later, had taken the initiative in drawing up the educational sections of the charter.[58] The Merchants' Club had sought the advice of the country's leading educational administrators in devising provisions that would lead to businesslike operation of the schools. In December 1906 the club held a discussion on how to create a more efficient administrative structure for the school system; the three invited speakers were Edward C. Eliot of St. Louis, James J. Storrow of Boston, and Nicholas Murray Butler, president of Columbia University. Butler had strong opinions on how the schools should be organized; he did not confine himself to propagandizing for his views but also played an active role in organizations such as the National Education Association in trying to insure that public school officials followed policies that met his approval. Butler believed that the key to the development of a good school system was the creation of a strong superintendency.[59] If a strong superintendent could be placed in charge, he told the Merchants' Club, and could be given the full authority due a member of a learned profession, then nine-tenths of the troubles of the school system would be over. Butler ridiculed the idea that public schools could be democratized through teachers' councils or any other means. He told the businessmen and their invited guests, the members of the board of education, that if he were a board member, he would do his best to see that any teacher who joined a labor organization was fired. It was absurd to talk of democratizing the schools; he would as soon talk about "the democratization of the treatment of appendicitis."[60]

Butler's views were akin to those embodied in the Harper Commission's report. The Merchants' Club drew up charter provisions that were broadly based upon the commission's recommendations. The charter proposals called for increased administrative centralization and the appointment, rather than election, of board members. No provision was made for teachers' councils or other means of teacher participation in policy making.[61] The Chicago Teachers' Federation opposed the charter provisions as it had opposed all previous attempts to implement the Harper Commission proposals.

The Chicago Federation of Labor agreed with its affiliate, the CTF, in attacking the educational provisions of the charter. The CFL maintained that the proposed changes in the school system were apparently designed to make the public schools "a cog in the capitalistic machine, so that the children [would] reach manhood's estate content in a condition of abject servitude."[62] The only purpose of creating the new, centralized system of authority would be to give a "reactionary mold to the minds" of the future workers. The labor federation had earlier called for the charter convention to include a provision for the election of school board members, but this was not adopted by the convention.[63] At the CFL meeting at which the charter "was raked fore and aft and steps were taken to defeat its adoption at the polls," the labor federation also criticized the charter for other provisions that struck it as undemocratic.[64] The CFL objected to the proposal to increase aldermen's terms from two to four years, arguing that it was reactionary because it removed the public servant still further from the "correcting hand of the electorate." The CFL also objected to the lack of provision for women's suffrage, the omission of the rights of referendum and initiative, and to revisions in the Civil Service laws that made it easier to fire employees charged with inefficiency. The labor federation adopted a motion calling for a campaign against the charter among all its constituent unions.

The charter's advocates also could not count on solid support from businessmen. Although businessmen had been active in the campaign to initiate the charter, some objected that the charter's passage would result in increased taxes. The Chicago city government, however poorly organized and corrupt, at least had the merit, from the business point of view, of keeping taxes low, partly through a very lax tax collection mechanism. The charter provided for a new taxing mechanism that was potentially costly in the long run. Disputes over the possible effect on the tax rate made it difficult for the Chicago business community to reach a unified position on the charter; the Chicago Association of Commerce held a meeting on the subject that ended inconclusively. Frank G. Hoyne, the 1906 president of the Chicago Real Estate Board and a member of the charter convention, argued against the adoption of the charter; his views represented a line of thought "held among the city's real estate interests." Hoyne reminded his fellow businessmen that "the foundation of a city rests upon its realty and the latter, therefore, should not be overtaxed. . . . Before government came property. If the charter passes, the tax rate under it will be excessive and burdensome."[65] Other businessmen spoke for the charter, and the executive committee of the Chicago Association of Commerce decided that, given the division of opinion, the association should take no stand on the charter question.[66]

The vote on the charter posed difficult questions for Chicago's reform advocates. Many of the middle-class professionals who had for years called for civic reform remained strongly committed to the charter. Typified by Charles Merriam, they argued that the charter represented a significant step forward, providing a means by which Chicago could shake off the control of the legislature and adopt an efficient administrative system.[67] Merriam considered the confused and overlapping system of local governing bodies in Chicago to be one of the key sources of corruption and of poor government. Even though he acknowledged the charter's flaws, he actively campaigned for its passage.

Others were far more critical of the charter and urged its rejection. While agreeing with Merriam that boss rule and inefficient government were Chicago's biggest problems, they contended that the passage of the charter might bolster instead of weaken boss rule. Harold Ickes, for example, who later became secretary of the interior under Franklin Roosevelt, argued that the new ward boundaries specified in the charter guaranteed a continuation of corrupt ward politics. Further, unlike Merriam, he expressed more sympathy with the anticharter arguments advanced by the labor movement. In one of three debates on the charter sponsored by the City Club, Ickes specifically noted the undemocratic nature of the charter's educational provisions: the charter would make "the entire school system an adjunct to the political machine" by providing that the mayor could remove school board members at will.[68] Other reform leaders, such as Louis F. Post and Raymond Robins, who had worked closely with Merriam in the past, were still more critical of the charter. Robins scorned the process by which the 74 charter representatives (who included himself and Merriam) had been selected; while the charter was allegedly designed to bring about "good government," the very political officials whose power would be undermined by the emergence of good government had chosen the charter representatives.[69]

Robins had closer ties to the labor movement than Merriam did; the latter often identified more strongly with the more liberal wing of the business community. Their division on the charter question reflected a deeper underlying split that beset the "good government" groups of Chicago. The reformers frequently faced political situations where the issues had already been defined by the polarized forces of labor and business. This left the reformers with the uncomfortable option of finding a compromise position (which was often difficult, as Jane Addams and later Superintendent Ella Flagg Young found) or of simply adopting different individual stances. The complex battle over the charter threw into relief the division among the reformers over whether more efficient government justified reforms that moved further from the idea of popular participation; the battle also highlighted division among businessmen on whether a possible rise in taxes could be justified by a more smoothly functioning government.

The fate of the charter was sealed by the intrusion of a still more explosive element into the controversy over its passage. Immigrant groups, formed into an umbrella organization called the United Societies, passionately opposed any restrictions on drinking liquor. The only immigrant groups that tended to align themselves with the prohibitionists were the Lutheran Scandinavians. Nearly all eastern and southern Europeans, as well as the Germans, viewed any attempts at prohibition as an assault on their culture.[70] In May 1907 the United Societies opened a campaign against the charter out of fear, caused by a remark by the mayor, that the charter's passage might result in a ban on Sunday drinking. Over the summer the United Societies and other ethnic bodies distributed reams of propaganda opposing the charter; as one of the leaders of the United Societies put it, the "really good people" went north or to the sea shore to escape the heat at that season. "When they returned," he boasted, "they could not understand why Germans, Bohemians, Poles, Danes, Norwegians and Italians should be so unanimous against the charter."[71]

The efforts of the charter advocates were futile against the combined opposition of the labor movement, businessmen worried about the tax rate, and the ethnic societies. On September 17, 1907, the charter went down to a resounding defeat, losing by more than 60,000 votes out of roughly 180,000 votes cast.[72]

Plans for restructuring the school system had thus repeatedly failed, but the Commercial Club made one final effort to implement the provisions of the Harper Commission's report. Theodore Robinson, a member of the school board and the chairman of the Commercial Club's education committee, prepared a new bill with the club's approval; it called for increased powers for the superintendent and a reduction of the school board to 15 members.[73] The bill was presented to the state legislature at the 1909 session. With the aid of two liberal school board members, Raymond Robins and John J. Sonsteby, the Chicago Federation of Labor and the Chicago Teachers' Federation successfully lobbied against the bill, which died in committee before reaching the senate floor.

Cooley and the Creation of a Strong Superintendency

Superintendent E. Benjamin Andrews had originally been hired with the hope, on the part of William Harper, at least, that he would act to implement administratively the plans for a more centralized school system. Step-by-step administrative changes might result in a more centralized system without provoking the immediate political conflict and bitter debate that resulted from the presentation of bills in the state legislature. Andrews proved to be so lacking in tact and political finesse, however, that he did not succeed in tightening the superintendent's authority, but his successor, Edwin G. Cooley, proved more adept in this regard.[74]

Cooley, who later became the Commercial Club's educational advisor and the author of the Cooley vocational education bill, demonstrated in the nine years (1900–1909) that he held the superintendency of the Chicago schools that he was an experienced political infighter. While Andrews had issued directives to the school board and teachers and passively expected to be obeyed, provoking observers to suggest that he would be better off in the more rarefied reaches of university administration, Cooley was under few illusions about the political forces he would confront.[75] From the beginning of his tenure as superintendent, he set about increasing the effective authority of the office and engaged in a series of prolonged and strategic battles with both the board of education and the teachers.[76]

Before Cooley's installation as superintendent, the board of education and 14 district superintendents shared much of the real operating power in the school system. The district superintendents operated semiindependent fiefdoms; they were never shifted from their districts and had sweeping authority within them to dictate the course of study and the appointment of teachers.[77] Over the course of several years, Cooley succeeded in having the number of district superintendents reduced to six, and by frequently shifting them from one district to another, he limited their ability to build up personal followings that would allow them to challenge the central office. District superintendents no longer retained the power to determine the curriculum; they became, to a much greater extent, agents of the superintendent's will rather than independent centers of authority. As Cooley cut the power of the district superintendents, he also began the process of creating his own central office staff. He appointed three assistant superintendents who operated out of the headquarters office and were responsible directly to him. The assistant superintendents soon superseded the district super-

intendents in power, and their appointment marked the beginning stages of a bureaucracy under the superintendent's immediate control.

Cooley also moved early to establish his authority to appoint
and promote teachers.[78] When Cooley assumed office, the district
superintendents and the members of the board of education drew
up the teachers' appointment lists. Individual board members
and influential school system officials were often besieged with
job seekers, and the appointment system offered numerous opportunities for favoritism and graft. The Harper Commission
had recommended that the superintendent make the decisions
on hiring and firing teachers, and although the recommendation
was not legally enacted, Cooley pressed the board into passing a
resolution stating that selecting teachers was a function of the
superintendent.[79] The resolution also required that the names of
any officials recommending particular candidates for office be
publicly listed; this was intended to reduce the amount of behind-
the-scenes patronage maneuvering. Cooley shocked the board of
education by later listing the names of several of its members as
having been among those who had tried to influence his selection of candidates.

Cooley intervened directly in the operations of the board of
education by insisting that the number of board committees be
sharply reduced. The Chicago school board had operated with as
many as 70 committees, and the board's functioning was marked
by confusion and overlapping assignments among members and
committees. Under Cooley's direction, the number of committees
was reduced to four, responsible for school management, buildings and grounds, finances, and compulsory education.[80]

Cooley's tightening of the administrative structure of the
school system achieved his main goal of making the superintendent the chief educational policy maker. Previous superintendents had often been politically adrift between contending
forces on faction-ridden boards, but Cooley early assumed the
reins of authority. In so doing, he altered board members' expectations of the role of the superintendent and created lasting
changes in the perception of the office. One indicator of the increasing importance of the superintendent as the originator of

policy was the frequency with which the superintendent's name appeared in board of education minutes. Some previous superintendents had barely figured in the minutes, but after Cooley took office, "from July 1st [1900] on, the reports of the school management committee consist of requests for the approval of the recommendations of the superintendent of schools."[81] Other board committees and the board as a whole soon followed the school management committee in looking to the superintendent to initiate policy decisions. On occasion, the board resented some of Cooley's directives, but its fundamental approval of the new centralization was indicated by its offer to Cooley of an unprecedented five-year contract beginning in 1902.[82]

Cooley's initial success was a result not only of his political skills and backing from the powerful business interests who later hired him as their educational advisor, but of the fact that he was working with a board of education appointed by a fairly conservative mayor, Carter Harrison. After 1905 Cooley had to contend with a far more liberal and antagonistic mayor who appointed seven school board members who often opposed Cooley. Cooley's position was further weakened because he had by then gained the intense enmity of the Chicago Teachers' Federation, which galvanized opposition to him in the labor movement as a whole. The disputes that arose between Cooley and the liberal board members, and between the liberal board members and the teachers, in the last five years of Cooley's tenure as superintendent are significant for what they reveal of the conflicting values among the different groups.

The composition of the school board and the general political climate of the city changed after Judge Edward Dunne defeated Carter Harrison in the 1905 mayoralty election. Harrison had been responsible for appointing the original conservative Harper Commission, and Harper's letters to E. Benjamin Andrews indicate that Harper believed the mayor to be a reliable ally. In contrast, Dunne was a liberal reformer whose chief campaign issues were immediate municipal ownership of public utilities and the need to move the school system in a less authoritarian direction.[83] The Chicago Teachers' Federation enthusiastically supported Dunne, both because of what it viewed as his general progressive program and because he was the federal judge who had ruled in favor of the CTF in its celebrated tax suit against the board of education; Dunne had ordered the board to disperse in the form of higher salaries to CTF members the extra funds gained through the CTF's successful fight against tax dodgers. Margaret Haley, the famous leader of the CTF's tax fight, spoke for Dunne at rallies throughout the city, and he publicly thanked her after his victory.

The teachers' hostility to Cooley sprang from several sources. On a general level, the CTF had waged numerous battles against the enactment of the Harper Commission recommendations, and the teachers did not want to see the report implemented through administrative means. They distrusted Cooley's centralization of power in his own office. On a more specific level, Cooley ignited the teachers' fervent opposition through the promulgation of a plan to promote teachers on the basis of "efficiency" ratings. As with most features of Cooley's program, this had originally been suggested in the Harper Commission report. Cooley argued that teachers would stop trying to do their best unless they were rated on their efficiency; the gearing of pay rates to the efficiency scores would provide "every teacher an opportunity for self-improvement and an incentive to use the opportunity."[84]

The teachers retorted that Cooley's supposedly impartial rating system was subject to gross favoritism and that the secrecy of the system violated teachers' democratic rights. Cooley's plan called for the teachers to be rated by their principals, with a provision for adjustment of the ratings by district superintendents to insure that marks would be "equalized" between different principals. The teachers were not allowed to see their ratings at any point, and this "secret marking" system aroused intense suspicion and resentment.[85]

The new school board members that Mayor Dunne appointed after his election in 1905 were drawn from the city's progressive leaders. Dunne appointed board members in both 1905 and 1906 as two sets of board positions became open.[86] Nearly all the Dunne appointees were well-known social reformers, including Jane Addams, Louis F. Post, Raymond Robins, Dr. Cornelia De Bey, and John J. Sonsteby.[87] Jane Addams became head of the important school management committee in a move that delighted the Chicago Teachers' Federation. Addams had long had close ties to the leaders of the CTF, although she sometimes felt ambivalent about the CTF's militant prolabor stance. Haley later wrote that she had suggested to Dunne that he appoint Addams.[88] In 1902, Addams had aided the CTF leadership, although reluctantly: John Fitzpatrick had invited the CTF to affiliate officially with the Chicago Federation of Labor, and the issue was debated at a mass membership meeting of the CTF. The leaders of the teachers' group, Margaret Haley and Catharine Goggin, favored affiliation but feared some membership opposition to so unorthodox a move. Addams gave what was intended to be a neutral speech summarizing the pros and cons of affiliation, but when pressed from the floor, she admitted that she thought that labor affiliation would supply a "very much needed element of strength to the teachers in their struggle on behalf of the children, the schools and themselves."[89] Addams later said she felt she had been pressed to take too strong a stand and "had been put on the defensive ever since in that matter."[90] She complained to Margaret Haley that she spent most of her time at a White House luncheon justifying her remark to President Roosevelt. In spite of such occasional differences, however, the teachers considered Addams a reliable ally at the time of her appointment; she provided an important link between the world of the middle-class reform community and that of the unionized teachers.

The relationship between Addams and the leaders of the Chicago Teachers' Federation underwent considerable strain, however, early in her term on the board. The tension that developed sprang in part from different personal modes of responding to situations (Addams was a conciliator while Haley was more aggressive), but more fundamentally it developed because of somewhat different perspectives on the part of Addams and the CTF's leaders. These differences in emphases and priorities were characteristic of differences between the city's liberal reformers and trade unionists generally.

The immediate source of tension between Addams and the teachers centered on Addams's response to a modification of the teachers' promotion plan submitted to the board in May 1906 by

Superintendent Cooley. Cooley called for a program under which teachers would have to take either an exam or five outside courses of 36 hours each before they could become eligible for salary increases. At the time Cooley submitted his proposal, the board of education was divided between Dunne and Harrison appointees, and Addams's vote was necessary for the proposal's passage. Addams voted for the promotion plan on May 23, to Margaret Haley's great indignation.[91]

Addams was torn between, as she put it, the needs of "democracy" on the one hand and "efficiency" on the other.[92] As head of the school management committee and a noted figure in the city, she found herself in an acutely uncomfortable position between the polarized contestants. She wrote in her autobiography, "I certainly played a most inglorious part in this unnecessary conflict; I was chairman of the School Management Committee during one year when a majority of the members seemed to me exasperatingly conservative, and during another year when they were frustratingly radical, and I was of course highly unsatisfactory to both."[93]

Addams distrusted the superintendent and the conservative board members who had worked to centralize the school system. They were, she wrote, "honest men," but they "unfortunately became content with the ideals of an 'efficient business administration.'"[94] They became so imbued with the "commercialistic ideal" of high salaries for top officials, combined with low pay for everyone else and maximum "output," that the schools were losing their democratic character. The growing bureaucracy was necessary and "well-intentioned," but it was needlessly self-assertive. The teachers, on the other hand, were unduly impatient and aggressive in their assertion of their rights. The proposal for promotions based on study and examinations provided "undoubted benefit," and it was "most impatiently repudiated by the Teachers' Federation."[95]

Addams was particularly sensitive to criticism of her role on the school board because she felt that the new school board members were popularly viewed as tools of the teachers' federation.[96] She hastened to say, "During my tenure of office I many times talked to the officers of the Teachers' Federation, but I was seldom able to follow their suggestions."[97] Addams's uncomfortable position between the conservative, business-oriented school board members and the militant teachers reflected in microcosm the problems of the middle-class reform movement as it strove to secure its visions of both social justice and social efficiency. The teachers' opposition to the efficiency ratings followed both from their distrust of the fairness of a system based on subjective, secret ratings and from the long-held union principle that merit pay was divisive and destructive of collective solidarity. Addams wavered uncomfortably between the union position and the social efficiency position, finally declaring that the whole conflict was unnecessary. If only both sides could have been reasonable, an accommodation could have been reached, but as it was, "Both sides inevitably exaggerated the difficulties of the situation and both felt that they were standing by important principles."[98] On the school board, Addams found that attempts at mediation "were looked upon as compromising and unworthy, by both partisans." In her frustration, she found herself "belonging to neither party" in this and future conflicts during her tenure.[99]

The teachers' federation, for its part, was profoundly disappointed in Jane Addams. The teachers accused her of "having had her opportunity and thrown it away" and declared that she had been swayed by the businessmen on the board.[100] Margaret Haley later wrote that when she heard that the report had been adopted by the board of education and that Addams had voted for it, "I experienced one of the keenest disappointments that had ever come to me in my life." Haley insisted that Addams had previously declared her opposition to tying salary increases to performance on outside exams or to taking external classes, stating rather that teachers had to have an internal source of motivation.[101]

After Mayor Dunne appointed the second round of board members in July 1906, the conflict over teachers' promotion was temporarily resolved in the teachers' favor. The board began to revise some of Cooley's programs, and he was faced for the first time with an effective challenge to his authority from the board. A subcommittee of the school management committee, chaired by Louis F. Post, undertook a *Special Report on the Promotional*

Examination and Secret Marking of Teachers. The report attacked Cooley's scheme of efficiency ratings, declaring that the new system had inherent problems of favoritism. The subcommittee declared that it was at a loss as to how Cooley's plan could eliminate political influence from the school system. Principals could arbitrarily give teachers efficiency marks which could still more arbitrarily be equalized by district superintendents, all without the knowledge of the teachers. There was, the subcommittee concluded, no assurance against favoritism on the part of the people who conducted or supervised the marking process. Such a system could only serve to excite "demoralizing suspicions" on the part of the teaching force.[102]

The newly constituted board of education voted to eliminate the secret ratings and also took a number of other steps that met with the teachers' approval. The board that had been appointed in 1905 had already voted to withdraw an appeal of Judge Dunne's decision in favor of the Chicago Teachers' Federation in the tax-fight case; the new board also moved to establish a system of teachers' councils with official standing as advisors to the board of education on curriculum and related teaching matters.[103] One of Cooley's close assistants, Charles D. Lowry, wrote more than 35 years later that the teachers' councils were a "doleful farce." Lowry referred back to Nicholas Murray Butler's 1906 speech to the Merchants' Club, commenting that truly did he remark when he learned of the proposals for the democratization of education, "You could as reasonably democratize the operation for appendicitis."[104] The teachers, however, considered that the plan for a council system was a step in the right direction of reducing the superintendent's unilateral authority.

The reforms came to naught, however, when Dunne was defeated for reelection in 1907. The newspapers and the business community had generated a sustained campaign against Dunne, arguing that he was selling out to pressure from organized labor. The Chicago newspapers published many editorial attacks against the new board of education and its proposals for "school democratization." Jane Addams wrote that "the newspapers had so constantly reflected and intensified the ideals of a business Board . . . that from the beginning any attempt the new Board made to discuss educational matters, only excited their derision and contempt."[105] Cooley's associate Lowry noted with satisfaction that the "destructive activities" of the new board "were given wide publicity and were the subject of much adverse criticism."[106] In the campaign, Dunne was defeated by Fred Busse, who was strongly favored by business leaders. The *Chicago Association of Commerce Bulletin* reported glowingly on the results of a meeting between Busse and business leaders shortly after his election:

> On Saturday evening, April 20, Mayor Busse, his entire
> cabinet, and seventy-five representative Chicago business-
> men dined together at the Athletic Club. . . .
>   Both the men who were there and the things which were
> said caused President [David] Forgan [of the Association of
> Commerce] to remark to the *Bulletin* that it was a meeting
> auspicious of the new era now dawning in the civic history
> of this city. It was a conference of the new municipal
> authorities with the city's business interests, and its effect
> upon a participant was inspirational. No partisan note was
> sounded to check the growing hope that it is possible
> to conduct the municipal business of Chicago as if it were a
> vast institution in trade or manufacture.[107]

One of Busse's first actions was to try to take immediate control of the board of education. In the past, although the mayor had the power of appointment to the board, the members once appointed were not subject to immediate removal by the mayor. Busse, however, demanded that 12 of the 21 members resign immediately. They protested and took their case to the courts. In January 1908 the Illinois Supreme Court ruled that they had been improperly removed and ordered their reinstatement.[108] In the interim, however, the new board, dominated by Busse appointees, had begun undoing the work of the previous board. Jane Addams had felt too burned by the early conflicts to take a stand on the battle between the Busse and Dunne appointees, but she commented sorrowfully that "during the months following the upheaval and the loss of my most vigorous colleagues, under the regime of men representing the leading Commercial Club of the city who honestly believed that they were rescuing the schools from a condition of chaos, I saw one beloved measure after another withdrawn."[109] Lowry reported that Superintendent Cooley once again took charge as the dominant force in running the city's schools: "Business again came to the board through the reports and recommendations of the superintendent. . . . Honors came to Mr. Cooley in recognition of his work."[110]

Because she believed that the teachers needed allies and she favored Dunne's progressive stand on the municipal control of public utilities and public transport, Margaret Haley had been one of Judge Edward Dunne's prominent supporters when he first ran for mayor in 1905. After Dunne's defeat in 1907 and the renewed conservative dominance of the school board, she commented on the need for a broad progressive movement to bring about changes both in the schools and in the community as a whole. Too often this movement had been divided: "It is a pity," she wrote, "that the progressive movement outside of the school has so little grasp and no touch with the same struggle going on in the educational field." But it was equally a pity that the teachers themselves were "frequently out of touch with the great movement for democracy outside of the schools."[111] The appointment of Jane Addams, Louis F. Post, and other progressive leaders to the school board had represented a confluence of the two movements (in spite of differences in emphasis and tactics between the teachers' leaders and the liberal board members), but it was only a short time before businessmen again were able to assert their control. Had the people of Chicago understood the significance of the merger of the movements inside the schools and in the community as well as the business interests had, Haley said, they would not have been persuaded by the hue and cry raised by the newspapers against the Dunne board. As it was, however, the teachers faced a return to sharp conflicts with the board of education over teachers' working conditions and benefits and over the control of educational policy.

The Attack on the Teachers

Cooley resigned in 1909, citing health reasons.[112] The tone of Cooley's February letter to the board made it apparent that the years of controversy had reduced his energy for further battles. He immediately joined a textbook firm, inspiring criticism from the labor movement, which had already objected that Cooley was too close to the textbook companies. The board of education deliberated at length on the choice of a new superintendent. Six months after Cooley announced his decision to leave, the board was still wrangling over the choice of a successor, with the *Tribune* commenting that the board meetings were "like a Bear Pit."[113] Ultimately, the board made a surprising choice. In spite of its hostility to the unionized teachers, expressed through such means as raising the salaries of most school employees except the teachers, the board appointed a superintendent who eventually antagonized most of the businessmen on the board while supporting the teachers.[114]

Ella Flagg Young, who was 64 when she was first appointed by the board, had been a disciple of John Dewey at the University of Chicago and was widely recognized as both an excellent teacher and an outstanding administrator. Young had come up through the ranks of the Chicago school system, starting as an elementary school teacher in 1862, progressing to the principalship of a new training school for teachers in 1865, and becoming assistant superintendent in 1887. After resigning her assistant superintendency under Benjamin Andrews in 1899, she obtained a Ph.D. under Dewey at the University of Chicago. She was then appointed to a professorship at the university, a post she left to become the head of the Chicago Teachers' College in 1905.[115]

Young combined a strongly held educational philosophy with administrative ability. She was poised, self-confident, and politically astute enough to rise to the top job in a male-dominated system. She was interested not simply in holding title to positions but in exercising as much power in them as democratically possible in the service of her goals.[116] As she proved throughout her career, she was more than willing to resign a position if she believed she could not act freely in it. Young had excellent rapport with the Chicago Teachers' Federation; her ideas on how to teach effectively and her intimate knowledge of the Chicago school system won teachers' respect, as did her commitment to improving the working conditions of the teaching force. Far from disapproving of the unionization of teachers, from the turn of the century on she had encouraged teachers to organize to fight for their interests.[117] Catharine Goggin, second only to Margaret Haley in influence in the CTF, particularly admired Young. Their acquaintance stemmed from the 1870s, when Goggin had first been a student at the practice school supervised by Young, and had continued when Goggin became a teacher at a school supervised by Young when she had become assistant superintendent.[118]

While a strong leader, Young believed that school systems should be run in a democratic rather than autocratic fashion. Her dissertation at the University of Chicago, *Isolation in the School*, developed her idea that teachers required not external pressure to perform well, but internal motivation and a good working environment that led to a spirit of collective endeavor.[119] Young's beliefs were congenial to John Dewey, who later wrote that he had learned a great deal about education from her. He commented that what he chiefly got from Mrs. Young was "the translation of philosophic conceptions into their empirical equivalents. More times than I could well say I didn't see the meaning or force of some favorite conception of my own till Mrs. Young gave it back to me."[120]

Young was willing to put her ideas into practice. When Superintendent Andrews's autocratic governance brought him into conflict with the teachers, Young resigned as a district superintendent.[121] She was offended by the way his centralizing impulses had reduced her and other administrators to the status of "ignoble subordinates" who lacked the ability to carry out their goals. She was not willing, in the words of the editor of the *Chicago Teacher and School Board Journal*, to "sit at her desk from month to month . . . and draw her salary" but find that her opinions were ignored. She was already sufficiently valued that her resignation caused a civic outcry, being treated as "a public misfortune" that was "near being a kind of local educational calamity."[122] (Andrews, for his part, expressed in a not very clear way his view that Young's opposition was tied to the effort to fire him. He wrote to William Rainey Harper that "whatever the origin of Mrs. Young's involvement, it is now being used in the most evident manner to further the boss interest." This, Andrews concluded, would set back all efforts to implement the Harper Commission proposals, but was not surprising, as "Mrs. Young has been a foe of the Commission from the beginning."[123]) Young's resignation sparked protests from the teachers, who viewed Young as their champion and an exemplary educational administrator. Several thousand teachers signed a petition, addressed to the workingmen of the city, that called for Young's return. The petition stated that Young had resigned in order to "impress on the minds of the citizens of Chicago the danger that lurks in the present movement of Mr. Andrews." Although the petition was presented to the school board and the protest received much attention in the press, Young was not recalled to her position.[124]

Young's selection as superintendent by a conservative board appears to have been a result both of her remarkable personal qualities of leadership, which were recognized by nearly all who came in contact with her, and of a desire to diminish the polarization that existed in the Chicago school system.[125] Margaret Haley declared that Young had been selected because she could get along with the teachers.[126] Young had high credibility among the teachers, and the board members may have hoped that, while Andrews's and Cooley's aggressive tactics had failed to bring order into the school system, Young might succeed with a more subtle approach. Young was to discover, however, as had Jane Addams, that the middle ground shrank beneath her when conflicts developed between the board and the teachers.

No major controversies marred Mrs. Young's first three years in office.[127] Young worked to reduce class size, and she continued her efforts to see that teachers were properly trained. She believed that students could not learn well if they were hungry or uncomfortable, and she emphasized the need to see that children were properly fed and schoolrooms well ventilated. Under her direction, schools were designed with good lighting and workable floor plans; she fervently opposed the graft that usually accompanied Chicago's school building programs. In keeping with her ideas on the value of teacher participation in educational decisions, she recommended to the board a system of teachers' councils that would meet on school time.[128] In March 1913 the school board accepted her recommendation.[129] Young did not have in mind agencies designed to transmit orders from the top; she once remarked that she well remembered how when she was a teacher, "we went meekly to the institutes that we were summoned to attend by the superintendent."[130] In order to make sure that administrators did not repress teachers' initiatives, she insisted that principals not be present during council meetings, having already written in her dissertation that at teachers' councils "the voice of authority of position not only must not dominate, but must not be heard."[131] Victor Olander of the Illinois State Federation of Labor later remarked that when it came to understanding the importance of teachers' councils in the educational process, Young had provided an education for him.[132]

In 1912, Young ran into her first serious political trouble with the board. Rumors floated through the city's educational circles that Young had lost the confidence of Mayor Harrison. Harrison denied these rumors, sending Young a letter of reassurance. It was clear, however, that the board was beginning to take a more dubious view of the superintendent and that her honeymoon period was over. Young's fight against the Cooley vocational school plan helped increase board doubts about her.[133] She strongly supported vocational education throughout her career; she believed that students needed a mixture of academic and manual subjects in order to hold their interest and provide them with useful training. She joined with the Chicago Teachers' Federation and the Chicago Federation of Labor in fighting the Cooley Bill because its provisions for a dual school system struck her as undemocratic.[134] Young served as a member of the Illinois State Federation of Labor's 1914 Committee on Vocational Education and signed its report strongly attacking the Cooley Bill.[135] Young said that she opposed the Cooley Bill because she did not believe "in training the young to belong to a lower industrial class"; this comment won the criticism of the *Daily News,* which declared that Young was stirring up class antagonism.[136] Board members began to criticize Young's recommendations on policy and personnel. In 1912 Catharine Goggin wrote to Margaret Haley that Young was becoming increasingly concerned about her position via-à-vis the board, and that in particular she was worried over the board's growing tendency to appoint special committees that might diminish her authority.[137]

In 1912, an episode occurred that highlighted Young's difficulty in trying to retain the confidence of both the teachers and the board. In 1907 the CTF had won a provision that established a reorganized pension fund; the fund was placed under the control of six trustees drawn from the teaching force and three representing the board of education.[138] Members of the board of education had expressed a desire to gain greater control of the pension fund. When Young had been interviewed for the superintendency in 1909, one board member had asked her where she stood on the question of expanding board of education representation among the pension trustees. Young replied that expanded representation might help give the fund a sounder base and that she thought the teachers could be brought to see the advantages of this. In 1912, Young's words were recalled to her by Alfred Urion, president of the school board and corporation counsel for Armour and Company. Urion told Young that he wanted her to persuade the teachers to accept more school board representation on the pension board.[139]

When Young told Margaret Haley that she had already committed herself to Urion's position, Haley expressed surprise and disappointment. The CTF became suspicious of the efforts to revise the makeup of the trustees when they found that one board member actively promoting the change, William Rothmann, had kept all the interest from a police pension fund he had formerly supervised. Under Urion's proposed plan, Rothmann would have headed the pension board because he chaired the school board's finance committee.* The teachers disregarded an effort by Young to work out a compromise that would have

---

*At the same time that he was the president of the board of education, Urion was the attorney of record for Armour in a tax suit brought by the teachers against Armour and 19 other major corporations. The teachers claimed that the corporations had been escaping taxes on a valuation of $250 million a year because their capital stock was not taxed. Rothmann also had a certain negative interest in the teachers' tax suit. His law partner, Roy O. West, was the president of the Board of Review, and the tax suit was directed against West's failure to assess the corporations (Margaret A. Haley, "Alderman Kennedy's Four Points," *Margaret A. Haley's Bulletin*, October 21, 1915, p. 6).

given the teachers higher salaries in return for accepting the alteration in the pension board's structure. They voted to reject any revisions in its composition. The conflict moved to the state legislature, where Haley's and Urion's forces fought for opposing bills. Haley's bill ultimately won, although Young testified for Urion's.[140] Young's relations with the teachers were not soured by their difference of opinion on this issue, but it appeared that she had been pitted against the teachers. It also became evident that where the teachers felt their vital interests were at stake, even Young's influence was not enough to make them change their position.

Tension between the CTF and the school board did not abate during Young's tenure. The differences between the opposing parties were too great to be bridged by force of personality, however widely Young's educational expertise and leadership qualities were admired. Mayor Harrison played an ambivalent role; although he had informed Young in July 1912 that he supported her, in that month he appointed several conservative board members who disagreed with her views. These board members, who included William Rothmann, were intent on destroying the influence of the Chicago Teachers' Federation. In January 1913 Harrison appointed Jacob Loeb, a real estate developer strongly opposed to the CTF, to fill a special vacancy on the board, thus increasing Young's troubles.[141] Harrison is reported to have observed in 1913, "I told [the board] that the time to kill that Federation was when it first started and before it had grown so powerful."[142] He appointed board members who did not share his view that the federation was too powerful to kill.

Young's basic attitudes were at odds with those of the majority of members of the board of education. She had been hired in spite of philosophical differences between her and many board members; as polarization continued between teachers and board and Young failed to exert a moderating influence, board members became increasingly critical of her. In controversies such as that over the pension fund the teachers demonstrated that in spite of their admiration for Young they would go their own political way, and Young demonstrated that in spite of disagreements with the CTF she would not join in a vendetta against the teachers.

The ideological differences between Jacob Loeb, who became president of the board, and Ella Flagg Young were expressed clearly in a spontaneous debate between them which took place at the 1916 convention of the National Education Association, after Young had retired. When Loeb finished reading a speech that indirectly but clearly attacked the Chicago Teachers' Federation, Young jumped up to reply.[143] She said that she had originally been dismayed by the CTF's affiliation with the Chicago Federation of Labor, as she thought that this made the teachers seem "grasping" and out for their own influence. But she had come to understand the CTF's reasons for joining with the labor movement:

> I was not large enough in the beginning to see, I had not the insight to see, that these women were realizing that they had not the freedom, the power, which people should have who are to train the minds of the children.

The affiliation with the CFL brought them respect and power:

> When they were affiliated with the Labor Union I was sorry. I thought they had made a great mistake . . . and on general principles I would be willing to make that statement today. But what affected my general principles and brought me down to something special? It was this. They found that in order to get anything done they must have voting power behind them. And they found that the people, the men, in their own station and rank in life, the college-bred men, were not ready to do anything for them; therefore they were compelled to go in with those who had felt the oppression and the grind of the power of riches. That is why they went into the Federation of Labor.

The bitterness between the teachers and the board had been brought about, Young concluded, by "class antagonism." When the teachers had brought corporate tax dodgers to book in their first great victory, the hostility of the city's powerful against them was assured.[144]

As the realities of Young's political position became clearer, her support within the board of education began to erode. She was unanimously reelected superintendent in December 1912, but only weeks later the board moved to undercut her authority. Board members objected that the elementary school curriculum had been filled with "fads and frills" at the expense of the three R's. The board voted to remove control over the course of study from Young.[145] Later both Loeb and Rothmann repeatedly approached Young and asked her to demote teachers who were federation leaders; in particular, they asked her to demote or dismiss teachers who had fought against the board-sponsored pension fund bill in the legislature.[146] Young resisted this pressure, but she felt increasingly badgered by the board members. Her cherished idea of giving teachers a voice in educational policy languished, and instead she found herself fighting a rearguard action to protect the teachers from attacks.

In July 1913 Young resigned. According to Haley, she "explained to Mayor Harrison that she did so because she refused to yield to the insistent demands of Loeb and other members of the Board that she penalize teachers for what she considered an exercise of their rights as citizens."[147] Young had sufficient popularity and political standing that Mayor Harrison came under immediate pressure to use his influence to get the board to retain her. Delegations of women visited the mayor, telling him of Young's contributions to public education. Harrison announced his support for Young and pressured his board appointees to persuade her to withdraw her resignation. In the face of public outcry and the mayor's actions, the board voted 14–1 on July 30, 1913, to ask for Young's return.[148]

Young retained her post in the belief that she had received a mandate that would enable her to regain some of the freedom of action she had lost the preceding year. Only five months later, however, in December 1913, Young resigned again when the board split evenly on whether to reelect her as superintendent.[149] She was shocked by the board's lack of support. She believed that she could not continue to serve as superintendent if she no longer had the authority to act as operating head; while conservatives in Chicago had long argued for increasing the power of the superintendent, in the rare circumstance of a liberal superintendent they responded by trying to strip the superintendent of customary aspects of power. Young had too strong a personality, and was too sure of what was intended, to accept this.

The December resignation led to an even larger groundswell of protest against the board from Chicago's reform-minded citizens and from the teachers than had occurred the first time. Jane Addams, Mrs. George Bass (president of the Chicago Woman's Club), and other civic leaders met with Mayor Harrison and urged him once more to use his influence with the board to insure that Young would return under acceptable conditions. Harrison issued a statement saying that he was sorry that the men he had appointed should have resorted to "underhand methods" to bring about Young's resignation.[150] Young's supporters organized a mass meeting on December 13, 1913, which attracted several thousand people. The speakers at the protest meeting represented a cross-section of Chicago's "good government" leaders, including Jane Addams, George Herbert Mead (of the University of Chicago and the City Club), and Harriet Vittum (president of the Woman's City Club). Margaret Haley was a featured speaker; she believed that Young had been driven out because of her refusal to bow to pressures to move against the CTF.[151] Haley called for an elected board of education to reduce business influence on the board.

Mayor Harrison again tried to get the board to reinstate Young. Unlike later mayors, who often claimed they had no direct power over school board affairs, Harrison acted decisively to force the board to accept Young. He removed five board members who had voted against her, and the newly constituted board voted in her favor. Young returned to office once again; she served two more years, from January 1914 to December 1915 before retiring. In returning, some later commentators thought that Young had committed the only violation of her principle of not serving as titular head of any agency she could not in reality control.[152]

Young's last years in office were marked not so much by resumption of direct attacks upon her as by a sustained board assault on the Chicago Teachers' Federation. In 1915, the opening stages of the assault began. A new mayor, William Hale Thompson, won the 1915 election; while declaring that he would stay aloof from school board matters, as they had brought only trouble for the three preceding mayors, Thompson indirectly aided the board members who were committed to destroying the CTF. He delayed making new appointments to the board in July, as was normally done, leaving the old board members free to press their case against the teachers.[153] Jacob Loeb sponsored a new regulation forbidding teachers to join unions or organizations affiliated with unions or "teachers' organizations which have officers, business agents or other representatives who are not members of the teaching force."[154] This direct attack on the federation was intended to sever its ties with the organized labor movement of the city. The CTF was supremely well organized and forcefully led, but Loeb and the others on the board of education were aware that the teachers greatly magnified their strength through their direct connection with the city's militant labor movement. The Loeb Rule was designed to break this united labor front.

Superintendent Young was dismayed by the passage of the Loeb Rule. After the board voted for it, Jacob Loeb was asked who would enforce the rule and find out which teachers were in violation. He replied that it would be the duty of the superintendent. When reporters asked Young if she would enforce it, she replied that it would be the duty of the board.[155]

The teachers and the Chicago Federation of Labor made immediate efforts to build public protest against the Loeb Rule. The board of education had passed the Loeb Rule on September 1, over Young's opposition. Nine days later, the Chicago Federation of Labor called a mass protest meeting at the Auditorium Theater. Over four thousand people jammed the theater and listened to speakers denounce the attack on the teachers' federation. The CFL had persuaded Samuel Gompers to come to Chicago to speak against the Loeb Rule, and John Fitzpatrick and John Walker, president of the state labor federation, joined Gompers in denouncing the board of education. Louis F. Post, the former school board member who had often worked with the teachers and the CFL, and who, in 1915, was assistant secretary of labor, also came to Chicago to speak at the rally. Post declared that the fight that had been going on for 18 years over the city's schools was not just a Chicago fight. It was, rather, part of a larger struggle between special interests and the common people. Businessmen had tried to turn the schools into factories, and the way they had chosen to do this was to increase the power of the superintendent and then to turn the teachers into completely subordinate employees.[156] Margaret Haley called once again for an elected school board to insure that the public would have some control over school matters.

Less than a week later, the Chicago Federation of Labor called a membership meeting on the Loeb Rule. Superintendent Young appeared at the meeting and received great applause.[157] John C. Kennedy, alderman for the city's twenty-seventh ward and a member of the Socialist party, also addressed the CFL. He told the CFL members that they needed to fight for control of the schools; organized labor had been largely responsible for the establishment of the public school system over the opposition of business, and labor would have to continue that struggle. Businessmen were only interested in preparing children to assume factory jobs; the business leaders had tried to change the school system "from a system of education for the development of the child, to a system to prepare the raw material for their factories and their shops and their mines and their stores. . . . They have wanted to give only such courses and to give such preparation and such training to the children as would be useful to these business concerns in turning out a maximum amount of goods."[158] It would depend on the forces of labor whether children of workers would receive a real education or would be "turned out as a machine made product." "That is the fight in which organized labor is engaged at this time," concluded Kennedy, and this fight was a continuation of the initial struggle to establish free schools.

The CFL adopted a resolution attacking the Loeb Rule by "unanimous rising vote." The resolution stated that "organized labor hereby expresses its determination that the rights of labor and of citizenship shall not be abridged or annulled by the Board of Education, and that the Teachers' Federation, an organization of demonstrated effectiveness in the protection of the public from grievous mismanagement or corruption in present or future Boards of Education, shall not be destroyed."[159]

The labor federation began an intensive campaign to press the city's aldermen to agree that they would not confirm the appointments of any school board members who opposed the right of teachers to belong to a labor organization. The CFL specifically called upon aldermen not to confirm any board of education nominees who did not state in writing that they would vote to rescind the Loeb Rule. The labor federation's letter to the aldermen said that "on behalf of the 250,000 organized men and women of Chicago, who with their families constitute one-third of the city's population and who certainly represent the entire working population," the aldermen were urged to acknowledge the right of teachers to form labor unions, a right that was "generally conceded throughout the civilized world and should obtain in Chicago."[160]

Scores of the CFL's individual union affiliates passed resolutions attacking the Loeb Rule and sent letters to their aldermen demanding that the rule be rescinded. Copies of such resolutions are extant from, among others, the Carpenters and Joiners Union, the International Association of Bridge, Structural and Ornamental Iron Workers, the Electrical Workers, the Steam and Operating Engineers, the Cigar Makers Union, the United Garment Workers, the Painters and Decorators Union, the Metal Polishers Union, and the Chicago Elevator Conductors' and Starters' Union. The Joint Council of Teamsters, declaring that it represented 19,000 workers in the city, adopted a representative resolution declaring that "labor's stake in education is of prime importance and subject to constant attack," and that teacher affiliation with organized labor would help to safeguard labor's education interests.[161]

The teachers won the first round on the Loeb Rule through court intervention. On September 23, 1915, they won an injunction against enforcement of the rule on the grounds that it was arbitrary and discriminatory. Under the rule as written, teachers would be prohibited from belonging to the National Education Association or the Illinois State Teachers' Association because these groups had paid staff members.[162] Loeb had stated that, in spite of the way the rule was written, it was intended to apply only to membership in the Chicago Teachers' Federation. The Superior Court of Cook County did not find this verbal emendation sufficient and on these narrow grounds ruled in favor of the teachers.[163]

The attack on the teachers did not relent, however. Mayor Thompson decided three days after the court ruling that he still supported the Loeb Rule, whether or not the courts found it legal. The state senate established a special committee to investigate Chicago school affairs; because it was established after the official adjournment of the legislative session, the committee was formed illegally, but senators pressed ahead with an investigation that turned into a steady attack on the CTF.[164] Ella Flagg Young was called as a witness, and, with almost complete polarization between the teachers and the board, she made clear her fundamental sympathies with the CTF.[165] The Illinois Manufacturers' Association (IMA) sent a letter to the board of education hailing the Loeb Rule because it would sever the teachers' federation from the schools on the grounds of being controlled by union labor. The president of the Illinois Manufacturers' Association also wrote to Mayor Thompson urging him to stand fast in trying to "separate the teachers of the schools from the Teachers' Federation" because of its labor ties.[166] The manufacturers' association urged employers around the state to bring pressure on the mayor to continue the attack on the CTF.[167] On September 29, the school board passed a new version of the Loeb Rule, revised to avoid the legal difficulty. The new rule applied specifically to teacher membership in labor organizations, thereby removing the problem of having inadvertently prohibited teachers from belonging to such professional organizations as the National Education Association.

The passage of the new rule delayed the real battle until the end of the school year; no teacher could be fired for violating the rule until the expiration of contracts in the spring. The labor movement continued to organize protests against the rule in the interim. On October 4, 1915, over 5,000 union members and teachers showed up at a city council meeting to protest the rule; the turnout was in response to a CFL resolution calling on the membership to attend the meeting "as a committee of the whole" when it deliberated on school board nominees.[168] The workers were unable to enter the council chambers, however, because the mayor had arranged for city employees to occupy all the seats beginning in mid-afternoon.[169]

Loeb responded to the labor protests by declaring that the labor movement was trying to foment class prejudice.[170] He reported that labor representatives were holding protest meetings all over the city and were illegitimately interfering in educational affairs. He quoted disapprovingly from a speech given by Victor Olander:

> "We know that back of the alleged author of the Loeb Rule
> stand the same interests and the same powers that have
> been preying upon the people of this country from one end
> of the land to the other. Back of it stand the powers that
> have stood for child labor, that have stood for long hours for
> working women and short pay for men, that have stood for
> all the unspeakable conditions that we have to fight against
> in this country."[171]

Loeb rhetorically asked Chicago parents whether they wanted this type of propaganda broadcast through the city and called upon them to support his antifederation policies.

In May the teachers won yet another court order against the Loeb Rule, but Loeb, who had become president of the board, adopted a new tack. He presented a list of 71 teachers whom he said he wanted fired, and the board agreed to fire 68 of them.[172] The group slated for firing included all the officers of the Chicago Teachers' Federation, all the teachers' representatives to the city and state labor federations, and four of the six union pension fund trustees. Only 20 of the fired teachers had ratings of "inefficient," which was the ostensible reason the board took action against the teachers. None of those rated inefficient was a member of the teachers' federation.[173]

The board's frontal assault on the union aroused a storm of protest both from the labor movement and from the civic associations.[174] The two groups worked together in sponsoring mass meetings of protest. On July 17, 1916, the civic associations took the lead in calling a protest meeting where the key speakers included noted civic reformers Jane Addams, Charles Merriam, and Helen Hefferan.[175] Mary McDowell, a settlement worker, chaired the meeting, and Victor Olander and John Fitzpatrick wrote sections of a printed statement that was distributed to the audience. The gravity of the situation led some of the city's reform activists to believe that longer-range organization was needed. Helen Hefferan, a leader of the Woman's City Club and president of the Illinois Congress of Parents and Teachers, called for the creation of a new citizen's group to protect the public schools from such blatant political manipulation as that exhibited by the board of education. The June 17 mass meeting proved to be the actual founding meeting of the new Public Education Association, although the new group was not officially incorporated until November. The Public Education Association included representatives from 28 civic organizations; its roster of members included such well-known figures as Jane Addams, Grace Abbott, Margaret Dreier Robins, George Mead, Charles Merriam, and Allen Pond, an architect who was a leading member of the City Club. John Fitzpatrick and Victor Olander were members, although the group was primarily representative of the city's middle-class reform constituency.[176]

Leaders of the Illinois Manufacturers' Association immediately formed a competing public school association, the Public School League. The IMA had been founded in the late 1800s, and by 1901 it represented 250 of the largest manufacturers in Illinois. Although it was a state-wide organization, all but 75 of its members were concentrated in Chicago.[177] The IMA had been organized around antiunion activities; on occasion, it actively intervened to break strikes, and it recruited its members on the basis of opposition to restrictions on child labor, women's eight-hour day laws, and such legislation as workmen's compensation that required acknowledgment of employer responsibility. In an era when the Civic Federation had pioneered in the development of programs designed to coopt conservative labor officials, the IMA remained sworn to a position of total hostility to unionism. In Chicago, the Commercial Club had learned from its experience with the Cooley vocational education bill that directly promulgating business programs for the schools had its disadvantages, and it did not play an aggressive role in fighting for the Loeb Rule, but the IMA had no hesitation on this score.

Part of the IMA's eagerness to plunge into educational matters may have stemmed from the long-standing school ties of one of its most important members, J. Ogden Armour. Armour joined the IMA when it was a newly formed, struggling organization, and he remained committed to it for the rest of his life.[178] Armour's chief counsel was Alfred Urion, who, in addition to supporting the Loeb Rule, had authored the legislation to take control of the teachers' pension fund away from the teachers.[179] The IMA's basic concern went deeper than this personal connection, however: the Chicago Teachers' Federation represented the type of politically oriented activist union that most aroused the manufacturers' hostility.

The IMA secured a state charter for its Public School League (PSL) before the competing Public Education Association was officially incorporated.[180] Two of the PSL's directors were former IMA presidents, Charles Felt and Laverne Noyes. The PSL explicitly stated that its raison d'être was the destruction of the Chicago Teachers' Federation. Carl Scholz, president of the Public School League and head of the Rock Island Mining Company, wrote to Harry Judson, president of the University of Chicago, on November 20, 1916, trying to persuade him to contribute to the PSL. In his letter, Scholz called Judson's attention to the "high standing of the members of the executive committee both in the interest of the public and in the business world," and urged him to contribute because "you as a taxpayer are perhaps aware that a few persons opposed to all of your business interests have control of the public schools at this time."[181] Judson delayed answering for three months and then replied that because there were two competing educational groups, he did not feel that he should participate in either one. This cautious reply received an immediate response from Scholz, who explained that the PSL differed from the Public Education Association in being dedicated to the elimination of the teachers' federation. Scholz wrote, "The organization of which I am the president, takes the stand that any efforts to improve materially the conditions now existing in the Public Schools of Chicago must be based on the entire elimination of the Teachers' Federation and its politico-labor activities."[182]

Organizational Reform

The Public School League's strategy consisted of working closely with the mayor in order to gain influence over the appointment of new school board members. The Public Education Association, in contrast, focused its energies on persuading the legislature to adopt a new school reorganization plan for Chicago. The actions of the board of education had convinced the PEA members that only a reorganization of the Chicago school system could avert political manipulations such as those engaged in by the Thompson-controlled board. They engaged the support of Ralph Otis, the school board member who had originally voted for the Loeb Rule but had come to regret the consequences when the 68 teachers were fired, and they drew up a reorganization bill to present to the legislature.

The PEA's organization plan, incorporated in the Otis Bill, emphasized reliance on neutral experts in running the schools. Because of long-standing union sensitivity to granting the superintendent unilateral authority, however, the Otis Bill provided for a three-person executive branch of the school system. The superintendent would be joined by a school system attorney and a business manager, each preeminent in his own sphere. Years later, the original author of the Otis Bill explained the rationale behind the reorganization plan to the City Club: "The primary idea . . . was to place the administrative phase of school affairs in the hands of experts, removed from political influence, and subject only to the approval or disapproval of a board of education, in matters of policy. Thus all details of the actual work would be in the hands of specialists."[183] The attorney who drew up the bill, Angus Shannon, explicitly stated that it was intended to provide a system of school governance analogous to the commission form of city government. In each case, government by experts was intended to replace government by political figures.

The Public Education Association printed a series of four

pamphlets designed to build support for revisions of the school law. The pamphlets summarized the middle-class reform position on the needs of the school system. They employed the rhetoric of social efficiency and expert governance, calling for democracy in measured quotients so as not to jeopardize efficiency. The first pamphlet declared, "The people want the board of education to organize the schools so that they shall employ the most expert people who can be secured."[184] This expert direction could only be provided if there was controlled turnover in the administrative ranks: "There should be as great a degree of permanence as possible in the school organization. To be sure, there must be enough change in people to insure progressiveness in policy, but there should not be so much change as to jeopardize efficiency."[185] Further, the board of education should be small enough to insure its noninterference in the administration of the schools, which was properly the responsibility of the superintendent. The third PEA bulletin explained that a large board inevitably tried to usurp the functions of the superintendent, "with those deplorable results which must follow when untrained men undertake to do the work of specialists." The necessary skill and training in education was not possessed by laymen but was, rather, the product of "careful preparation for, and experience in, a highly technical and specialized profession."[186] The PEA recommended against paying salaries to board members because dedicated and experienced civic leaders would not be lured to membership on the board by payment of a stipend, and such payments might only encourage the type of amateur board that was inclined to meddle in the superintendent's business.[187]

The Otis Bill contained one provision that was of crucial importance to the teachers: it provided that teachers would receive tenure after a three-year probationary period. The Chicago Teachers' Federation had been very hard hit by the concerted drive against it on the part of the board of education, the mayor, and many business leaders. The arbitrary firing of the 68 teachers weakened the federation's status as an organization able to protect its own against retaliation. The CTF could not look to national teachers' organizations for aid because the American Federation of Teachers was then a nascent organization with no national ·strength and the National Education Association remained wedded to the interests of the elite educational administrators. Margaret Haley's confidence appears to have faltered as she surveyed the forces ranged against her pioneering union. Under the repeated attacks, CTF membership had dropped by half in the years 1915 and 1916.[188] Much of the organization's income had gone to pay salaries to the fired teachers. Under the circumstances, Haley put the union's short-term interests above its leaders' frequently stated long-range goals.

This focus on the tenure issue led the Chicago Teachers' Federation to accept provisions in the Otis Bill that they would have rejected in previous years. The teachers had long been scornful of demands for "educational efficiency" and control by experts, viewing such goals as being more suitable to business concerns than to working-class educational needs. In the political climate of Chicago in 1917, however, the leaders of the Chicago Teachers' Federation evidently believed that their militant organization could be swept under or slowly bled to death by combined business and political pressure. An alliance with the middle-class reform groups, who were aroused by the frontal nature of the attack on the teachers, appeared essential to the leaders of the CTF, and this alliance would have to be based on terms acceptable to the civic reformers. The Otis Bill provided for an appointed rather than an elected board, contained no provisions for teachers' councils, and justified increased powers to the superintendent on the basis of presumed expert knowledge. The teachers had long-standing positions that were at variance with each of these aspects of the Otis Bill. They nonetheless accepted the bill and worked for it behind the scenes in order to gain the tenure clause.[189] The Otis Bill was also easier for the teachers to accept, because of its provision for a three-headed executive board, than were the Harper Commission proposals for a superintendent with concentrated powers.[190]

The 1917 session of the legislature passed the Otis Bill over two other competing school reorganization proposals.[191] The Otis Law was intended to bring rational, expert direction to the Chicago schools and to end the unsavory political wrangling and corruption that had marked school affairs, but, ironically, the law produced the opposite effect. In later years, even its original supporters acknowledged that the provision for a tripartite executive only encouraged board of education interference, under the guise of "coordinating" the work of the three experts, with the work of the superintendent. The full implications of the Otis Law for the Chicago schools were not realized until the 1930s, however, when the same civic organizations and, in some cases, the same individuals who had devoted their energies to the passage of the Otis Law made its repeal a top priority.

The middle-class groups deeply distrusted Chicago's machine politicians and resented the way board of education posts were handed out as rewards of spoils system politics. They wanted the school system removed from politics and placed under the control of neutral administrators. Business groups, in the past, had often indicated general support for these goals through their sponsorship of Harper Commission proposals for a stronger superintendent insulated from pressure through a long contract, but they were not averse to working with the machine politicians when the opportunity arose. The civic reform groups generally had neither access to the machine bosses nor any desire for their cooperation. Their only opportunity to work with politicians came on those rare occasions, like the election of Edward Dunne in 1905, when a reformer might briefly occupy the mayor's office. The ties between the businessmen and the politicians, although erratic, were generally stronger.

The Public School League's relationship with Mayor "Big Bill" Thompson appeared to offer it the opportunity for substantial behind-the-scenes influence. Jacob Loeb, who articulated an ideology of business control of government, joined the PSL in supporting Thompson in the 1916 Republican primary against reformer Charles Merriam.[192] Loeb and the Public School League received personal assurances from the grateful Thompson that they would be consulted on all future school board appointments. After the election, however, Thompson reneged on his promise. He evidently resented the businessmen's expectations that they could help select school board members; patronage was the lifeblood of Chicago machine politics and granting the businessmen control over school board appointments represented a substantial concession.

The passage of the Otis Law in the spring of 1917 meant that 11 new school board members had to be selected for the new, smaller board to replace the original 21 members. On Saturday, May 19, Thompson stunned Loeb and the Public School League by suddenly naming 9 nominees. Loeb called a meeting of the original 21-member board on Tuesday and issued a vitriolic denunciation of the mayor for this betrayal of his pledge. Loeb declared that "the mayor had on several occasions promised the executive committee of the Public School League not to make new appointments without giving the League an opportunity to investigate and pass on their fitness." He charged, "William Hale Thompson, mayor of Chicago, broke faith with the Public School League." The mayor had repudiated his promise to the League because he "resented the advice of men of the highest standing in the business and professional world." Instead, Thompson had decided to follow the "dictation of a political boss."[193]

After Loeb's bitter public denunciation of the mayor, the break between them was final. Thompson, ever a political opportunist, immediately castigated the Loeb supporters on the old board as being mere puppets of the city's businessmen.[194] The old board of education continued to meet while the city council delayed confirmation of Thompson's new appointees. The old school board members went to court and won reinstatement on the grounds that the Thompson appointees had never been officially approved by the city council. The wrangling between contending boards continued unabated for two and a half years. The passive superintendent, John Shoop, died in 1918 after three years of reduced activity because of illness, and the contentious, ever-changing school boards were confronted with the task of selecting a new superintendent. A commission appointed by the board of education to recommend a new superintendent reported in favor of the selection of Charles E. Chadsey, Detroit's superintendent of schools. The commission chose Chadsey because he was a tolerant man who would "maintain the system without friction."[195] Chadsey needed all the tolerance he could muster, because after his selection by the Loeb-controlled board, Thompson ran his 1919 campaign with the promise to "kick Chadsey out." Upon his reelection, Thompson appointed a new school board, which promptly locked Chadsey out of his office. Chadsey, astounded by the treatment he had received, followed the precedent of numerous school board members and went to court. The court ruled that under the Otis Law he had a four-year contract and could not be fired. The Thompson-controlled board, forced to accept Chadsey as nominal superintendent, then stripped him of all his powers. Chadsey again appealed to the courts, and they ruled that the board had acted illegally in depriving him of the authority granted him under the Otis Law. The court sentenced six board members and the board attorney to jail terms for their roles in reducing Chadsey to a figurehead. Chadsey, after a prolonged and ludicrous battle, had finally won uncontested authority, but he was by then so disgusted with Chicago politics that he immediately resigned to head the School of Education at the University of Illinois.

The civic reform groups that had lobbied for the Otis Bill in the hope that it would replace machine politicking with rational discussion of the governance of the public schools watched in dismay as years of comic-opera battling between school boards followed the bill's passage. Although they had opposed Loeb in his effort to fire the teachers, they rallied behind him in his battle with Thompson's political machine. Loeb retained the support of the Public School League, with the result that he was supported by the two groups that had opposed each other only a few years before. Their support was given on different grounds, however. The secretary of the Public School League wrote during one of the conflicts over whether Loeb would be reappointed to the school board that the real issue remained domination of the school system by the Chicago Teachers' Federation:

> The name of Jacob M. Loeb will come before the City Council on Monday evening next . . . for confirmation as a member of the new Board of Education. The Chicago Teachers' Federation, Miss Margaret Haley, John Fitzpatrick, Ed

Nockels, and the Chicago Federation of Labor are making
a desperate battle against Mr. Loeb's confirmation.

The issue is whether or not the Chicago Teachers' Federation shall dominate the Board of Education. Mr. Loeb
has had the courage to make a fight for the school children
and for a school system that shall not be dominated by
any clique of labor agitators.[196]

Similarly, school board member Ralph C. Otis, who had often
quarreled with Loeb over the attack on the teachers, forgot his
differences with him during Loeb's fight with the mayor. At the
special board meeting where Loeb lambasted Mayor Thompson,
Otis immediately presented a resolution commending Loeb for
his courage. Previous differences, Otis said, sank into insignifi-
cance when contrasted with Loeb's "shocking revelations" of
Thompson's political designs on the school system.[197]

Other Loeb supporters declared their support in spite of his
position on the rights of labor. James Minnick, the superintendent of the Chicago Tuberculosis Institute, a body whose reform-
minded president had committee suicide in protest against political interference in an effort to rid the city of tuberculosis, wrote,
"I do not like Mr. Loeb because of the fight that he has made
on the school teachers but now that he is fighting the administration it seems to me that he ought to be supported." Minnick
also observed, "Certainly the type of people whom Mayor Thompson has appointed on the new School Board are not there because
of their knowledge of educational methods but evidently because
they were the easy tools of the administration."[198] Minnick urged
that influential groups come to the support of Loeb to prevent
the buildup of such a powerful machine in the school system
"that in spite of all the exposition of their rascality they will be
able to keep in power."[199]

Few Chicago businessmen ever exhibited a sustained interest
in civic reform of a sort that would enable them to maintain
close ties with the city's civic associations. Julius Rosenwald, the
immensely wealthy founder of Sears, Roebuck, was an exception
to this pattern. Rosenwald worked very closely with Charles
Merriam on a variety of projects to clean up the city's govern-

ment. Although Rosenwald had been attacked by labor groups for the below-subsistence wages paid to young female clerks at Sears, Merriam hailed him as a social statesman who brought breadth of vision to the world of Chicago politics.[200] When Merriam was a city alderman, he had headed a committee to investigate corruption and waste in granting public contracts and public business. Rosenwald created the Chicago Bureau of Public Efficiency in 1910 to carry on the work of the Merriam Commission in rooting out public waste.[201] The Bureau of Public Efficiency surveyed city agencies to determine if they were spending public funds wisely, and its rhetoric of social efficiency endeared it to the more conservative wing of the middle-class reform movement.

Rosenwald contributed $5,000 to a legal fund established to pay Superintendent Chadsey's court costs in his battle to maintain his authority against the Thompson-controlled school board. One of the men involved with the Chadsey defense, Wallace Heckman, wrote to Rosenwald in 1925 that the final litigation had ended and that the battle was well worth the expense: "This piece of work carried through by your group seems to have been worth while. It gave to Thompson's regime its first serious jolt. In the height of his high-handed career your action halted him. . . . The benefit goes beyond that particular case. It stood, and will stand, as a permanent warning and assurance."[202]

The middle-class reformers and their powerful ally, Julius Rosenwald, joined the IMA-controlled Public School League in fighting Thompson's control of the schools. The labor movement remained aloof in this battle, not being attracted to any of the parties. The Chicago Teachers' Federation distrusted Superintendent Chadsey because he was so passionately championed by Loeb, and it did not share the reformers' desire to see him installed as a blow at the machine.[203]

The CTF and the CFL Part Company

The passage of the Otis Law had required labor acquiescence to the goals of the middle-class reform movement. In this respect, it represented a defeat for the Chicago Federation of Labor and the Chicago Teachers' Federation, although both groups ultimately supported the Otis Law because of its tenure provisions. The Chicago Teachers' Federation also suffered what proved to be a more major defeat in the aftermath of the Loeb Rule controversy: the teachers' federation withdrew from the Chicago Federation of Labor. The passage of the Otis Law had guaranteed tenure to teachers in the future, but it had not required rehiring of the 68 teachers Loeb had already fired. Margaret Haley abruptly led the teachers out of the Chicago Federation of Labor in May 1917 in what seemed an obvious move to make peace with Loeb and win the teachers back their jobs. Reportedly, John Fitzpatrick urged Haley to take this step in the belief that the ties between the teachers' federation and the CFL were so close that they could continue to work together even in the absence of formal affiliation, as reported by a teacher with long connections to the CFL.[204] Later Haley wrote that "John Fitzpatrick knew that the Loeb rule was intended to break up the organization of the Chicago Teachers' Federation; that the important thing to the teachers was to preserve their organization."[205] This was evidently also Haley's view of the situation; she believed that the teachers' federation had been subjected to so many attacks that as a matter of expediency it should withdraw from the CFL while maintaining its working relationship with the labor federation. Leaving the national American Federation of Teachers, which the CTF had helped form as recently as 1916, was not a difficult step for the Chicago Teachers' Federation, because the national organization was so small and so weak, and it appeared that the CTF could still maintain its more significant local labor ties.[206]

The CTF's disaffiliation from the CFL did not have immediate consequences, but in the long run it clearly weakened the relationship between the teachers and the main body of the Chicago labor movement. Margaret Haley's CTF was made up of elementary school teachers; the smaller high school unions, notably the Federation of Women High School Teachers and the Chicago Federation of Men Teachers, did not disaffiliate from the CFL in spite of the passage of the Loeb Rule. They were never attacked as the CTF had been, evidently because, in the words of one of the leaders of the women high school teachers, "We were too insignificant."[207] Although these unions continued to participate in the Chicago Federation of Labor while the CTF was formally outside, Haley remained more influential with the leaders of the CFL (see "Labor Refuses to Endorse McAndrew Salary Schedule: Men's Federation Appeals in Vain; Fitzpatrick Assails McAndrew," *Margaret Haley's Bulletin,* May 15, 1927, p. 245, for an example of her ability to persuade Fitzpatrick to take a position over the objections of the other teachers' unions). Over time, however, the other teachers' unions superseded the CTF as significant elements of the labor movement.

Haley rebuffed attempts in the mid- and late 1920s to have the teachers' federation reaffiliate with the CFL. She held back even though the school board rescinded the Loeb Rule in 1922.[208] At a January 12, 1924, meeting of the CTF, a long-time member of the teachers' union asked from the floor why the CTF didn't reaffiliate. Although the speaker was greeted with applause, Haley tried to cut her off with the remark that the subject was not under discussion.[209] The questioner had commented that the officials of the Chicago Federation of Labor were still nursing a forlorn hope that the CTF would rejoin the labor federation, but that they thought the CTF was waiting too long. The questioner's remarks appear to be borne out by statements made by CFL and ISFL officials at teachers' federation meetings over the next few years. Labor officials repeatedly but diplomatically urged the CTF to rejoin the labor body.[210] Victor Olander stated in 1925 that he was speaking officially for the labor body in urging the teachers' unions to begin to work together; no response was forthcoming from Haley. By 1927, spokesmen of the Chicago Federation of Labor, including John Fitzpatrick, while still displaying a very high regard for the CTF, were finding that there were points on which they agreed more with the high school teachers' unions and where they tried to dissuade the CTF from following particular policies.[211]

Haley continued on her independent course in spite of these pressures from the CFL. As the 1920s wore on, Haley appeared to become increasingly rigid as she tried to duplicate the CTF's earlier dramatic success in its tax fight; she tried pursuing the same tactics of legal action, publicity, and political intervention, with less favorable results. The CTF became increasingly isolated, and Haley suffered from organizational parochialism and jealousy as the other CFL-affiliated unions ultimately combined in the 1930s to form a strong and united teachers' union.* The CTF's disaffiliation from the CFL proved to be a far more significant step than it evidently appeared to either Haley or Fitzpatrick when it was carried out in 1917.

Conclusions

Whatever their political proclivities, few would have disagreed that the Chicago school system stood in need of organizational reform at the turn of the century. Board members hired teachers on a patronage basis; the board of education itself operated with a multitude of ill-organized, overlapping committees. The superintendent's powers were not clearly defined, and he often found himself contending with district superintendents who had built up semiindependent fiefdoms in their local areas. The issue of how the school system was to be reorganized could not be divorced from politics, however. With Chicago's teachers already unionized and aggressive by 1900, conservative business interests in the city had strong reasons for wanting a new form

---

*Haley grew more and more detail-obsessed, with her reports full of specific examples of how board of education members and others had violated rules of procedure or honesty. Chicago Teachers' Federation meetings also increasingly became forums for Haley to express her views, with little discussion from the floor (see stenographic reports of meetings, CTF Papers, Chicago Historical Society). There are several possible explanations for why Haley began to lose her political touch. One is that objective conditions just became too hard; the CTF had been the subject of assaults for so long that its leaders began to lose their confidence that they could find bold or innovative solutions. Another is that Haley personally became more rigid as she grew older. A third possibility is that the death of long-time CTF activist Catharine Goggin in an accident in 1916 resulted in the loss not only of a talented and dedicated organizational leader but of a leader with a good tactical sense. Haley and Goggin had worked in partnership since the early 1900s; while Haley received far more press attention and clearly enjoyed the public role more, it is possible that Goggin in fact had a clearer sense of what the CTF should do to preserve both its health as an organization and its social principles. Goggin's writings reveal a woman with strong political convictions and a deep commitment to the labor movement (Catharine Goggin, "The Chicago Teachers' Federation," *CTSBJ* 1 [May 1899]: 257–259; see also "Chicago Notes," *CTSBJ* 1 [April 1899]: 186).

of organization that would both serve to get the schools operating on a more efficient and economical basis and hold the teachers in line. The businessmen consistently favored reorganization plans that would give the superintendent added power. The schools were to be run like businesses, with power flowing from the top down. Teachers were not to make demands; they were to follow orders. The superintendent was to receive both the symbols of power, in terms of increased salary and professional deference, and the reality, in terms of increased control over hiring and firing and a firmly defined position as the decision-making educational expert.

By the time the various business-sponsored reorganization plans were put forward, both the labor movement as a whole and the teachers in particular were already sufficiently politicized and attuned to school issues that the plans met immediate and fierce opposition. Neither side was under any illusions about the importance of the reorganization proposals. The teachers defined the issue as one of democracy in the schools. The Chicago Federation of Labor agreed with this analysis and argued that if the teachers were submerged in a top-down school system, it could only bolster efforts to run the schools like factories. Both the city and state labor federations interpreted the plans for school reorganization in class terms. They believed that increased power for the superintendent would increase business influence over the schools. The very ideology of professionalism in school administration could be used to justify efforts to strike at the Chicago Teachers' Federation. This centralization meant not only that the teachers could find their own power diminished but that a voice for democratization of the school system could be stilled.*
The teachers had an ideology in this period that emphasized the

*See John Walker's remarks at the CFL's mass meeting to protest the Loeb Rule (CFL, "Verbatim Report"). Walker told the audience: "We know what it means, the difference between school teachers who are free and untrammeled and independent, who have the right to act towards the school system as their knowledge of it and judgment leads them to believe is right, and, on the other hand, school teachers who will be held in the hollow of the hands of the direct representatives of the business interests [applause]. We know what it means, the difference between the type of citizenship that will come from one school as compared with that of the other [applause]. And they know it even better than we do."

need to make the school system more open; this paralleled a political perspective that called for greater democracy in the political sphere through such measures as the initiative and the referendum. The teachers identified with the labor movement and with the labor goal of a broad liberal education for working-class children. In the eyes of the Chicago Federation of Labor, if the teachers were suppressed, this would be a threat to labor efforts to make the school system more responsive to working-class children.

The intensity of the class disputes over the schools was reflected in a range of measures adopted to try to restrict the power of the Chicago Teachers' Federation. The passage of the Loeb Rule made it clear that conservative board members and business allies saw the teachers' alliance with the labor movement as a fundamental source of conflict and challenge in the school system. The ultimate inadequacy of Haley's response, after a strong fight, reveals in turn that Haley overestimated her ability to keep the Chicago Teachers' Federation going on the basis of an informal alliance with the labor movement.

Several questions remain about the events of this period. First, if superintendents generally shared conservative business assumptions, how to explain the emergence of Ella Flagg Young as superintendent? A talented administrator who rose through the ranks, she retained basic sympathy with the Chicago Teachers' Federation throughout her professional life. She predicated her educational philosophy on the idea that teachers had to be given responsibility; if they were reduced to ciphers carrying out orders from above, they would lose the initiative that made for good teaching. Her selection as superintendent appears to have stemmed from a desire by the board of education to hire someone who could deal with the teachers' federation and reduce the conflict in the system. Board members may also have believed that, since she was 64 when she was first appointed, she was in any case unlikely to be in office long enough to do anything dangerous.

The record of events following Young's appointment indicates that board members grew increasingly dismayed with what they had done. Appointing Young created great political problems for them; the teachers had an ally who resisted attempts to blacklist them politically or to challenge the teachers' federation. Once appointed, Young was sufficiently politically skillful that it was difficult to remove her. Twice she resigned when board members restricted her power. Twice she was brought brought back by a groundswell of opposition to the board. School board members, when faced with this stubborn and popular opponent, forgot their strictures on the need for centralization and increased power for superintendents. Instead, they tried to undercut Young by taking the power of determining the course of study from her and by attacking her personnel policies. She held on, but ultimately the board was able in any case to mount a decisive attack on the teachers.

A second question concerns the role of the middle-class reform advocates who had helped the labor movement defeat the Cooley Bill. Why were they unable or unwilling to protect the teachers from the onslaught against them? Part of the reason was that many of them had a fundamentally ambivalent attitude toward both the teachers and the labor movement. Although willing to acknowledge that the society stood in need of reform and that the labor movement might aid this process, many of the reformers remained suspicious or hesitant about movements from below to change the society. They favored order and incremental change, not disruptive challenges predicated on the power of numbers that called into question principles of efficiency. While the reformers were sincerely committed to change, they proved unreliable allies for the labor movement because they did not share the same assumptions. Compared to the labor movement, they had a narrow view of the need for social reform. The ambivalent stance of the middle-class reformers led on a practical political level to the types of vacillations that Jane Addams went through and on a more abstract level to the development of middle-ground ideological positions. George Herbert Mead, a noted professor at the University of Chicago and chair of the City Club's education committee, perfectly expressed this ambivalence. He wrote that the Chicago Teachers' Federation was an "irresponsible" organization—irresponsible because it organized along trade union rather than professional lines—yet it was a necessary organization given the conditions that teachers faced.[212] The teachers needed it, yet in an ideal world, it would not exist. The attempt of the City Club to mediate the differences between labor and business on the Cooley Bill reflected another example of the attempt to find compromise where, sometimes, no compromise was possible.

The middle-class reformers were dismayed by the Loeb Rule, which struck them as undemocratic and coercive. They joined the labor movement in denouncing it, but they put most of their energies into trying to secure the passage of a school reorganization bill that they hoped would lead to more orderly and efficient administration of the schools. The teachers felt sufficiently weakened by the attacks upon them that they ultimately accepted a reorganization plan drawn up by the progressives that violated some of their long-standing principles about the need for teacher participation in policy making.

The machine itself remained the wild card in the political calculations of all groups. Flamboyant politicians such as Mayor Thompson were devoid of political program or principle. Their actions were unpredictable because they were so rooted in expediency that their evaluation of a given situation might change at any moment. The Illinois Manufacturers' Association found to its cost that an alliance with a politician such as Thompson was a risky venture. In later years, with the development of a stable machine, such an alliance became more productive.

During the years before and immediately after World War I, the main line of controversy around the schools remained that between labor and business. In spite of tensions between labor representatives and progressives, these two groups often found themselves in agreement, as during most of the time that the liberal Dunne school board was in power. In the 1920s, the differences between the labor movement and the middle-class progressives became more acute and decisive. The superintendency of William McAndrew epitomized social-efficiency goals almost to the point of caricature. When centralizing impulses were clothed in the rhetoric of professionalism, the progressives and the labor movement parted company. McAndrew held the support of both the business community and of the progressives in battling the teachers and the labor movement. He was defeated only through the intervention of politicians bent on winning easy popularity and publicity. Chicago's school politics approached the bizarre during the 1920s, but underneath the absurdity of the particular events that surrounded McAndrew's superintendency lay a more fundamental set of issues, and it is to a consideration of these that we now turn.

5 | THE POLITICS OF EFFICIENCY

THE SCHOOLS OFFERED tempting prospects to Chicago's politicians. The board of education spent millions of dollars annually on buildings and services and it also controlled a large supply of teaching and blue-collar jobs. In a city where corruption was the lifeblood of the political system, the schools offered opportunities that could not be overlooked. Although the civic associations had won the passage of the Otis Law, with its provisions for a strong superintendent with a guaranteed tenure of four years, the school system was rocked by scandal in the immediate aftermath of the law's passage. The school board members appointed by Mayor William Thompson stole city funds with abandon and siphoned millions from the schools to their own pockets. Thompson and his chief political henchmen were said to have informed their board of education appointees, "We're at the feed box now—and we're going to feed."[1] The weak superintendent, Peter Mortenson, made no attempt to control the graft as the school board members, called a "plundering crew" by the Municipal Voters' League, abandoned any pretense of serving the public interest.[2]

The behavior of the school board and of the mayor reinforced Chicago's reform-minded citizens in their belief that to avoid such depredations in the future a strong, professionally oriented superintendent would have to assume control. The schools would be vulnerable to political interference and graft as long as those who ran the schools did not operate out of a secure sense of professional ethics and technical expertise. Although in 1909 a superintendent had been found in Ella Flagg Young, who combined these qualities with a strong belief in the right of teachers to organize and to have a voice in school system affairs, school administrators were increasingly coming to define professionalism in such a way that it automatically excluded the rights of those in the lower ranks of the hierarchy to determine policy.

Instead, administrators declared school administration to be a specialized function beyond the grasp of either teachers or parents; only those with specific credentials and training could assume control of the schools, and only they knew what policies would result in the maximum learning at the least cost.

The civic associations had supported the Chicago Teachers' Federation through many of its battles with school boards and superintendents for higher salaries and for greater autonomy within the school system. As Jane Addams had written, the teachers stood for "democracy" in the schools, and this goal, while not one to receive unquestioning support, appealed to many of the reform-oriented middle-class groups. It was part of Margaret Haley's skill as a political leader that she was able to gain the support of many who did not automatically identify with the labor movement. The teachers gained this support in part because they presented their demands in broad terms; they did not just want more money, they wanted to make sure that large corporations paid their share of taxes; they did not just want better and less harassing working conditions, they wanted better education for the city's students. The alliance between the teachers and the civic association leaders had been strained in the past (as when Jane Addams and Margaret Haley disagreed on the best means of evaluating teachers' performance in the classroom), but it had also been durable and successful in gaining victories in such areas as the abolition of child labor. The emergence of increasing professional consciousness among school superintendents and administrators, however, raised the potential of a more direct clash in values for the reform-oriented civic leaders. Against the value of "democracy" as defined by the teachers and other labor groups could be weighed the value of not only "efficiency" but "professionalism." This marked a new development in relations between the teachers and the reform leaders, a development that had concrete effects in the 1920s as the civic leaders supported a superintendent who embodied the new spirit of professionalism at the same time that he moved energetically to limit the voice and the prerogatives of the teachers.

The broader labor movement in Chicago sided with the teachers in their resistance to the new policy directives of Superintendent William McAndrew. This was done not simply out of loyalty to a fellow group of workers, as the teachers had come to be perceived in spite of their white-collar status, but out of a conviction that the superintendent advocated policies that would be damaging for working-class education as a whole. Labor opposition to the superintendent became particularly explosive because it revived the sentiments aroused by the Cooley Bill and the Loeb Rule. In the labor view, a superintendent was once again doing business's bidding and restricting opportunities for working-class children, but this time the superintendent hid his allegiances behind the ideological cloak of professionalism. The labor movement was not able to count on support from the civic associations, however; in their desire to limit political intervention in the schools and to see a strong and professional administration emerge, the associations backed a superintendent who made no bones about his belief that teachers were lazy and unqualified to participate in educational decision making. The latent differences between the labor movement and the civic associations emerged clearly during McAndrew's tenure as superintendent, leaving the labor movement to seek allies in other circles.

McAndrew and Efficiency Engineering

After the open plundering of the schools immediately after World War I, outraged citizens' groups had succeeded in 1922 in obtaining a grand jury investigation of the board of education. Jacob Loeb testified for the prosecution against his former colleagues, and ultimately several board members, including the board president, were sentenced to jail terms.[3] Mayor William Thompson was, temporarily at least, politically discredited, and a reform candidate, Judge William E. Dever, won the 1923 mayoral election.

Under the influence of the new political regime, a reconstituted board of education decided to restore public confidence in the schools by appointing an uncompromising, strong-willed, efficiency-oriented superintendent, William McAndrew. McAndrew, who had been associate superintendent of the New York City public schools, agreed to come to Chicago to "put the schools on their feet."[4] He arrived determined to operate the Chicago public schools according to strict criteria of efficiency, but his effort to do so provoked a storm of political protest that ended in his ouster in 1927. The battle over his superintendency was frequently ludicrous—the *New York Times* declared that the trial that resulted in his removal from office could be compared only to the Scopes trial in Tennessee—but beneath the buffoonery attending McAndrew's ouster lay more fundamental issues of class politics.[5] McAndrew's four years in Chicago in the role of the expert, impartial, technocratic superintendent were marked not by smooth administration but by a restoration of the city's schools to the position of focal points of class antagonism.

William McAndrew arrived in Chicago with, he thought, few illusions about Chicago's political system or its schools, and little doubt about what needed to be done to set them right. McAndrew later informed his close friend, Charles Judd, head of the University of Chicago's School of Education, that he had agreed to come to Chicago only on the board's repeated assurances that it would "clean up" the administration of the schools.[6] McAndrew believed that the first and most important element in the clean-up campaign was the acknowledgment of the superintendent as the unquestioned authority in all educational matters.[7] The superintendent, and the superintendent alone, had the professional training and expertise to determine the city's educational priorities. The superintendent should make the educational decisions, and his programs should be carried out through the medium of a strict line-and-staff organizational system.[8] Neither the teachers nor the board of education nor the parents were entitled to interfere with the superintendent's plans for maximizing the efficiency of the city's schools. The schools' efficiency could be measured, and the job of the board of education was to check on the superintendent by evaluating educational progress through the appropriate tests. If efficiency was found lacking, the board was entitled to hire a new superintendent, who would then implement his own expertly determined educational program. McAndrew did not describe the school's goals in the philosophical and broadly humanitarian terms of a John Dewey; instead, he declared that the aim of the school system was "to produce a human, social unit, trained in accordance with his capabilities to the nearest approach to complete social efficiency possible in the time allotted."[9]

To McAndrew, these points were self-evident. In retrospect, he identified the board's failure to understand that only the superintendent had the knowledge and authority to develop educational programs as the chief fault of the Chicago school system. Using the medical analogy popular with educational administrators, he wrote that "the whole Chicago tragi-comedy is inevitable so long as one board passes on to its successor the outworn fallacy that a superintendent is the board's . . . executive to carry out their policies. He isn't. . . . They can't say what medicines shall be used or what operations shall be performed. Somebody had to tell 'em that."[10]

The depth of McAndrew's convictions about the need for efficiency and the implications of these convictions were not immediately apparent when he first arrived in Chicago, and he was warmly greeted by the teachers and many citizens who hoped he would end the rampage of graft and restore the schools to their proper position. The teachers were pleased that the regime of the Thompson-controlled board had ended, and they viewed McAndrew's appointment as a positive step.[11] McAndrew was also warmly received in other quarters. The business manager of the University of Chicago wrote to Julius Rosenwald that the $5,000 Rosenwald had contributed to Superintendent Chadsey's legal defense was money well spent because it was probable that the successful legal conclusion of the Chadsey case had "led to the selection later of McAndrew, a distinct advance."[12] It was only a few months after his arrival, however, that support of the teachers and the labor movement for McAndrew changed to hostility, due to his rapid moves to concentrate power in his office and to reorganize the school system in accordance with his efficiency notions, as well as his frequent acerbic remarks about the incompetence and laziness of the teaching force.

McAndrew's first conflict with the teachers arose because of the unilateral manner in which he tried to push through two proposals for school system reorganization: the introduction of junior high schools and of platoon schools. Teachers' councils in the schools raised questions about the reorganization plans, at which point McAndrew moved to effectively abolish the councils. This in turn introduced an element of controversy which became still more bitter than the original disputes. The conflicts over the school-reorganization plans were quickly generalized into conflicts over the class purposes of the school system, and the teachers' council conflict became an issue of basic questions of authority and teachers' rights.

Teachers' councils had a long history in the Chicago school system. Their vitality depended in part on the attitude of the superintendent; Superintendent Edwin Cooley had been hostile to the idea of the councils and worked to abolish them, while Ella Flagg Young had encouraged the councils as a way of having the teachers contribute their views on educational programs.[13] They had later been revived by the weak Superintendent Peter Mortenson, evidently in the hope that he would gain support from one element in the school system.[14] The teachers at the councils were free to raise any matters of administration, curriculum, or general educational policy that concerned them. Principals and other supervisors were barred from attending the local school councils, to insure that the teachers would feel free to speak their minds. By the time Superintendent McAndrew arrived, the teachers considered the councils established institutions and were highly resistant to any efforts to weaken or abolish them.

McAndrew, for his part, could not comprehend how institutions that so violated the principle of expert direction could ever have been established. He viewed the Chicago Teachers' Federation as a threat to the proper working of the school system. When he first came to Chicago, McAndrew told the board of education that the Chicago schools would remain a laughingstock as long as the board acknowledged that the teachers had any legitimate voice in determining educational policy. "I saw no reason to avoid telling them," he wrote, "that they and their schools were jokes and bywords the country over for the reasons that the board was afraid of teachers and principals' organizations and of other things."[15] This fear, McAndrew believed, had bred paralysis, but McAndrew himself had no doubts about the need to "escape from the weird [teachers'] federation project" of board-sanctioned councils.[16]

The conflict over the teachers' councils involved points of principle that neither side felt inclined to compromise: McAndrew believed the councils infringed upon his authority and the teachers thought they provided a hard-won degree of democracy in the running of the schools. The councils had never, in fact, functioned very effectively, but McAndrew's attack on the very idea of teacher participation in educational decision making elevated the councils to symbolic importance. Although McAndrew made it clear that he believed as a matter of basic organizational principle that the councils should not exist, his attack on the councils intensified after they raised questions about his plans for restructuring the schools.

Superintendent McAndrew proposed a scheme for the reorganization of the schools shortly after he arrived in Chicago. The Chicago schools remained overcrowded, with more children legally bound to attend than there were seats. McAndrew felt that large class sizes were not a problem for efficient teachers and that an elementary class of 45—the average size in Chicago at the time—was not unduly large.[17] The problem of lack of actual seating space, however, required a solution. McAndrew proposed two organizational changes that were designed to make more effective use of existing resources while also increasing the school system's ability to offer differentiated school programs. The two proposed changes were the introduction of junior high schools and the switching of regular elementary schools to "platoon schools." The teachers' councils raised questions about both these plans, which led McAndrew to declare that the councils were no longer officially sanctioned institutions. Each of McAndrew's proposed moves aroused an uproar and brought the Chicago Federation of Labor into vehement opposition to the superintendent. As George Counts wrote in his classic study of McAndrew's administration, both planned changes in the organization of the schools

generated an enormous amount of hostility and precipitated
a fight of the most violent and partisan character; and
in both cases the alignment of forces was much the same.
Ranged on the side of the opposition were a large fraction
of the teaching staff, many ordinary citizens, and the solid
cohorts of organized labor. Ranged on the other side were
the members of the supervisory and administrative staffs,
the business interests, the professional people, and the
educated classes generally.[18]

Tracking and School Reorganization

The root issue behind the controversy over the introduction of junior high schools and platoon schools was whether
all children would receive a common education or whether they
should be tracked into differentiated educational programs.
This in turn ignited a protest over a second fundamental issue: who had the right to determine school policies? Should
the superintendent make the educational decisions, or did teachers have a right to a voice? Historians of education have demonstrated that there was a pronounced move toward tracking
and the development of varied curricula in the Progressive Era
as the schools expanded to absorb millions of immigrant children.[19] The ideology of social efficiency, with its emphasis on measurement and testing, lent itself to the encouragement of programs for children based on their particular tested capabilities.
McAndrew believed that all children should attain "100% efficiency" in the basic subjects of reading, writing, and arithmetic, and that this goal could be easily reached if teachers
were competent and hard-working.[20] The conviction that students would attain superior and easily measured results if teaching were handled scientifically led naturally to a conviction
that teachers had to be tightly supervised to insure that they
turned out well-trained students. During McAndrew's superintendency, the two issues that had led to the most bitter conflicts in Chicago's history, the rights of teachers and the class
bias of the school system, merged into one as the Chicago labor movement argued that McAndrew wanted to constrain both
the teaching force and the education of working-class children.

The Chicago Federation of Labor, sensitized by the battle over the Cooley Bill, denounced the plans for both junior highs and platoon schools on the grounds that they were intended only to provide cheaper and less complete education for children from poor and working-class families. Although some of the teachers' organizations favored the plans for junior high schools, or at least adopted a wait-and-see attitude, McAndrew's plans for platoon schools evoked outrage from both the teachers' groups and the CFL. In platoon schools, elementary school children were to rotate from classroom to classroom and from teacher to teacher throughout a lengthened school day. Children were no longer to be taught in self-contained classrooms; instead, individual subject specialists would teach them for brief periods during the day and the children were to engage in structured work and play activities in addition to their regular classroom studies.[21]

Platoon schools had a complicated history. John Dewey and his daughter Evelyn had published a book in 1915 in which they hailed the efforts of various local school districts to move children from isolated academic studies to greater participation in the life of the community. The Deweys argued that children should not study academic subjects in a merely formal manner but should be taught in ways that integrated the traditional curriculum with practical learning. Children could learn basic principles of arithmetic, for example, by taking part in cooking classes and dividing or expanding recipes, or they could learn hand skills by making useful objects for the school. John and Evelyn Dewey had particular praise for the schools of Gary, Indiana, which had introduced "work-study-play" schools (later called platoon schools) in 1907. These schools, the writers suggested, lived up to the ideal of merging academic and practical learning in a way that produced benefits for the children themselves, for the teachers, and for the community.[22]

Platoon schools thus won endorsement as progressive educational innovations from the most influential of educational theorists. Critics charged, however, that the reality behind the schools was far different from the idealistic portrait painted by the Deweys. Although in superficial respects the schools conformed to progressive principles, labor leaders argued that the prime motives behind their introduction were the desire to save money and to introduce children early to differentiated school programs.

Labor suspicion of the platoon schools was intensified because of the circumstances of their introduction in Gary, Indiana. Although a number of cities across the country introduced platoon schools on a limited basis, Gary had taken the lead in switching to platoon schools on a large scale.[23] (Chicago had actually operated a small number of platoon schools before McAndrew's arrival, but the board had made it clear that these schools were operated solely because they helped relieve overcrowding, and it did not propose them as a permanent or superior form of school organization.) In Gary, Superintendent Willard Wirt, a man with strong right-wing political connections, introduced platoon schools when he assumed the superintendency in 1907. The plan received enthusiastic backing from United States Steel. Because the schools were adopted under conservative auspices in a town dominated by a fiercely antiunion steel company, labor leaders viewed the schools with pronounced skepticism, which deepened when Superintendent McAndrew tried to revamp the Chicago schools in a similar manner.

In Gary, students were moved from classroom to classroom from their first year of schooling in order to insure that at any given moment no part of the school building would be left unused. Fewer school buildings were required because more students could be accommodated in any one building than under a conventional plan. The auditorium of a school, instead of being used only for assemblies and school programs, became a way station in the shuttling of students, and thus less classroom space was needed. Every day an individual student would be assigned to spend an hour or more in the auditorium in the company of several hundred others. The assembled students would do choral music, listen to records, or hear speeches from visiting businessmen or other dignitaries. During half of the lengthened school day the students engaged in supervised play or study in the school cafeterias, gymnasia, and common rooms. Girls took cooking classes in which they prepared the daily lunches that were served in the cafeteria; boys took woodworking classes in which they made benches and other items used in the school.[24]

Labor representatives were critical of almost every feature of the platoon school plan.[25] Businessmen liked the platoon schools, C F L officials charged, because they held out the promise of being cheaper than regular schools. Public school costs could be lowered because overcrowding could be solved through the heavy use of limited school facilities. Various features of the Gary plan were described as having been adopted because they would reduce costs rather than because they were educationally justifiable.[26] The use of older children to teach younger ones, a basic feature of the Gary schools (and one that was criticized even by those who were generally favorable to the plan), reduced teaching costs but was not necessarily educationally effective.[27] Similarly, having children prepare school meals might not be so much educational for them as it was cost effective for the school system. In their basic features, the Chicago Federation of Labor maintained, the platoon schools resembled schools that were on half-day sessions due to overcrowding, except that students were provided with more structured activities during their out-of-classroom period, and they switched classrooms while in school. The alleged virtue of flexibility in the curriculum was, in labor's view, less a virtue as a threat, as it held out the potential of having even very young children divided up into different academic programs that would ostensibly be matched to their abilities.*

McAndrew's proposed restructuring of the Chicago school system also included plans for a junior high school system to replace eight-year elementary schools. The labor and teacher reaction to this proposal was not as immediately hostile as it was to the platoon school idea, but resentment over McAndrew's dictatorial approach, combined with suspicion over his efficiency goals, led both teachers and labor representatives to question the reasons for the introduction of the junior highs. In March 1924 the

*See Public Administration Service, *The Public School System of Gary, Indiana* (Chicago: Public Administration Service, 1955), for a report on the destructive effects of the platoon school system in Gary, where it was employed for 50 years. Adoption of the platoon school allowed for reduced school costs, but students did not gain the advantage of flexibility in their school programs. Instead, they often wasted time sitting in auditoriums and common rooms with no planned educational activities.

elementary school teachers' councils met to consider McAndrew's reorganization plans. Five of the elementary teachers' councils, which were bodies made up by the local councils, approved the introduction of the junior highs, six opposed the new schools, and 28 councils requested that McAndrew answer five specific questions about the functioning of the planned junior highs.[28] The councils emphasized that they did not disagree with the idea of junior high schools in principle but that they needed more information to know exactly how the junior high schools would work in Chicago. The teachers expressed concern that the junior highs could result in a "cleavage along class lines," with students slated for industrial life leaving school at the end of junior high while the more prosperous continued on to high school.

The Elementary Teachers' General Council, a delegated body that represented the group councils and reported the teachers' views to the superintendent, met with McAndrew for the first time on March 22, 1924. The general council extended cordial greetings to the new superintendent but also asked him to answer the specific questions about the junior highs that had been formulated by the local and group councils.

McAndrew replied to the request for further information by saying that he did not yet know enough about the junior high school system himself to answer any questions.[29] The March teachers' councils meetings could not have been agreeable for him; in addition to questioning the value of the junior highs, all 39 elementary teachers' councils adopted resolutions opposing platoon schools.[30] McAndrew nonetheless left the meeting with the remark that he hoped the teachers would have a pleasant vacation in case he did not see them again.

McAndrew's remark, although courteous, was surprising, as he would normally meet with the councils again before vacation. It proved to be a warning of what was to occur. A month after the councils had questioned his educational plans, McAndrew issued a memo stating that it was up to him to decide when to call the councils, and that "this [did] not appear to be a good time."[31] A month after this opening salvo, McAndrew took an action that precipitated a direct confrontation between him and the teachers. He declared that in the future teachers' councils would no longer have the right to meet on school time. The teachers and the Chicago Federation of Labor interpreted this as a reaction to their rejection of his plans and as a signal of open war.[32]

By striking at the teachers' councils themselves, McAndrew was making it clear that he would brook no interference in his running of the schools. The teachers found themselves confronting an attack on what they viewed as one of their basic prerogatives. While the Loeb Rule had been aimed at the Chicago Teachers' Federation as an organization, McAndrew's refusal to call the councils was aimed at a long-standing mechanism for the expression of teachers' views. The councils had a long history; they had never worked particularly well as policy-making bodies, but their very existence had served to legitimate the idea that teachers had a right to influence school policy.[33] McAndrew, by his contemptuous dismissal of the councils, served notice that the teachers would not hold any rights by tradition; the very idea of teachers' councils that operated outside the control of supervisory staff was repugnant to him. The battle that erupted over the teachers' councils highlighted basic differences in attitudes toward authority, expert direction, and democracy, and it marked the last great fight of the Chicago Teachers' Federation.

The CTF immediately organized its forces for the same kind of political battle it had engaged in many times before. It called a series of mass meetings, addressed by labor leaders such as Victor Olander, that were designed to rally the troops. The teachers' councils themselves put out reams of material on the value of the councils. Their leaders argued that McAndrew was obligated by board of education rules to call council meetings. When they were able to prove that teachers' councils were mandated by board rule, McAndrew did reluctantly call a meeting. Immediately afterward, he succeeded in altering board rules to change the nature of the councils: from bodies in which teachers had deliberated without principals present, in accord with Ella Flagg Young's notions, he arranged for new councils that would include all the supervisory staff. McAndrew responded to the argument that teachers would be afraid to speak their minds with the comment that "if anyone should be so inaccurate as to charge Chicago teachers with general faults, timidity would not be one of them."[34] McAndrew's new council would be, in the words of board member James Mullenbach, a labor arbitrator in the men's clothing industry, nothing but a "hand picked" body for the superintendent.[35]

When the teachers lost the organizational battle to keep the original councils, they kept up a barrage of propaganda on why teachers and the labor movement should resist McAndrew's centralizing tendencies. They emphasized the hallowed nature of the councils in Chicago, quoting from a report sent out under Jane Addams's name when she was head of the school management committee in 1907. The report insisted that teachers had a right to a say in school decisions: "Even if it were true that all goodness and wisdom in affairs educational dwell with the school authorities, the fact remains that in the end their decrees must be executed by teachers."[36] The teachers and their supporters also referred to Ella Flagg Young's advocacy of the councils and her insistence that teachers meet without the dampening presence of the principals.[37] More recently, the teachers could point to the support given the councils by Superintendent Peter Mortenson, McAndrew's predecessor. Mortenson lacked McAndrew's aggressive spirit and his centralizing drive; he had emphasized the value of the councils, declaring that they offered him a chance to rely on the collective wisdom of the teaching force.[38]

The teachers' ideological defense of the councils helped rally supporters in the labor movement, but it was not ultimately successful. Board member James Mullenbach commented sorrowfully on the demise of the councils and the uproar that it caused, expressing the opinions of those who retained a belief in the teachers' rights even in the face of the efficiency ideology: "I am certain in years to come, when the historians of educational development look back upon it that it will be of immense interest to the folks to read of the tremendous reaction that took place in the school system of Chicago in 1924 and 1925, when the school councils . . . were suddenly and ruthlessly withdrawn and, . . . in my judgment, destroyed."[39] He felt ashamed, he went on, that the teachers in Chicago had less say "about the conditions and the policies of our educational system than the humblest sewing girl working in the manufacture of our men's clothing has to say about the condition under which she works."[40] His words had little impact on either board conservatives or board members who identified primarily with the progressive tradition. Helen Hefferan, for example, who occupied an important position as chair of the school management committee and who had behind her years of activism in the city's reform groups, voted for McAndrew's plan for a new council system that included supervisors. McAndrew's ideas of school reform appealed to progressives who favored greater centralization and efficiency in the schools, even at the cost of aspects of democracy. In the progressives' relatively uncritical identification with superintendents whom they classed as reform oriented, the Chicago progressives were similar to those of other cities.[41]

Meanwhile, the school board pressed ahead with McAndrew's plans for junior high schools. A board of education committee appointed in December 1923 to report on the desirability of junior high schools recommended that they be established in Chicago.[42] The board so voted without responding to the teachers' queries about whether the schools might increase the class cleavage within the system. The school management committee did agree to a labor request for a public hearing on the junior highs and the platoon school plan, but the hearing only intensified distrust between the two sides. John Fitzpatrick and Victor Olander both testified at the hearing and were dismayed by what they interpreted as a rude and indifferent response from Hefferan and other board members.[43]

The board of education committee that reported in favor of the junior high schools emphasized the flexible programs that would be possible in such schools. The committee explained that one major advantage of the junior highs was that they would allow the development of differentiated curricula, which was difficult when seventh- and eighth-grade pupils were still attending elementary schools. The committee concluded that "the grouping of pupils according to their abilities to progress, which is possible in junior high schools, is . . . an important consideration."[44] The junior high schools would also allow for the fuller development of vocational guidance, which would enable students to make the appropriate job decisions. This was particularly important for students of junior high school age. As the committee observed, "Pupils of the early adolescent age are passing through a critical period and are in special need of guidance and counsel with respect to vocational and educational information and opportunities."[45] The committee recommended that the junior highs be built to accommodate 1,200–2,000 pupils, because they would then be small enough to remain neighborhood schools but large enough to allow for differentiated programs.

The committee seemed unaware that the labor movement viewed each of these stated advantages with suspicion. The haste with which the junior high school proposal was passed further increased the fears of labor leaders that the junior highs might be another, more sophisticated, version of the Cooley plan to create a class-divided educational system. The Chicago Federation of Labor's newspaper, the *New Majority,* published a front-page article titled, "Labor Suspects New Junior High; Chicago Board of Education, by Snap Judgment, Throws Schools into Uproar." This article expressed the labor suspicions about the new schools, stating: "Sudden decision by the Chicago board of education, without consultation or public hearings, to establish junior high schools has thrown the school system into a furore again, especially in view of the fact that simultaneously there is an effort going forward to fasten 'platoon schools' on the Chicago system also."[46]

The labor suspicion arose primarily from McAndrew's "highhanded, imperious method" of destroying the teachers' councils just before deciding to install the junior highs. His refusal to consult with either the teachers or the public reinforced labor's suspicions. Fundamentally, however, the labor movement was most deeply wary that the new junior high schools would in some manner be a more sophisticated method of creating the type of tracked school system that Edwin Cooley had tried to introduce. As the *New Majority* article stated, "The principal fear of labor and the teachers is that the new schools will introduce a caste system of vocational training like that sought to be forced onto the school children in the 'dual' vocational schools some years ago under the leadership of E. G. Cooley." Although the new junior high schools might have some educational advantages, the labor movement should approach the new schools with caution. The proposal of establishing the junior high schools and then developing the curriculum was a risky one, because labor had found that "usually school policies antipathetic to the workers are fastened on them by encroachment—a little at a time—and that at least the general principles of a junior high curriculum should be determined before the schools are fastened on the system, never again to be detached."[47]

Labor opposition to the junior high schools was more a reflexive reaction to the statements about the differentiated curricula and the method of introduction of the schools than it was to any obvious inherent disadvantages of the schools themselves. The supporters of the junior high schools were often explicit in stating that the new schools would allow for greater tracking; this reinforced labor suspicions.[48] Occasionally there was agreement in the labor ranks that separating seventh or eighth graders from the younger pupils might prove beneficial, and the CFL-affiliated Federation of Women High School Teachers came out in favor of the junior highs. The high school teachers' councils also took a more positive stand toward the junior highs than did the elementary councils.[49] The suspicion generated by McAndrew and the fact that the city's major business organizations supported the junior high schools led labor representatives to reject the idea of the schools in the absence of any clear evidence that they were damaging. Once the junior high schools were in fact established, however, it became apparent that the new form of grade division did not have the deleterious consequences that had been feared. Ironically, by the 1930s the labor organizations had so accepted the junior high schools that when a business-controlled "economy" committee struck them from the school system, the CFL protested.[50]

If the CFL was hesitant about the junior high schools, it was completely hostile to the introduction of the platoon system. Platoon schools became to the labor movement in the 1920s what the Cooley Bill had been in the pre–World War I years—a symbol of business attempts to remake the schools to create docile students at low cost. The *New Majority* scorned the idea of establishing platoon schools because they were cheaper. An editorial on April 26, 1924, declared, "It makes no difference whether [platoon schools] are cheaper or dearer. . . . The discussion should not hang on matters of expense. It only serves to conceal far greater concerns."[51]

For the Chicago labor movement, one of the greater concerns was the introduction of intelligence tests into the school system. Superintendent McAndrew wanted to introduce these tests in conjunction with the platoon schools and junior highs. There was a much expanded use of these tests in the Chicago school system during his term in office. While Superintendent Mortenson had reassured the teachers in 1923 that intelligence tests were only being used in Chicago on an experimental basis, McAndrew was vigorous in promoting them.[52] The *Chicago Schools Journal,* a publication of the board of education, began to carry an increasing number of articles on the merits and advantages of IQ testing, beginning in Mortenson's term and accelerating when McAndrew assumed office.[53] Advocates of the tests favored not just using them as a gauge of the range of ability in a classroom or as a diagnostic tool in dealing with a particular child but as a means of dividing students into different tracks. Such use of the tests, the Chicago Federation of Labor argued, was inherently inhumane and resulted in the treatment of children as numbers, a favorite goal of the efficiency engineer. "It is a monstrous thing to do to a child, to label him as less bright than another, even if the tests are reliable, which is challenged. It smacks too of the quackery of the efficiency engineer . . . and certainly it is the reverse of democratic to group kids in a caste system of intelligence."[54]

Labor representatives rejected the idea that intelligence tests measured children's inherent abilities and argued that instead they transparently reflected the student's class backgrounds.[55] The real educational question was not how to measure students' intelligence levels but how the teachers treated children; even if the plans for giving children IQ tests were defeated, workers should still oppose the platoon schools because, with students moving from room to room, teachers would never be able to pay attention to children as individuals. For education to be productive or meaningful for young children, the teachers had to become acquainted with them. Elementary teachers did not need profound knowledge of specialized subject matter, and therefore nothing was gained by having experts teach each individual subject. What was important was that the teachers should be skilled at teaching and should have small classes.

The CFL returned to the theme it had first developed in the battle over the Cooley Bill—the argument that employers wanted the public schools to be authoritarian and impersonal because that would accustom students to the environment they would later find in their work situations. Students' educational experiences would consist of low-cost preparation for routine and repetitive jobs in factories; their creativity would not be encouraged in the schools any more than it would be in the work place. The Chicago Federation of Labor declared that McAndrew and the school board wanted to make the schools resemble factories. "No more important issue, of immediate concern" was before the workers of Chicago than this attempt to "make the school system over into a replica of the Ford automobile plant, pouring little children into the hopper at one end and grinding them out at the other end as perfect parts of an industrial machine." The students would be "calculated to work automatically, smoothly and continuously for a short period and then go on the scrap heap, to be replaced by other cheap, simple parts, exactly like them." Just as the labor representatives often referred to plans to introduce platoon schools as efforts to "Garyize" the schools, so they tied the features of Detroit as a city to the attempted "mechanization" of the school system. "Ford's highly systematized factor is at Detroit. There is an efficiency-shark, machine-organized school system at Detroit. Is it an accident? Could anything more dramatically illustrate how this mechanized platoon system, with its precision, standardization, 'efficiency' as its gods, has its birthplace in the . . . inhuman . . . undemocratic industrial machine?"[56]

The Chicago Federation of Labor, in echoes of the "fads and frills" debate of the beginning of the century, argued that businessmen were only too ready to cry economy where the public schools were concerned because their own children attended private schools. The drive to "Garyize" the schools stemmed from more than a simple desire on the part of businessmen to avoid increased taxes, however. As industry was increasingly subdivided, there was less and less need for well-educated workers; indeed, educated workers could become a menace to plant stability by raising questions and asserting their rights. The CFL argued that businessmen promoted mechanical education of the sort offered in platoon schools because they did not want working-class children to learn to think critically. In one of many editorials on the Chicago public schools during the battles over efficiency programs, the CFL argued that, ideally, efficiency engineers would like a society organized in such a way that workers were never required to think during the performance of their tasks. "There is a classic anecdote in the annals of efficiency engineering. It is said that a large manufacturer once remarked that he did not want intelligent workers. He wanted only those who could perform a few simple operations in his machine-run industry and who would develop automatic regularity in the repetition of those motions." This manufacturer, although repudiated by his efficiency comrades, "gave the snap away. Workers properly educated will be able to think."[57] Management of the educational system, while technically in the hands of the government, was controlled by employers through their control and domination of the major political parties. They had no desire to see workers trained to question the status quo, so "it is to their interest to prevent the education system from educating—that is, training . . . to think." In their outlook, "only the sons of the few in power must be trained to think, and even they must not think too much or too well."[58]

The CFL voted to undertake a sustained campaign among the city's working-class population against McAndrew's innovations of platoon schools, junior high schools, and intelligence tests. The CFL worked with the teachers' groups in sponsoring a mass protest meeting in October 1924 that was attended by more than 4,000 of the system's teachers.[59] Oscar Nelson, a city alderman and a vice president of the Chicago Federation of Labor, addressed the crowd in terms similar to those of the CFL's protest statements: the business interests were "not only interested in escaping taxation, and for this reason want economy in the public schools, but those same financial barons are equally interested in seeing to it that the future citizens, the children, do not receive too much of an academic education." The meeting voted to condemn intelligence tests "as a sordid scheme to deprive the children of workingmen of a thorough education, with the anticipation that they can be handled better if they have but little schooling when entering the industrial field."[60]

Vocational guidance programs increasingly came under fire as a means of shunting working-class children into dead-end jobs. The intelligence tests were likely to provide only a means of adding a scientific gloss to a class-biased process. Schools, through their vocational guidance departments, were becoming "human feeders for factories and manufacturing establishments." It was becoming more and more apparent, in the eyes of the CFL, that the modern movement for vocational guidance was "fast degenerating into a control of the public schools by big business."[61] The Illinois State Federation of Labor joined the Chicago Federation in writing a comprehensive report on McAndrew's proposals, taking particular note of the connection between vocational guidance and IQ tests, and emphasizing the class-biased nature of both. The report was the labor federation's most serious and full-scale analysis of educational questions, and a key section dealt with reasons for opposing the new intelligence tests.

The Illinois State Federation of Labor report cited a board of education document that ranked the mental ability required for various occupations. The board of education report stated that the most intelligence was required for professional and business occupations and the least for unskilled labor. Students pursuing courses leading to these different areas of work showed mental ability levels that corresponded to those of the people then employed in the occupation. The labor report commented,

> The alleged "mental levels," representing natural ability, it will be seen correspond in a most startling way to the social levels of the groups named. It is as though the relative social positions of each group are determined by an irresistible natural law.

The labor federation report rejected the "natural law" thrust of the board of education document. On the contrary, the report stated, all that the intelligence tests measured was social inequality.

> The selection of courses is naturally determined very largely by the social and economic status of the pupil . . . /T/he so-called "mental level" ascertained by the "intelligence tests" corresponds in an astounding exactness with the social and economic status of the family. Has a new natural law been discovered which binds each individual to a place in society and against which protest or struggle is hopeless?

The board of education report was not offering anything new but was merely bringing into America "the ancient doctrine of caste." In fact, the Chicago school board and other school boards, in "yielding to the pressure for classification," were "submitting the school children to the degrading influence of class propaganda."[62]

The labor representatives rejected the idea that the proposed intelligence tests rested on any scientific principle. The labor movement had fought the Cooley Bill because it was intended to separate children into academic or vocational programs, and the intelligence tests seemed merely a new way of achieving the same goal. The difference was that nearly all of Chicago's middle-class civic leaders agreed with the labor federations that the Cooley Bill was undemocratic, but the intelligence tests struck many of these leaders as genuinely scientific. Thus, they were much less ready to desert the superintendent and stand with the labor federations in opposing the tests than they had been to battle the Cooley Bill earlier. McAndrew, with his conviction that his actions rested on unshakable professional premises, appeared to them to have sound reasons for rejecting the labor objections.

McAndrew's Response to the Labor Attacks

Superintendent McAndrew was not a man to bow to pressure. This won him the grudging admiration even of Margaret Haley.[63] He did not trouble to hide his opinion that the teachers and labor leaders had no business meddling in educational affairs. During a board of education hearing on junior high schools, called at the request of John Fitzpatrick and Victor Olander, he made a point of his deliberate nonattentiveness by reading a newspaper throughout the hearing.[64] He replied to a long and careful report on the history of the teachers' councils with an abrupt note of dismissal addressed to a minor functionary.[65] McAndrew was so sure he was following the approved scientific course that questions of tact or compromise seemed irrelevant to him. In the face of a growing uproar, he simply continued with his plans to revamp the Chicago schools in order for them to meet what he considered to be impartial, unalterable criteria of efficiency.

McAndrew believed that all aspects of the educational process could be measured and analyzed. He employed efficiency rhetoric not as a convenient rationale for accomplishing his goals but because to him it represented a genuine creed. A memo he sent to William J. Bogan, division superintendent in charge of high schools, indicates that he thought techniques of measurement could be usefully applied to almost any teaching situation. The memo begins with the announcement that an opportunity to "sweep up some old inefficiencies in your high schools which have changed principals" had arisen because the new principals could employ the new techniques. McAndrew had visited two high schools and had been "appalled" by what he saw of the teaching technique. McAndrew suggested a remedy that was very much in keeping with his general approach. He recommended that Bogan read a book on the *Practice of Teaching in the Secondary Schools* by Dr. Henry Morrison. Morrison's treatment of "Sustained Application" could be of inestimable value to the new principals:

> Take for instance the scoring of group control. An observer sits in an inconspicuous place in the front corner of the room, notes number in the class and the number of pupils in attention at the end of the first minute, second minute, third minute, etc.; multiplies the number of minutes by the number of pupils, which gives the maximum pupil minutes

attention; adds the number of pupils in attention recorded at the end of each minute and divides this by the maximum possible pupil minutes attention and gets the percentage of attention.

McAndrew concluded enthusiastically, "This is one of the simplest and quickest ways to enable the principal to make clear to the teachers the tremendous waste of class periods."[66]

Under McAndrew's influence, the school administration at all levels began employing the modish efficiency jargon. The Chicago Principals' Club prepared a series of articles on "The Chicago Public Schools: How They Teach Healthful Living and Help the Physically Handicapped" that was replete with taken-over business phrases. The little booklet was dedicated "to the stockholders in the public schools by the Chicago Principals' Club." The introduction regretfully remarks, "Too seldom is the stockholder in the public schools aware of how this corporation is managed, for what the funds are spent, how the raw material, the pupil, is being treated in order to secure the finished product, the man or woman, the citizen."[67]*

McAndrew's system of school administration went beyond mere rhetoric, however. He believed that the teachers should be subject to "close supervision." He informed principals that they had the "hand of iron" and should use it.[68] He criticized teachers not only for laziness—a laziness that should be overcome through administrative vigilance—but also for their deportment and mode of dress. In response to teacher complaints of low pay, McAndrew replied that teachers might consider how they looked to the public: "If you talk about the slowness of our profession to gain public esteem, I'm ready to wager you that the retardation has not been so much on account of slovenly teaching as it has been due to the ungroomed appearance of teachers."[69] The teachers in Chicago had enjoyed a sense of influence over educational matters through their strong union, but McAndrew

*Some forms of rhetoric die hard. The *Annual Report of the Superintendent of Schools*, 1951–52 was titled "Report to the Stockholders." The report asked, "Are you a student, a parent, a resident of Chicago? Then *you are a stockholder*— a stockholder in one of the biggest businesses in Chicago—Public Education. . . . Will you join us in going over our accounts?" (Chicago Board of Education, *Annual Report of the Superintendent of Schools* [Chicago, 1952], p. 2).

was determined to end the teachers' voice in policy making. McAndrew had been brought to Chicago, he stated in a speech to the University of Michigan Club, to weaken the Chicago Teachers' Federation. He told his audience that he had been brought in as superintendent for the purpose of "loosening the hold of this 'invisible empire' within the schools, a weird system, a selfish system, doing everything to indicate a selfish purpose and demanding the right to govern the schools."[70]

Margaret Haley commented bitterly on McAndrew's "daily demands for reports, graphs, statistics, tests in so-called fundamental subjects, records of 'civic services' by the children to which teachers were required to certify," which "flowed from the superintendent's office in an unending stream." The teachers' real objection, however, was to McAndrew's often stated assertion that teachers required close watching to make sure that they performed all of their assigned duties with efficiency and dispatch. "Over and above all the congestion and the constant distraction of over-reporting . . . is an intensely sharpened system of supervision and inspection that harrasses principals, teachers and pupils alike."[71]

McAndrew was capable of contemptuous dismissal of labor objections to his system of school administration; he was more responsive to business requests that the schools be organized to increase the efficiency of their future employees. He solicited business opinions on the efficiency of the schools, sending out letters to the Association of Commerce under the heading, "Customers' Estimate of Service."[72] McAndrew won praise both from major business organizations and from the city's conservative newspapers.[73] The organized teachers had long been a thorn in the side of Chicago's businessmen, who welcomed the new superintendent's efforts to remove the federation's influence from the schools. Businessmen also appreciated McAndrew's campaign to drill students in basic skills while avoiding emphasis on other kinds of academic subject matter. McAndrew developed a "100% mastery" program under which students were to reach 100 percent efficiency in reading, writing, and arithmetic.[74] Chicago's business leaders, McAndrew emphasized, had often complained that the products of the public schools were too lacking in basic skills to make good employees. McAndrew's program consisted of constant drill in the fundamental subjects. He reported happily on vast improvements in students' accuracy scores; he declared, for example, that in February 1924 only 66 percent of roughly five thousand eighth graders tested could correctly do a simple problem in arithmetic, while by June 95 percent of the students tested added a sum correctly. This improvement McAndrew attributed to his and the principals' closer supervision.[75] Teachers objected that the improved scores that McAndrew boasted of resulted largely from principals and district superintendents adjusting ratings to improve their chances for promotion. Individual teachers also reported that lagging students had been sent from the classroom on testing days.[76] McAndrew did not accept the teachers' argument that the schools needed more resources, an argument that had frequently led the teachers to attack Chicago's many corporations for not paying their full share of taxes. Instead, he placed all the responsibility for improving education on the teachers, an orientation that was compatible with the predominant business view in Chicago.

In a characteristic gesture that appealed far more to businessmen than to the Chicago Federation of Labor, McAndrew decided in May 1926 to organize a "Citizens' Sampling Day" to demonstrate the efficiency level of Chicago elementary school pupils. Students were chosen by lot from the elementary schools and then required to answer the questions of a group of leading citizens. The citizens were to ask questions "on the basis of what abilities they think our human output should possess."[77] The citizen examiners included representatives from the Chicago Association of Commerce, the Union League Club, the Woman's City Club, and the City Club. The children were gathered into a large hall at the Fullerton Art Institute; the leading citizens, designated the "customers," asked them questions to see how the "human output" met their requirements.[78] Elmer Stevens of the firm of Charles A. Stevens and Brothers proposed the first test for the children: "The community expects the public-school output to have clean clothes, clean teeth, clean hair and clean skin." The children were duly inspected to see how they met this requirement. Mrs. Ignace J. Reis, president of the Chicago Council of Jewish Women, required the children to write five of the most important qualities of a good citizen. The president of the Chicago Bar Association had the children write him a letter to test their penmanship, and the best and poorest of the letters were thrown on a screen. The children faced a startling range of other requirements, including being asked to "make a rapid sketch" of a figure skater, dissect and analyze a speech on "what the public expects of its schools," finish sewing a boy's safety-patrol belt (with the explanation, from Mary McDowell, a noted settlement worker, that "all work . . . is noble"), and to answer a series of questions from E. R. Vornholt, of the Western Union Telegraph Company, on "Preparation for Life." The questions included, "Who pays for educating you?" and in what occupation or business the children thought they could best serve. A spelling test was introduced with the remark, "Good spelling is still the sign of good breeding," and the Sampling Day concluded for the no doubt exhausted children with a description of the character traits of five hypothetical citizens, with the children required to select the one who best exemplified the traits of good citizenship.

McAndrew had originally asked John Fitzpatrick of the Chicago Federation of Labor to participate in the Citizens' Sampling Day. With his customary tactlessness, McAndrew's letter to Fitzpatrick ended with the lines, "You are a stockholder in the public schools. The output should be brought up to your requirements."[79] Fitzpatrick's reply was scathing:

> I cannot understand how the Board of Education, who have such a tremendous responsibility in legislating for our public school system, would permit such a monstrosity in education as your "sampling day."
> I cannot understand what you and your assistants are thinking about when you talk about "output, customers, stockholders and sampling day" unless you imagine that you are running some kind of a mill or factory while you are grinding out a certain kind of product or material and you are going to get the "stockholders and customers" together and bring forth your "samples" as an exhibit of your "output."

. . . This "sampling day," as you present it, is nothing
more or less than an exhibition of the effort and result
of eight years' schooling to make the youngsters think and
act alike. . . . And the customers will be shown that the
products of our public schools jump when the string is pulled
and they will be splendid material to draw upon for employees in stores, offices, shops, factories, or elsewhere.

The parents are not consulted as to whether or not they
are satisfied with the kind of schooling their children are
getting. But why should they be consulted? The schools
are not being run for them but for the "stockholders and
customers."[80]

Fitzpatrick ridiculed McAndrew's plan of throwing portraits
of famous people on a screen and having the children identify
them and their contribution. He proposed an alternate test that
would still use the portraits and the screen. Fitzpatrick said that
he would "be glad to sponsor a test like this: First, throwing the
picture of the *Daily News* and the *Tribune* upon the screen and
seeing if the youngsters can tell out of how much money they
cheated the school fund by holding much valuable land leases on
school property and dodging taxes." Fitzpatrick's other proposed
tests included throwing the picture of Ella Flagg Young on the
screen to see if the children could identify her as the initiator of
the teachers' councils McAndrew had abolished, and showing
the pictures of the officers of the U.S. Gypsum Company to see
how many of the children knew that they had paid $40,000 in
taxes when they should have paid $600,000.[81] Understandably,
Fitzpatrick's tests were not employed at the Sampling Day. As
Victor Olander told a meeting of the Chicago Teachers' Federation, McAndrew believed that Fitzpatrick's questions were "very
complicated for young children."[82]

McAndrew and the Civic Associations

While McAndrew's relations with the labor movement
reached a point of outright hostility, he preserved close ties with
the city's civic associations and leading individuals active in
educational and political circles. They generally approved of his

efforts to introduce control by experts and "scientific" means of developing differentiated education. The occasional alliance between the labor movement and the civic associations was severed as labor's hostility to McAndrew increased. The middle-class groups joined the business organizations in supporting the efficiency-oriented superintendent in his plans for platoon schools, junior highs, and increased educational measurement and testing.[83]

The Chicago Teachers' Federation had made a policy of working with women's clubs since early in the century. In March 1902 the CTF formally affiliated with the Illinois Federation of Women's Clubs, and Margaret Haley developed a theory of "coordinated reform" that called for joint efforts by labor, the teachers, and the women's clubs to reform society.[84] These three groups represented, respectively, the factories, the schools, and the home, and in working together they could constitute a formidable alliance. This alliance had, in fact, often operated in Illinois and Chicago politics and had won reforms in such areas as the revision of child labor laws and improvement of working conditions. The alliance had undergone strain, but it had never been severed. In 1924, however, the Woman's City Club came out strongly in favor of both the junior high schools and the new platoon schools, and the teachers active in the club immediately resigned their membership.[85] The teachers were particularly angered because the Woman's City Club had not followed the usual policy of referring the matter first to the club's educational committee, where it could have been discussed and debated. Rather, the club's executive board had decided on a strong pro-McAndrew stand independently and did not allow membership debate. The teachers felt that the influential husbands of some of the executive board members might have helped persuade them to take the aggressive stand. Later, when McAndrew, then fighting for his hold in the superintendency, wrote a letter of support for the incumbent mayor, William Dever, the Woman's City Club distributed copies of the letter to every principal.[86]

The Chicago Bureau of Public Efficiency, not surprisingly, supported McAndrew, and lent its executive secretary, Harris Keeler, to the board of education's commission to study platoon schools. The teachers refused to participate in the commission, declaring that it was a foregone conclusion that it would decide in favor of the platoon schools.[87] In 1923, the bureau prepared a pamphlet urging the public to vote no on a proposed tax increase for school buildings. The Chicago Federation of Labor had strongly endorsed the tax increase, declaring that the city's schools were grossly overcrowded, with many children on double shifts, and that the increase was needed to gain sufficient seats and smaller classes. In the eyes of the CFL, the city was "up against an educational emergency" because of the overcrowding, and the entire front page of the CFL newspaper was devoted to urging a "yes" vote on the tax increase.[88] The Bureau of Public Efficiency declared that such an increase was not needed because the board of education might decide to adopt platoon schools, which would limit the need for new buildings, and, perhaps, require buildings of a different design.[89] The labor federation's fears that the adoption of platoon schools would provide a justification for reducing school funding appeared to be justified; "efficiency" presupposed better use of existing resources and thus could provide a powerful rationale for not increasing the resources devoted to education. The more conservative wing of the middle-class civic associations could find common ground with businessmen in developing this line of argument.

The middle-class civic associations formed a loose organization during the 1920s for the purpose of promoting their educational policies. The group, called the Joint Committee on Public School Affairs, included almost all the well-known civic associations, with representatives from the Chicago Woman's Club, the League of Women Voters, the YMCA and YWCA, the Settlement House Board, the City Club, the Woman's City Club, the Union League Club, and the Chicago Woman's Aid.[90] The Joint Committee on Public School Affairs continued to support McAndrew throughout his tenure as superintendent, as did the liberal civic associations more generally.

The civic associations supported McAndrew because they identified with his goals of efficiency and measurement. No one better developed the educational theory behind such programs than Charles H. Judd, dean of the University of Chicago's School of Education. Judd worked to promote increasing professional consciousness among the nation's educators and he exemplified the new style of university-trained educational authority. He was a personal friend of McAndrew and respected his abilities as an administrator and educational expert. Judd had supported the Chicago Teachers' Federation in its fight against the Loeb Rule, going so far as to speak at a mass protest meeting organized by the labor movement in June 1916.[91] Although he was basically sympathetic to the teachers' struggle for job security, he believed in McAndrew's educational principles and supported him in his contentious career in Chicago. He endorsed platoon schools, arguing that it was desirable to have a differentiated curriculum. Increased division of labor and specialization in the society made it necessary for schools to respond by training students to fill particular kinds of occupational and social roles. The platoon schools allowed pupils to move from "opportunity to opportunity" as the pupils shifted from room to room.[92]* Tracking in the schools was not undemocratic, because it would allow students to be trained for the tasks they were best suited for. Similarly, Judd believed that teachers could only benefit from the "measurement movement in education." Chicago, fortunately, had a superintendent in McAndrew who believed in "helping teachers in their work by testing their results." In adopting these testing procedures, the superintendent was "following one of the most important trends in modern school supervision."[93]

Judd's analysis of trends in American education provides an instructive contrast with the views of the labor representatives. Writers on education from the city and state labor federations

---

*Labor leaders had objected that the constant shuttling of platoon schools might make elementary-age children nervous and tense. McAndrew wrote to Judd that he wanted Judd's graduate students to undertake an evaluation of the platoon schools that had been introduced in Chicago. No doubt knowing Judd's views on the desirability of room changes, he inquired sarcastically: "Has your laboratory any neurometers by which the nervous condition of platoonized and nonplatoonized children can be compared? Or has your neurasthenic department any criteria for estimating nervous conditions of children?" (William McAndrew to Charles H. Judd, November 18, 1926, Charles H. Judd Papers, Department of Special Collections, University of Chicago Library.)

agreed that the modern movement toward an increased division of labor underlay changes in school organization. To the labor movement, however, both the increasing specialization of industry and the increasing differentiation of public education were pernicious. Judd identified both as positive and necessary features of an advancing industrial society; the plethora of specialized jobs and educational programs offered each working person an opportunity to find the appropriate niche in the industrial and educational worlds. Judd utilized the rhetoric of attention to each child's individuality that had been popularized by John Dewey, but in a very different context. To Judd, recognition of each child's individuality meant early identification of the child's abilities and interests through testing programs; the tests would reveal which form of education would be most appropriate for the particular child, and he or she would then follow either an academic or vocational program. The labor movement did not view the educational changes as following from any necessary adaptation to industrial conditions; rather, it saw attempts to reorganize the schools as a conscious policy on the part of businessmen to promote cheap and narrow education. In the view of the labor movement, the schools did not merely acknowledge differences in individual aptitudes and interests; they worked to create and make rigid those differences through class-biased programs. Businessmen did not need or want workers with high levels of education in factory jobs, and the reorganization of the schools would serve to confine working-class children in limited programs designed to stifle creativity and genuine learning. The "measurement movement" in education would only serve to diminish the independence of the teachers while providing a justification for sorting working-class children into vocational programs, a process that would begin in the elementary grades if the platoon schools were adopted.

The very definition of efficiency adopted by the labor movement and the middle-class reformers was at variance. Margaret Haley had early argued in a speech at the National Education Association convention that genuine efficiency should be measured by the degree of social justice achieved. Industrial workers made up the vast majority of the population, and no society could be said to be just or efficient of it did not fulfill the needs of the majority.[94] The labor movement had fought for the general social welfare through its efforts to end child labor and improve working conditions. These efforts of the labor movement to raise "the standard of living of the poorest and weakest members of the society" should be supported and aided by the teachers. The teachers, who occupied a critical position in educating the next generation, should help train future members of the working class in the power to think and "to select the most intelligent means of expressing thought in every field of activity." In this sense, "the ideals and methods of the labor unions are in a measure a test of the efficiency of the schools and other social agencies."[95] The teachers could help to promote an intelligent, socially commited labor movement that would encompass the majority of the population, and the success and ideals of this movement would constitute one true test of the efficiency of the public schools. Few definitions of efficiency could have been further removed from those of William McAndrew and some of the middle-class efficiency advocates.

On a concrete level, the ideological differences between the labor movement and the middle-class civic activists were reflected in growing labor hostility toward the role of school board member Mrs. Helen Hefferan. While the teachers' federation and the labor movement as a whole had had occasional differences with Jane Addams and other liberals appointed to the board of education by Mayor Edward Dunne, there had also been a basic harmony of views on many points. In the 1920s the labor movement found far fewer points of agreement with progressives, who found congenial the school administrators' growing emphasis on efficiency. When issues were posed in terms of efficiency and scientific direction, the tenuous alliance of labor and civic activists, which held together on points of teachers' rights and lack of rigid class-based tracking systems, began to collapse. Hefferan, for example, had exemplary credentials in the city's liberal community. She had a long record of activism, having served as vice president of the Woman's City Club and president of the Illinois Congress of Parents and Teachers. Her political attitudes were marked by great consistency throughout her long career on the board of education: she opposed political intervention in the schools, supported the right of experts to make educational decisions, opposed graft, and favored more funding for the schools on the basis of equitable taxation.* Even those opposed to her, such as Alderman Oscar Nelson, the vice president of the Chicago Federation of Labor, acknowledged her ability.[96] During the financial crisis of the board of education during the 1930s, she and the labor movement found themselves on the same side, but during the 1920s she aroused labor indignation because of her general support of Superintendent McAndrew's efficiency goals.

Although the labor movement identified Hefferan with McAndrew, it is interesting (and indicative of the genuinely middle position of Hefferan and others with views similar to hers) that McAndrew also found her a thorn in his side. In a letter summing up his feelings about the political crises he had encountered in Chicago, McAndrew wrote to Judd that Hefferan was one of the board members who refused to give the superintendent adequate authority. She and others, he charged, had hired him on the basis of a specific understanding regarding the policies that he was to pursue with regard to the Chicago schools. The board members then chose to ignore or forget this understanding, leaving him with about "as much assurance of support from the Board as a farmer has from the wind."[97] McAndrew also charged Hefferan specifically with holding up his request for a testing bureau large enough to put into effect his plans for measured efficiency.

On July 26, 1927, the Chicago Federation of Labor unanimously adopted a resolution calling on Mayor William Dever not to reappoint Mrs. Hefferan to a school board seat. Copies of the resolution were sent to all the CFL's constituent unions. The resolution held Hefferan "more than any other member of the Board of Education . . . responsible for the adoption of the Platoon and Junior High School systems and for forcing these sys-

---

*She believed that schools were good insurance against social disruption and could not understand the blindness of those who did not want to fund public education adequately (Helen [Mrs. William S.] Hefferan, "The Present Status of the Continuation School Laws," *Woman's City Club Bulletin* 10 [September 1921]: 9).

tems permanently down the throats of the citizenry of Chicago over the protest of parents and teachers." The resolution went on to say that representatives of the CFL and parents of school children were "flouted and treated with contempt and their opinions disregarded and given no consideration when they appeared before Mrs. Hefferan in her official capacity."[98]

Hefferan, in the eyes of the Chicago Federation of Labor, identified so strongly with the rights of experts that she was willing to disregard the views of anyone without formal authority. Hefferan chaired the school management committee, and it was this committee that had responsibility for introducing many of McAndrew's innovations, such as the junior high school and platoon schools. John Fitzpatrick later testified before the city council, asking council members to refuse to confirm Dever's reappointment of Hefferan; Fitzpatrick testified that when he and Victor Olander had appeared before Hefferan's committee to protest the introduction of intelligence tests and platoon schools, she had listened politely, but immediately after they finished she read a prepared statement explaining why she was committed to going ahead with the new programs.[99] This to Fitzpatrick was evidence of Hefferan's disregard for labor opinion. Hefferan also angered the teachers because she voted for Superintendent McAndrew's plan to replace the independent teachers' councils with what one CTF sympathizer described as a "hand picked" body, where a small number of administrators would outvote the teachers.[100] She also angered the teachers because in her capacity as committee chair she had responsibility for firing teachers who were deemed inefficient.[101] Even outspokenly conservative board members won no more hostility from the Chicago Federation of Labor and the teachers' union than did Helen Hefferan.[102] That hostility symbolized the growing rift between labor unions and those identified with progressivism.

McAndrew's Ouster

McAndrew believed that the school system could produce the maximum output at the least cost if politicians and subordinates did not interfere in the workings of the system. In

Chicago, this view quickly brought him into conflict with the highly organized teachers, but McAndrew's ultimate removal from office occurred when he became the target of the mayor, William "Big Bill" Thompson, in a bizarre clash that caught the attention of the national and international press. The mayor charged McAndrew with seeking to destroy American patriotism and to downgrade the contributions of non-British ethnic groups through biased presentations of American history. The mayor's charges against McAndrew gained public attention (his evident goal), but they represented the last hurrah of a faltering political figure. Thompson was the last of Chicago's mayors to ride into office on the strength of a personal machine, backed by a flamboyant personal presence and alliances with gangsters and the most disreputable of Chicago's businessmen. Succeeding Chicago mayors based their power on careful ward and precinct organization. Flamboyance and magnetism were not their stock in trade, at least for the next half century; rather, they built tightly disciplined political organizations that followed cautious and predictable policies. They were arbitrators and negotiators and could form stable coalitions based on interest-group bargaining. Thompson represented another era of Chicago's political leadership, and his clash with McAndrew provided a dramatic, if seemingly irrational, finale to the earlier period.[103] McAndrew probably became the mayor's particular target both because he had already antagonized a very considerable part of the population and because he was as adamant about the need to restrict political meddling in the schools as he was about other aspects of his administrative program.

William Thompson was mayor of Chicago from 1915 to 1923. He decided not to run for reelection in 1923 because he was sufficiently discredited after eight years of looting of the public treasury, school board scandals, and deals with figures such as utilities defrauder Samuel Insull that his prospects for reelection appeared uncertain. The Democrats had announced that they would run William Dever, a former judge with a restrained manner and a "good government" image against Thompson, and that his campaign would be based on criticism of the debauchery of the Thompson administration. Rather than wage a losing battle, Thompson withdrew, and the Republicans fielded a weak candidate in his place who lost to Dever.

Even as mayor, William Dever never had real control of the Democratic party organization. Patronage appointments remained in the hands of the behind-the-scenes party bosses, but Dever nevertheless exhibited some independence of his party backers by beginning a campaign to clean up the city by restricting bootlegging operations. Dever's growing commitment to enforce the Prohibition laws antagonized many former supporters. There is evidence that because of their own strong commitment to the unrestricted sale of liquor and their feeling that Dever had reneged on his original mildly "wet" stand, the powerful Democratic ward bosses and political leaders, particularly Anton Cermak, did little to turn out the vote for Dever in his 1927 reelection campaign.[104]

Dever also antagonized the teachers and the leaders of the Chicago Federation of Labor by his efficiency rhetoric and his refusal to back the teachers in their battle with McAndrew. Dever consistently maintained that he would not involve himself in school matters because it would constitute undue political interference. A year after Dever's election, the *New Majority* reported that Dever would not criticize McAndrew's unilateral abolition of the teachers' councils. The article concluded with restrained criticism of Dever for his refusal to "commit himself further to or to aid the teachers in their fight."[105]

In the fall of 1924, when the battle between the teachers and McAndrew had become a matter of considerable public attention, Dever still refused to take a stand. Victor Olander, secretary of the Illinois Federation of Labor, quoted the mayor as saying that he didn't want to get involved. Olander reported that Dever told him: "I will not interfere in the schools. People will claim that I am using the public school system for politics if I undertake to do anything. So I am not going to touch it. I have appointed what I believe to be a good school board, and I am going to leave matters with them."[106]

This stance of noninvolvement later became the characteristic response of mayors to Chicago school crises, but after Thompson's open intervention and manipulation of the schools, Dever's above-the-battle air appeared unusual. McAndrew responded positively to Dever's aloofness from school matters and later came out in public political support of Dever during his 1927 reelection campaign.[107]

Thompson sensed Dever's increasing political weakness and challenged him in the 1927 election. The Chicago Federation of Labor demonstrated how far it had moved from its Labor party politics of the postwar years when it officially endorsed Thompson. CFL vice president Oscar Nelson, always in the conservative wing of the labor organization, provided the weak justification that Thompson, renowned for the corruption of his administration, was not the representative of "big business," in contrast to Dever.[108] Margaret Haley, who had been the holder of the first membership card of the Cook County Labor Party, supported Thompson because she had been deeply antagonized by Dever's implicit support for Superintendent McAndrew. The CFL endorsed Thompson at least in part because it wished to defer to the wishes of the teachers in their struggle against the superintendent.

The CFL's endorsement of Thompson marked the beginning of a process of political accommodation that eventually brought it securely into the fold of machine politics. John Fitzpatrick and Victor Olander were not yet ready to take this step, however, and in spite of the official CFL support for Thompson, they refused to endorse him personally.[109] Fitzpatrick and Olander no longer believed that the CFL could oppose the national policies of the American Federation of Labor or maintain an independent party, but Fitzpatrick continued to speak of the necessity of ultimately building a third party. He told an audience of teachers in March 1928 that labor needed its own party, and he was scathing in his denunciation of the two major parties, saying, "Today we are dominated and controlled and dictated to by the political parties in power in this country, just as much as Mussolini operates his Fascism in Italy, or these other birds do their communism in Russia."[110] He reiterated his belief that labor had to counteract the control of the Republican and Democratic parties, saying that the Chicago Federation of Labor had tried to do this. "We developed a political activity here in opposition to the old parties, as a new instrument to define, safeguard and protect labor's interests, and in a short period of time we had worked wonders." He concluded by making it plain to his audience that in spite of setbacks he retained the conviction that it was possible for labor to succeed in building its own party. The labor party activists had had to forego their organizing for the time being, "but we have not surrendered our right to step into the open and to take over the reins of this government, not in the interests of greed or dollars but in the interest of men, women and children of today."[111]

The 1927 election campaign was one of the most unrestrained in American political history, with both sides engaging in ethnic slurs and insults, and the National Guard being put on standby to oversee the polling places. Thompson emerged the winner, at least partly because Dever did not receive strong support from the Democratic organization.[112] Thompson had gained adherents among the anti-Prohibition Democrats because of his repeated campaign assertions that he was "wetter than the Atlantic Ocean." The campaign had been marked by Thompson's attempts to introduce "America First" chauvinism into a local electoral battle, and he had succeeded in doing this through blistering attacks on Superintendent McAndrew for allowing "pro-British" propaganda into the schools. Thompson promised that, if elected, he would throw McAndrew out of office and end the use of unpatriotic textbooks in Chicago classrooms. His campaign statements on the pernicious British influence in the schools became wilder and wilder, culminating in a pledge to "punch King George in the snoot" as he attempted to capitalize on anti-British sentiment in Chicago's diverse immigrant communities.[113]

Superintendent McAndrew responded to Thompson's attacks by working actively for Dever; he wrote a letter of endorsement for the mayor that was distributed by the Woman's City Club to the principal of every school.[114] In spite of his strictures about keeping school administration and politics separate and his general refusal to brook political interference, McAndrew was the only Chicago school superintendent to plunge actively into partisan politics. It was clear in the aftermath of Thompson's victory, however, that McAndrew faced a formidable foe who was

determined to remove him from office with the maximum publicity and dispatch. Not one to run from a fight, McAndrew told
supporters that friends had originally predicted that he would
only last five weeks in the Chicago job; the removal effort was
overdue.[115]

Thompson gained control of the board of education soon after
his election, and the pliant board agreed to bring McAndrew to
trial on charges of insubordination. McAndrew had a valid contract and therefore could only be fired for cause, so the board
majority seized upon a dispute over the civil service status of
teacher clerks in the schools to accuse McAndrew of failing to
follow the board's wishes. The "trial," under the direction of
Thompson's crony Jack Coath, new president of the school board,
reached a depth of ludicrousness that the *New York Times* described as "a mixture of vaudeville, burlesque, and broadest
farce."[116] The board did not feel compelled to stick to the details of
the charges against McAndrew, but rather followed Thompson
in ranging far afield in search of evidence of McAndrew's pro-
British sympathies and attempts to poison the minds of Chicago's schoolchildren. On several occasions, the board invited
speakers to harangue the superintendent for allowing the use of
history textbooks that described George Washington as a rebel;
several speakers went through prolonged recitals on the dangers
of books such as those written by Arthur Schlesinger, Sr., and
other similarly unpatriotic historians. The *New York Times*
noted that the proceedings were often a source of amusement:

> "This is not a vaudeville show," says the president of the
> Chicago Board of Education, vainly rebuking the audience
> that assembles day by day to giggle or guffaw at the per-
> formances of "Driving George V from the Bookshelves." . . .
> The spectators appreciate it but it is getting a little ir-
> ritating to Americans who wish to believe that they live in
> a civilized country. The stupidities or drolleries of Cook
> County may become infectious.[117]

On occasion, the proceedings palled. Former Congressman
John J. Gorman appeared at the trial to testify that the University of Chicago history department was pro-British. At no time

during his lengthy and rambling account did he make any reference to Superintendent McAndrew, ostensibly the focus of the
proceedings. The *New York Times* reported that when Gorman
droned on for hours, "the defendant appeared to be asleep, as did
his counsel. President Coath said after the meeting adjourned
that he had counted five board members asleep at one time."
Coath was disturbed by the faltering entertainment value of the
proceedings. He remarked that "something has got to be done to
pep up this trial. It is beginning to fall flat and everybody goes
to sleep. I am in favor of cutting this history book stuff short."[118]

Thompson thrived on the publicity the trial generated, and he
produced ever more outrageous charges and denunciations. His
representative on the Chicago Library Board searched the library stacks for pro-British books and eventually emerged with
four musty volumes. Thompson denied that he had ever intended
to burn the volumes on the lakefront, as was reported in the
press, and instead took under consideration a plan to place them
in a locked cabinet along with other literature not deemed suitable for unrestricted public perusal. Rebukes, such as the one in
the *New York Times*, stated that "nominally, Superintendent
McAndrew of the public schools is on trial on charges of insubordination. In fact, it is Chicago as represented by its Mayor and
Board of Education that is on trial" failed to make an impression
on Thompson as he developed grandiose plans for a presidential
campaign.[119]

McAndrew responded to the proceedings with scorn. He read
newspapers during the trial until finally, six weeks after the
proceedings began, he walked out, saying that he would return
only when they got to the specifics of the charges against him.
McAndrew made no secret of his contempt for Thompson, but
he also lambasted the board members. Not only the clownish
Thompson appointees, but the original Dever members had
failed to understand their function and the role of the superintendent, McAndrew believed. He wrote to Charles Judd, "You
will realize that the advent of Wm. Hale Thompson boasting of
his immediate intent to guillotine the superintendent of schools
is not so bad as it seems. An avowed enemy is not nearly so
wearing as a group of well-meaning board members who con-

ceive their duty to prevent their executive from building up an efficient school system." McAndrew concluded that the board's failings were "not due to crookedness. They mean well but their conception of the function of a school trustee is that of the superintendent of a Sunday school."[120]

Chicago's liberal professional and political figures reacted with outrage to the school board's trial of the superintendent. Allen B. Pond, the former president of the City Club, referred to Jack Coath as "that unspeakable insect in the president's chair."[121] Charles Judd organized a national fund-raising drive among the country's school superintendents to pay the expenses of McAndrew's defense lawyers. Members of the newly professionally conscious body of superintendents responded to Judd's call for contributions and issued statements of support. The superintendent of the Philadelphia schools, Edwin C. Broome, wrote to Judd, "I am glad indeed that some of you have taken up the McAndrew case and are going to do for the educational profession what the American Bar Association would do for the legal profession should the position of a judge be similarly assailed."[122] The superintendent of the public schools of Elizabeth, New Jersey, was more succinct. He wrote, "This whole affair is a damnable outrage. McAndrew should fight for his tenure. Go to it."[123] In Chicago itself, Charles Merriam had been assailed during the trial proceedings for being a key perpetrator of pro-British propaganda. He told a reporter for the *New York Times* that he was neither worried nor suffering from loss of sleep over the charges. "'The McAndrew trial is funny,' the professor said, 'but I find the comic strips far more amusing.'"[124] Judd responded with similar scorn to the Thompson-orchestrated attacks upon him and the education school of the University of Chicago. The liberal professional community in the city, organized into the Joint Committee on Public School Affairs of Chicago, composed of 29 civic organizations, denounced the trial as an exercise in political self-aggrandizement on the part of the mayor.[125]

McAndrew made efforts to gain the active support of the business community, but the most important business leaders were reluctant to involve themselves in the controversy. McAndrew had worked closely with the city's business leadership in the past, but Thompson was noted for his vindictiveness, and few businessmen were willing to to out on a limb. McAndrew wrote to Judd that an intermediary had tried to get Clayton Mark, Theodore Robinson (both former heads of the Commercial Club's education committee), A. B. Dick, John Scott, and Clarence Pellet to "volunteer as laymen auditors to review the facts," but "only Clayton Mark volunteered. Herbert Perkins was secured by telephone at the last minute. Neither Mark nor Perkins are heated with a violent enthusiasm to perform the function desired."[126]

Businessmen were hesitant to support McAndrew publicly, evidently because of fear of the not-inconsiderable power of the mayor. M. A. McCherney, the secretary of board president Charles M. Molderwell, who coordinated McAndrew's trial fund, wrote in a letter to a businessman: "Practically all of the contributions I received to the McAndrew fund were given with the understanding that the names would not be used. . . . The balance of the subscribers were largely from representative business men of Chicago and for obvious reasons would prefer not to have their names used."[127] McAndrew would not deviate an inch from what he considered to be correct policies, but his friends in the business world not were so steadfast; their support was tempered with a realization of the practical need not to bring down the wrath of the politicians and the public upon their heads.

Few powerful voices were raised in McAndrew's defense, and the school board culminated the farcical proceedings by voting to fire him. McAndrew ultimately won a court judgment against the board, but by then he had long since left the city and taken up posts as editor of the *Educational Review* and *School and Society*.[128] He responded to his firing with his customary philosophic acerbity, remarking on his many predecessors who had been unceremoniously axed: "I knew before I went to Chicago that it was 50-50 that I'd get the Chadsey-Young-Cooley-Andrews-Lane *coup de grâce*. I can't work up any whine over it. No more'n a man who operates close to the hind legs of a mule has any kick when he gets his."[129]

Conclusions

McAndrew had been brought to Chicago both to re-store order after the depredations of the first Thompson regime from 1915 to 1923 and to complete the job of crushing the Chi-cago Teachers' Federation. The teachers' federation had enjoyed moments of victory from 1905 to 1907 when a liberal mayor, Edward Dunne, had appointed supportive board members. It had later received cooperation and aid from Superintendent Ella Flagg Young during her term from 1909 to 1915. From the time of the major attempts by the board of education to strip Young of her power, however, the teachers' federation had faced in-creasingly serious attacks. The passage of the Loeb Rule had capped the campaign to deprive the unionized teachers of their trade union allies; the hiring of Superintendent McAndrew, whose views on hierarchy and efficiency were well known to board members, represented an effort to move against the teach-ers from inside the school system. McAndrew defined his task as restoring the superintendent's power to make decisions without interference from either teachers or politicians. He was so im-bued with the efficiency ideology that he lacked the political skills to survive in his post.[130] In this respect, he resembled Super-intendent Benjamin Andrews more than Superintendent Edwin Cooley; while Cooley had been flexible enough to carve out a strong position for himself, neither Andrews nor McAndrew had a good tactical sense of how to operate bureaucratically. From the standpoint of conservatives who wanted simply to see the school system made more orderly and the teachers brought into line, both men pointlessly antagonized others whom they should have courted, including board members. In so doing, they in-vited their own defeat, even while powerful elements of the com-munity shared their goals.

The controversy over McAndrew is instructive when consid-ered in light of what has been written about the political pur-poses and coalitions that made up progressivism. Some of the revisionist authors have argued that middle-class progressives shared a business ideology;[131] other authors have argued in refer-ence to progressivism in general that, while the motivations of middle-class progressives may have differed from those of businessmen, they often ended up in the same political camp.[132] In Chicago, this was not valid as a general statement. Progressives differed from the city's business leaders in important respects. These ideological differences in turn led them to adopt different positions on concrete issues before the city. The progressives generally supported the teachers' right to organize, for example, and opposed the Loeb Rule. McAndrew's superintendency represented an occasion when they and businessmen jointly supported an educational administrator and a set of educational policies. This occurred in part because McAndrew couched his attack on the Chicago Teachers' Federation in terms that made it acceptable to most of the civic reform organizations. McAndrew had a clear perspective on what he was doing and he was able to explain his centralizing drive in a way that appealed to the progressives and enabled them to be split from their occasional alliance with the teachers. He similarly appealed to businessmen because of the fundamental conservatism of his efficiency-oriented ideology. McAndrew emphasized that he saw running the schools as being very much like running a business: the schools didn't need more money, assuming a stable tax base; they needed more efficiency. The teachers didn't need councils; they needed supervision. The students didn't need academic extras; they needed drill in the basic subjects. While progressives might not have been entirely comfortable with his abolition of the teachers' councils or other aspects of his program, the appeal of policies based on the twin grounds of science and professionalism was reflected in the steadfast support that reform organizations offered Chicago's embattled superintendent.

The teachers and the labor movement in general were on the defensive in the 1920s in Chicago. The reform organizations had helped the labor movement win educational battles over the previous two decades, but this support was no longer forthcoming. The teachers, on the firing line, still had aid from the labor movement, even though Haley had led the CTF out of the Chicago Federation of Labor. The CFL's support of the teachers was not merely the customary support given a beleaguered sister organization. McAndrew stood for political and organizational values that ran directly counter to those upheld by the Chicago Federation of Labor. The CFL weighed McAndrew's educational plans in light of their class implications. There was, to the CFL, nothing subtle about his plans for platoon schools or for the introduction of large-scale intelligence testing. They represented a more indirect and astute means of trying to achieve a class-divided school system of the sort that would have obtained had the Cooley Bill passed. The fight over the Cooley Bill had left the CFL ready to look beneath the surface of educational innovations to try to understand what impact they would actually have on the schooling of working-class children. This sometimes led the CFL to condemn innovations it later accepted, such as the junior high schools, but it also left it with an ability to place educational battles within a broader political context. The measurement movement in education, hailed by Charles Judd of the University of Chicago, did not represent progress to the CFL, but a backward step. Neither working-class children nor teachers had anything to gain from it, and both had something to lose. The teachers would lose in the form of increased supervision and rigidity in what and how they taught, and the students would lose in terms of their ability to get a full and democratic education.

McAndrew had reason to fear the independent organization of the teachers in Chicago. Because the teachers had their own educational ideology, one they shared with the labor movement, they had the will and the motivation to resist top-down plans for restructured schools. Through the 1920s, the teachers continued to contribute educational ideas to the labor movement, and the labor movement continued to support the teachers in their demands for economic security and a voice through the teachers' councils. A hierarchical form of organization over which teachers had no control would make easier the implementation of plans for a school system in which students would be tracked and sorted early. The drive to extinguish the vestiges of the teachers' influence within the school system was intimately connected to the drive to make the schools a more efficient mechanism for sorting students. It was understood and opposed on this basis by both the teachers and the labor movement.

While the labor movement remained sure of its educational goals and enunciated them forcefully during the 1920s, both the Chicago Federation of Labor and the teachers' organizations began to lose their assurance that they knew the best political means of winning their aims. McAndrew's tenure as superintendent coincided with the C F L's abandonment of its labor party efforts and its move for entry into the mainstream of Chicago's rough-and-tumble politics. After the heavy blows dealt Margaret Haley's C T F through the Loeb Rule, she was desperate for a victory against the autocratic superintendent and was willing to seek political allies where she found them—in this case, in the person of William Thompson, her erstwhile enemy during his first term as mayor. The labor movement's well-publicized opposition to McAndrew enabled Thompson to seize upon the issue during the course of his 1927 campaign and blend it with his own bizarre brand of American chauvinism in a drive calculated to win ethnic votes.

The opportunism of Haley's alliance with Thompson (the C F L-affiliated Federation of Women High School Teachers did not support Thompson) reflected a loss of certainty that the teachers could continue to win on their own. Progressive leaders were also dismayed by many of the events of the 1920s; they could find little in the artificial hysteria surrounding McAndrew's ouster that pleased them. His removal from office appeared to confirm their worst fears about the dangers of partisan intervention in educational issues. The 1930s brought a new set of political threats, however, that led the Chicago Federation of Labor and the civic associations back into an uneasy alliance. The depression changed the political configuration of Chicago in ways that had a lasting impact and brought about new modes of political organizing and responses to the schools. The developments surrounding the emergence of Chicago's Democratic party political machine will be explored in the next chapter.

6 MACHINE POLITICS AND SCHOOL CRISIS

THE NINETEEN-THIRTIES marked a fundamental shift in Chicago's line of development. The Great Depression brought massive unemployment to the city—an estimated half of the city's work force was unemployed—financial collapse to the board of education and other government agencies, and the entrenchment of the Democratic political machine. The Chicago Federation of Labor was challenged by the rise of the CIO in the city's industrial plants, and John Fitzpatrick increasingly moved the organization into close alignment with Democratic Mayor Edward Kelly. After decades of political factionalism and intra-party bickering, the Democrats swept the 1932 elections and incorporated both labor and business into a political coalition. The Chicago Democrats were aided by President Franklin Roosevelt's immense appeal, but they provided only tepid support for the New Deal and followed conservative policies within the city. Their local conservatism enabled them to win the support of such key business figures as Robert McCormick, publisher of the vehemently antilabor *Chicago Tribune*. In the new political constellation, the schools became the target of a business-sponsored cost-cutting drive that was opposed by organized labor, but with the contending groups embraced within the Democratic party, the conflicts were muted. In the years after 1932, the far-reaching power of the Democratic party leaders enabled them to serve as mediators in a nonideological bargaining process that led to reduced political mobilization on the part of the city's varied economic and political groups.

There were seemingly paradoxical elements in Chicago's political life in the 1930s. The same labor leaders who had earlier declared their allegiance to a labor party now supported a mayor who strove to cut back spending on all social services, including the schools. Businessmen allowed their own political organizations, such as the Commercial Club, to atrophy as they supported the same mayor, Edward Kelly, who was endorsed by the Chicago Federation of Labor. The very business leaders who called for efficient operation of all city services tacitly accepted the patronage-swollen payrolls of the school system's business administration. Even as instructional expenditures were pared, the school district janitors, who served as foot soldiers for the machine, were employed in numbers far beyond those required, and at some schools these janitors received higher salaries than did the principals. The only groups who pursued a wholly consistent course were the civic associations, which still strove to attain both high-quality (if stratified) and honestly delivered educational services. Unconstrained by support for the mayor, they remained free to criticize the depredations of the school system. Their goal of reaching a high level of professional administration during the 1930s appeared so remote as to be unattainable, however. The playing out of class forces in the city did not provide any mechanism by which the schools could reverse the downward spiral from within the city itself. When help finally came, it was from the outside, with the corrupt school board and superintendent challenged by national and regional professional associations.

Why did the Chicago Federation of Labor, still under John Fitzpatrick's leadership, cease to throw its resources into the types of social struggles that had previously engaged it? The accommodation with the newly entrenched Democratic party during the early 1930s was hastened by a range of factors both internal and external to the labor movement. Internally, the CFL had been weakened by the failure of the organizing drive in steel in 1919, by the continued hostility of Samuel Gompers and the AFL bureaucracy during the early 1920s, and by the faction fighting with the Communist-controlled Worker's party, which had disrupted the independent labor party founded by the CFL. The Depression made the CFL all the more a beleaguered organization; massive unemployment had a devastating effect on many of the unions that comprised the CFL's core.[1] Further, despite historic ties between the leaders of the CFL and those who tried to organize the mass production industries, bitter organizational and political rivalries ultimately developed between the Chicago Federation of Labor and the CIO unions.[2]

The essence of machine politics is the welding together of a diverse coalition within a centralized framework; it is essential to the smooth workings of the machine that the different groups incorporated within it make limited and narrow demands upon the political system.[3] Within the same decade, the 1930s, that witnessed the emergence of the militant CIO industrial unions, the organized labor movement in Chicago, or rather, the most influential sections of the organized labor movement, shifted from a general position of raising class demands to one of operating as a pluralist pressure group. As part of the CIO's massive organizing drive, the steelworkers, the meatpackers, and later, the auto workers in plants around Chicago were successfully unionized. Even the new industrial unions found their political role sharply constrained by Chicago's "forbidding local political culture."[4] Industrial unions must fight for benefits for more diverse constituencies than do craft unions; they are therefore more likely to pursue broad political objectives than are their more narrowly focused craft counterparts. In Chicago, bitterness between the unions affiliated with the Chicago Federation of Labor and those affiliated with the CIO hindered efforts to develop a common political program or to press for mutually beneficial social policies. The industrial unions ultimately accommodated themselves to the realities of operating in a machine-controlled city in which they remained a subordinate part of the labor movement, and they began to concentrate their political energies on the same kinds of demands that had come to occupy the unions remaining in the CFL. These demands centered on benefits for their members (through city help in negotiating contracts and promises from the mayor not to use police to break strikes) and gaining influence and prestige through the appointment of labor officials to public posts.

Chicago's school problems weren't solved during the 1930s, and there was no consensus on the proper educational direction; there were bitter disputes over educational funding and political manipulation of the schools, but the intensity with which the labor movement pursued its educational objectives diminished.

Before looking at the ways in which controversies over these issues were played out, it will be useful to ask why the Chicago machine gained its predominance in the city and how its rise affected the historical pattern of political confrontation.

The Rise of the Chicago Democratic Machine

Ethnic politics played a major role in solidifying the machine's hold in Chicago. Beneath the surface instability of the city's political life during the 1920s, ethnic voters increasingly shifted their allegiance to the Democratic party. Historians used to date the national Democratic party's triumph in creating an ethnic coalition from Franklin Roosevelt's 1932 victory, but further research into urban voting patterns indicates that the shift began in the nation's big cities in the mid-1920s.[5] Ethnic voters increasingly identified the Republican party with nativist prejudice against immigrants, while the Democratic party gained an image of championing the rights of recently arrived citizens. In Chicago, this national trend gained added impetus because many members of traditionally Republican ethnic groups, such as the Germans and Scandinavians, had been repulsed by the corruption and flamboyance of Republican Mayor William "Big Bill" Thompson.

Voters from recent immigrant backgrounds were brought into the Democratic party fold in large numbers in Chicago around the issue of Prohibition. The Democratic mayor who first consolidated the party machine, Anton Cermak, built his career around his attacks on the Eighteenth Amendment as a violation of individual liberty.[6] The issue of Prohibition was an ideal one for machine politicians seeking to build a diverse coalition. In machine politics, spoils and patronage claim far more attention than do issues or ideology.[7] The politicians are in a sense almost "apolitical." They seldom identify themselves strongly with developed positions on political issues, and the machine operates through interest-group bargaining and maneuvering within a centralized framework.

The Prohibition issue had enormous emotional saliency in Chicago. It helped to propel Anton Cermak into the mayor's office and to weld disparate ethnic groups together into a durable political coalition. Resistance to Prohibition became a symbol of resistance to attempts by Protestant, nativist Americans to impose their culture and values upon the immigrant groups. As late as 1930, first- or second-generation immigrants comprised roughly 65 percent of Chicago's population of three and a quarter million.[8] The immigrants overwhelmingly opposed Prohibition.[9] Cermak recognized the great partisan benefit that accrued to the Democrats because the Chicago Democratic party opposed Prohibition, and when some Republicans tried to circulate petitions for the repeal of the Eighteenth Amendment, he declared that "the issue is a Democratic one and we won't submit to its being carried off by outsiders."[10]

Concentrating on Prohibition as an issue not only was advantageous to Chicago's aspiring Democratic politicians because it enabled them to avoid issues with more fundamental class implications that might have split their constituency, it was also advantageous in that the politicians received material aid from the anti-Prohibitionists. The ethnic anti-Prohibition voters were organized into a massive conglomerate association called the United Societies that claimed to represent several hundred thousand voters; the association helped funnel money supplied by the brewers to the "wet" candidates.[11] From his election as secretary of this association in 1907 to the end of his political career, the United Societies remained a key source of Anton Cermak's power and political legitimacy. The United Societies successfully brought such disparate groups as the Poles, Czechs, Belgians, Hungarians, Germans, Italians, and French together around the free sale of liquor and opposition to nativist legislation.

The shift toward the Democrats gathered momentum at the end of the 1920s. Until then, both Chicago and Cook County had had Republican majorities, but this began to change as more immigrants became citizens and were able to vote. In the 1928 election, William Thompson and his faction of the Republican party initially appeared in a strong position because they controlled patronage and had the ability to intimidate such organizations as the Chicago Bar Association into supporting them. The bitter Republican primary of 1928, however, shocked many citizens when it exploded into violence. Those voters who had not been repelled by Thompson's corruption as mayor were scandalized when bombs were placed at the homes of opponents of the Thompson faction, and the electoral contest became known as the "pineapple primary" because of the homemade explosive devices. Thompson himself was not up for reelection until 1931, so he suffered no direct personal defeat, but his faction lost badly in the local contests.[12] The Republicans appeared increasingly vulnerable, an impression that was confirmed when the Cermak-led Democrats won a sweeping victory in the 1930 elections. Nearly all Democratic candidates for county and local offices won landslide victories, and the Democrats gained complete control of the county machinery.[13]

The 1931 mayoral election completed the victory of the Democrats. Cermak went into the election expecting to win, and Thompson, fearing defeat, lashed out in a wild display of political insults and ethnic slurs. Building his campaign around social prejudice only helped to further alienate many of his former supporters, however, and Cermak put together a strikingly diverse coalition that laid the basis for Chicago Democratic politics for decades to follow. Cermak assumed he had the support of the city's main ethnic blocs and, in contrast to his previous campaigns, he did not focus much of his campaign propaganda around resistance to Prohibition. In a career that had been built upon "wetness," there was no need to belabor the point. Thompson aided Cermak in this strategy by losing his usual political astuteness and attacking Cermak for his ethnic origin, an approach guaranteed to backfire in a city with an overwhelmingly immigrant population. (Thompson's most famous attack along these lines was his rhetorical question, "Tony, where is your pushcart at? Can you imagine a World's Fair Mayor with a name like that?")[14] In a very significant development, however, Cermak went beyond the immigrant groups to win the support of the city's business leaders and the most prominent middle-class "good government" independents.

Chicago's business leaders supported Cermak almost unanimously.[15] In terms of personal background, the business leaders had more in common with Thompson, who was from a wealthy and socially prominent family, than they did with the working-class, uneducated Democratic candidate. But Thompson's political instability alarmed businessmen, while Cermak had long cultivated business support. Cermak made it clear to leading business figures that he would follow conservative economic policies and would hold taxes down by limiting city services. In this respect, the businessmen considered him more reliable than the erratic Thompson.[16] Further, Thompson no longer had great power to intimidate businessmen into supporting him by implicit threats to use the city government against them, because Cermak was expected to win the election. Such powerful businessmen as Sewell Avery, president of Montgomery Ward, Silas Strawn, former president of the Commercial Club, and Robert I. Randolph, president of the Chicago Association of Commerce, supported Cermak's election bid. Julius Rosenwald, owner of Sears, Roebuck, and financial mainstay of the Bureau of Public Efficiency, endorsed Cermak. Antiunion leaders such as Robert McCormick, publisher of the conservative *Chicago Tribune*, and Thomas E. Donnelly, one of the owners of the huge, fiercely antiunion Donnelly printing company, joined in supporting Cermak's campaign.[17]

In retrospect, it is ironic that most of Chicago's independent "good government" liberals also supported Cermak. In later years, many of these same people viewed the growth of the machine as one of the city's greatest evils, but in 1931 they felt that Cermak represented the forces of efficiency compared with the flamboyantly corrupt Thompson, although they were not enthusiastic about Cermak's long identification with "wetness" as an issue. Jane Addams and Mrs. Louise de Koven Bowen both helped Cermak win the support of many of the city's politically active women leaders. Charles Merriam and Harold Ickes, probably the two most influential liberal figures in Chicago, offered their support to Cermak and worked for his election.[18]

Cermak took office as mayor of Chicago the year before Franklin Roosevelt's victory over Herbert Hoover at the outset of the Depression. Cermak had been lukewarm about Roosevelt and had, in fact, briefly supported a favorite-son candidate against him because he favored a confirmed anti-Prohibitionist such as Al Smith. Cermak had explained in 1931, "Of course, our first concern at the Democratic National Convention next year will be to get adopted for the platform a wet plank that will go far enough to be fully satisfactory to the wets. Then we will pick a candidate to fit the plank, and unless the fit is perfect we will not be for him."[19] As a consequence of Cermak's desire for a more anti-Prohibitionist candidate than Roosevelt, the relations between the president-elect and the mayor were cool. Cermak realized that Chicago, probably the city that was hardest hit by the Depression, would need federal funds to provide relief and keep the city from total financial collapse. The channeling of federal funds (and the maintenance of control over patronage from federal sources) would require closer relations between the leaders of the Chicago Democratic party and the architects of the New Deal. Cermak therefore traveled to Miami to meet Franklin Roosevelt and discuss forms of federal relief. While on this pilgrimage, Cermak was hit by an assassin's bullet intended for Roosevelt. The new boss of the Chicago Democratic party died a martyr after less than two years in office.[20]

The machine was sufficiently institutionalized that Cermak's death did not cause any severe disruption. Rather than hold a new election, the state legislature obligingly passed legislation allowing the Democratic-controlled city council to select the new mayor. After some back-room maneuvering, Edward J. Kelly, chief engineer of the sanitary district, was chosen by the Democratic caucus and ratified by the council. The Chicago Federation of Labor, not yet completely allied with the Democratic machine, remonstrated in an editorial titled "Chicago's Invisible Government" that a temporary mayor should be appointed and then a new election held, rather than going through the motions of a city council election.[21] Kelly, however, reigned over Chicago for the next 14 years, and, during his tenure as mayor, the Chicago Democratic party achieved unshakable political supremacy.

Economic Crisis and the Building of a Political Coalition

Immediately upon taking office both Cermak and Kelly were forced to deal with the city's economic crisis. Chicago, as a key center of industrial production and distribution, suffered a near-total economic breakdown during the Depression. The value of industrial output slumped drastically in the Chicago area, falling from roughly $5.4 billion in 1929 to $3.3 billion in 1936.[22] Chicago's unemployment rate approached 50 percent; an estimated 750,000 Chicagoans were out of work in October 1932; only 800,000 still held their jobs.[23] Many of those who were still employed worked part time, so the true unemployment rate was still higher. Thousands were evicted from their homes, and there were often clashes between the police and those being driven from their dwellings. The Unemployed Councils organized opposition to the evictions, and the clashes sometimes became bloody, as in a series of eviction riots in August 1931 that left several dead and many wounded. Massive unemployment weakened the unions, and even the fortunate workers who kept their jobs had to watch their wages plummet as the unions no longer had the strength to enforce contracts. As late as 1940, average weekly wage rates in Chicago were still below those of 1929.[24] The construction unions, previously among the strongest in the city, were particularly hard hit, as all new building programs were halted; with 40 percent of the union membership out of work, the building trades workers accepted slashing wage cuts.

The city's most immediate need was to gain relief for the hundreds of thousands of unemployed. Chicago's public and private agencies were not equipped to cope with the massive devastation of the Depression, and there was no realistic relief program. Hundreds of thousands subsisted from hand to mouth through a patchwork of programs, as the city's political leadership gradually realized the need for federal intervention. In keeping with his generally conservative social philosophy, Cermak had been ideologically predisposed against federal relief programs, but as the weekly relief bill mounted to a million and half dollars, he appealed for federal aid.[25] By the summer of 1932, he had fully committed himself to seeking a federal solution for Chicago's relief problem, and his trip to Miami was designed to press Chicago's case with President-elect Roosevelt.[26] The city was already receiving a disproportionate share of federal relief monies (by October 1932, Illinois had received half of the total federal relief money distributed to all states), but the need was still overwhelming.

The city's problems were compounded by the inefficiency and corruption of its tax-collection machinery. Under state law, the assessors were required to assess all property at 100 percent of its valuation, but in practice, the proportion of assessed to actual value varied greatly. Political favoritism was rife in levying taxes, and citizens had no confidence in the fairness of the city's assessment machinery. Matters came to a head in 1927 when the Cook County Board of Commissioners appointed a Joint Committee on Real Estate Valuation to review the practices of the assessors and recommend methods of levying taxes more equitably. The committee reported that the just completed 1927 assessment was the most biased of any it had reviewed and asked that it be declared invalid. After much political maneuvering, the state tax commission ordered Cook County to perform a revaluation of all property for the 1927 tax levy.[27]

Margaret Haley's Chicago Teachers' Federation hailed the revaluation as a victory; the CTF had long argued that the solution to the board of education's financial problems lay in reform of the tax machinery, but the revaluation ultimately worked to greatly increase the severity of Chicago's economic crisis. The revaluation proceeded extremely slowly and was still underway two years later when the Depression began to take its toll. Large property owners promoted a tax strike in the hope that either a tax bill could be avoided until the economy recovered or that the taxes would never be collected. In fact, the breakdown of the tax machinery did result in a smaller and smaller proportion of taxes being paid each succeeding year. By mid-summer of 1930, 80 percent of the 1928 taxes had been paid compared to only 60 percent of the 1929 taxes and 50 percent of the 1930 taxes.[28] Chicago, as Paul Douglas pointed out in 1939, had a tax delinquency rate nearly five times that of New York City.[29] Chicago's government was already in fiscal collapse during the opening stages of the Depression.

The city of Chicago and the board of education had long operated to increase revenues through a fiscal sleight-of-hand involving tax anticipation warrants. Rather than basing each year's budget on the amount of tax money actually collected, the budget was based on the taxes that were anticipated for the following year.[30] As the assumption invariably was that the tax take for the following year would be greater than that for the current year, this allowed the promulgation of a larger budget than would otherwise have been possible. This system made the board of education and the city in general highly dependent on the banks, however, as they had to be willing to buy the tax anticipation warrants, and it also necessitated the payment of large sums in interest. As the city's fiscal problems mounted and the banks themselves faced crisis conditions because of the economic slump, the tax warrants began to be offered on the market only to meet with no takers.

Business and the Machine:
The Bankers Assume Control

Cermak had enjoyed strong support from the city's business community because of his commitment to conservative social policies and keeping down taxes. Edward Kelly took office with the same kind of powerful backing that Cermak had received and quickly moved to demonstrate that he would follow the same policies. A *Fortune* article of August 1936 on the power of the Chicago machine remarked on Kelly's support among the business community: "As the friend of Colonel McCormick [Kelly] was acceptable to the State Street merchants as well as the [City] Council. The city businessmen expected him to continue the political cheeseparing and relatively solid financial administration that had made the rough Cermak palatable, despite his origins, to bankers from the Gold Coast and civic leaders from the better families, who maintain apartments on Lake Shore Drive or estates in Lake Forest."[31] *Fortune* further speculated on the reasons for Kelly's popularity among businessmen and concluded that the machine allowed business free play within the city: the machine "serves the economic lords of the community by keeping its hand off national business—and most of Chicago's business is national in scope. . . . Probably this is why influential first citizens of Chicago—such as Robert J. Dunham, former Vice President of Armour and Company—support Kelly unequivocally."[32]

Business leaders in Chicago supported the local Democratic

party in spite of its growing alignment with the New Deal. Colonel McCormick, publisher of the *Chicago Tribune*, had no difficulty in simultaneously supporting his close friend and early political protégé, Edward Kelly, on the local level, while attacking FDR and the New Deal on the national level. The business leaders evolved a close working relationship with the mayor that was based on a common approach to municipal politics. Mayor Cermak, in particular, was noted for his connection with Melvin Traylor, president of the First National Bank. He nominated Traylor as a favorite-son candidate at the 1932 Democratic national convention and relied on him for political advice. One Chicago historian described the connection between the mayor and Traylor as being that between client and boss: "When bankers and other big business men met to discuss public affairs President Melvin A. Traylor of the First National Bank sat at the head of the table. He was the banker-political boss. When it was the consensus of opinion that the city or other local municipality should do this or that Traylor invariably said: 'I'll see the Mayor and have him do it.' In such matters he was Cermak's boss."[33]

Chicago's business figures had faced many years of unstable political leadership, and they welcomed Cermak's efforts to centralize control and provide the city with conservative leadership on economic questions, even within the framework of continued and intensified operation of spoils politics. The Depression presented the city with a fiscal crisis and provided a powerful rationale for close cooperation between political and business leaders. It is noteworthy, however, that in contrast to the pre–World War I era, the businessmen acted largely through ad hoc "citizens' committees" and informal contacts with party bosses rather than through well-organized business clubs. With consistent and reliable access to the highest levels of the Democratic party, including the mayor himself, there was little need for formally organized business pressure groups. Such clubs only called attention to the businessmen's role and aroused potential opposition, while the same results could be achieved at less political cost through informal contacts. The Commercial Club continued to exist, but it ceased to be the central policy-formulating body for the Chicago business elite. The 1930s marked the beginning of the atrophy of the once powerful business organizations.

In the 1930s businessmen in Chicago used their ties with the machine and with the banks to mount a sustained drive to force slashing cutbacks in the educational budget. The school board faced a critical financial situation as early as 1929 as Chicago's tax machinery broke down and tax anticipation warrants could no longer be readily marketed. Teachers' salaries were paid late or not at all, and there was speculation that the schools would have to close in the fall of 1930 because of lack of funds.[34] In this crisis, business leaders formed the first of a succession of committees to deal with the school board's financial problems. The Joint Committee on Real Estate Valuation appointed 58 prominent businessmen to a special committee whose chief purpose was to market $74 million worth of tax warrants to keep the city and the school board afloat while a longer-range solution to the economic crisis was found. This committee was headed by Silas Strawn, a lawyer who, as a former president of the Commercial Club and a prominent Cermak backer, was influential in both the city's business and political worlds.[35] Strawn later went on to become president of the United States Chamber of Commerce. The Strawn committee quickly succeeded in raising the necessary funds, then formulated a series of recommendations regarding reform of taxation policies, its chief recommendation being that the board of education and other government bodies should be free to issue bonds without a referendum.[36]

Mayor Anton Cermak pressed the school board to make budget cuts, but the board, still controlled by Thompson appointees, insisted on independent management of school affairs. Following Cermak's assumption of office in April 1931, the teachers went unpaid from April to June. The board had no cash reserves left, but it refused to take any comprehensive measures such as reducing patronage-swollen expenditures for the district business office; instead, it stumbled along in the face of growing financial crisis while Cermak protested and tried to persuade the Thompson appointees to resign. Finally Cermak simply denounced the board members, declaring that "the majority of the Board, a holdover from the Thompson regime, may be chiefly concerned with saving itself and its friends. Chicago is concerned with saving its schools. The two objectives are miles apart."[37]

Under growing pressure, as Chicago's antiquated and corrupt tax machinery failed to yield revenues, the board slowly moved to make budget cuts.[38] Cermak lacked direct authority to force the board to follow his policies, but he worked closely with a newly formed businessmen's committee that wielded the economic clout to assure some measure of compliance. The new committee was formally titled the Committee on Public Expenditures but was more widely known as the Sargent Committee, after its head, Fred W. Sargent, president of the Chicago and Northwestern Railroad. The committee was formed after businessmen working more informally had been unable to get the school board to agree to a program of sweeping retrenchment. The businessmen intended the Sargent Committee to bring concerted pressure on government agencies to cut back expenditures. As Sargent explained to the press: "Unless the businessmen of Chicago can be awakened to this situation, unless they are united and coordinated in a militant drive, with the single objective of reducing governmental expenditures and balancing budgets, the prosperity of the city will be threatened for years to come."[39]

Although its members usually referred to the Committee on Public Expenditures as a "citizens' committee," Sargent was frank in stating that it was a committee of businessmen who were influential because of their connections with the city's banks. In an article titled "The Taxpayer Takes Charge," Sargent explained:

> Since March, 1932, Chicago has been steadily achieving a sharp reduction in the operating costs of its government through the cooperation of its various officials with an extralegal body of which I am the general chairman.

This "extralegal body" gained its power from its connections with the banks on one hand and the city officials on the other:

> Our committee found its power in the genuine eagerness of most of the officials to cooperate, plus the fact that banks

had decided that our committee's judgment could be trusted. To some extent, the banks have shown themselves willing to be guided by us. I do not mean that they have been disposed to put up any sum we might ask for—naturally not, since they are banks. But they have shown that they positively will not lend money for any municipal function which does not have our active support. This has been a powerful lever in dealing with the really small number of recalcitrants in public office who still cling to a faith in Santa Claus.[40]

Sargent expressed his satisfaction that the committee's relations with the city officials were cordial as the committee went about its business of advising the banks which municipal services should or should not be funded. "Fortunately," he wrote, "we find ourselves dealing with city officials who want our aid and who are willing to go a long way to get it."[41] The essence of the business program was, as Sargent put it, "retrenchment, and then more and more retrenchment," but the committee did not attempt to dictate the specific programs that should be cut.[42] Rather, "we have tried to indicate the size of the economies which must be achieved and left it to the responsible authorities to work out their own plans of economy."[43]

The committee's membership list justified Sargent's claim that the group acted as spokesman for the "big taxpaying organizations," although he hastened to add that it also spoke for "the myriads of less-articulate taxpayers." The Committee on Public Expenditures included Sewell Avery, president of the U.S. Gypsum Company and Montgomery Ward, Peter Carey, vice president of the Chicago Board of Trade, Charles S. Dewey, vice president of the Colgate-Palmolive-Peet Company, Stanley Field, director of Marshall Field, George A. Ranney, vice president and treasurer of International Harvester, Robert E. Wood, president of Sears, Roebuck, and Max Epstein, chairman of the board of the General American Tank Car Corporation.[44] The Chicago Principals' Club reported that out of the 28 leading members of Sargent's committee, only two or three had ever sent their children to the Chicago public schools.[45]

In addition, and critically, five of the committee members were

on the board of directors of one or the other of the main downtown banks, and two commitee members were on the boards of
two of the banks. These banks (the First National, the Harris
Trust and Savings, the Continental Illinois, and the Northern
Trust) were the institutions that would have to buy the board of
education's tax warrants.[46] The banks demonstrated their reliance
on the committee's judgment by refusing to purchase warrants
for any amount in excess of that which the committee deemed
adequate. There were frequent informal contacts between representatives of the five major banks in Chicago and the committee.
In an interview conducted in 1967, the former professional director of the Committee on Public Expenditures, John O. Rees,
described the contacts between the bank representatives and the
committee:

> There was a committee from each of the five loop banks—it
> was an informal committee—and I met with them prob-
> ably once a week to review what was going on and to in-
> dicate to them what my survey of conditions would indicate
> as what would be a safe margin for loans—whether fifty
> per cent or sixty per cent, or what have you—and there was
> once or twice where I stopped the board of education from
> borrowing a lot more than they needed to. The banks backed
> me up on it. They [the Board of Education] were going
> to sell a lot of tax warrants in excess of what they needed
> to, and I convinced them and the banks. They were figuring
> on borrowing six or seven million more than they needed.
> It was all sort of informal.[47]

The board of education could not readily ignore a committee
that was backed by the financial might of the city, and after an
attempt at getting federal funds failed, the Committee on Public
Expenditures began a concerted drive to force the board of education to cut expenditures sharply. The committee, led by Fred
Sargent, had a series of evening meetings with the board in July
1932. The board's financial position made it vulnerable to outside dictation, since for months teachers had either gone without
pay or been paid in scrip.[48] Cermak had already announced in
March that unless the "Thompson Board" made more cuts, there
was no possibility of selling warrants to the banks, so it was

clear that the mayor would not be a source of political support to the board; rather, he endorsed the efforts of the committee.[49] One board member, Orville Taylor, had declared a full year earlier that the board had no choice but to make the cuts desired by the mayor and the banks: "Whether we like it or not, we are in the LAP of the citizens' committee, upon whom the bankers are depending."[50]

When faced with the Sargent Committee's insistent demand for further retrenchment, the board reluctantly complied and ordered a series of cutbacks in the educational program. The Sargent Committee declared that the board could make the cuts where it wished, but that it would have to cut at least $15 million from the proposed $90 million budget.[51] The board cut the required amount under strong pressure from both the committee and Mayor Cermak. Cermak had declared, "If the reduction is not made then the responsibility for failure to secure more funds later must rest entirely upon the school board."[52] In December 1932, the committee demanded that still further reductions be made, and, in a series of closed meetings, one held in the mayor's office, the committee and the board worked out more budget cuts.[53]

The political equation in Chicago was dramatically upset when Cermak died from an assassin's bullet on March 6, 1933, but his successor, Edward Kelly, quickly demonstrated that he intended to follow conservative economic policies similar to Cermak's. Kelly, chief engineer of the sanitary district, had been indicted in connection with a series of scandals involving the district and had been required to pay over $400,000 in back taxes to the federal government, but his somewhat dubious antecedents were generally overlooked by the press.[54] Kelly was a close friend and protégé of Robert McCormick, the publisher of the *Chicago Tribune,* a friendship that arose from their acquaintance when McCormick was president of the sanitary district board. Cermak had distinguished himself from his predecessor, William Thompson, by his businesslike approach to city politics, his building of a powerful precinct-based machine, and his consistent and close working relationship with the city's leading business figures.[55] The new mayor intended to follow the same policies, and he symbolized his adherence to the principle of economy in government by receiving Fred W. Sargent as one of his first official visitors.[56]

Cermak had been handicapped by his inability to control the board of education completely because six Thompson holdovers remained in office, but Kelly had the opportunity to appoint seven new board members within a few months after he took office.[57] The seven Kelly appointees could usually count on the support of three of the other board members, leaving Mrs. Helen Hefferan, a Dever appointee, in a frequent minority position of one. The Kelly appointees were men who had connections with the party organization or were representatives of the city's main voting blocs. None of the first five appointees that Kelly named to the board in May 1933 had been to college and none had demonstrated any previous interest in public education.[58] Kelly gained political mileage from their appointments, however, because they represented diverse ethnic and religious blocs. The new board members included three Catholics and one Jew and were of Irish, Polish, and Czech background. James McCahey, the new board president, who was to hold his post for the next 13 years, was an Irish Catholic political ally of the mayor. The new board members were neither big businessmen nor professionals—the two groups that had supplied the bulk of board members in the past. Rather, they were primarily self-made businessmen who were economically successful but far from membership in the city's business elite (McCahey, for example, was a coal dealer). In this respect, too, the composition of the new board reflected changes that had come over the city since the consolidation of the Democratic party machine; prominent social origins counted for less than did skill in the rough and tumble of politics.

Kelly made it plain when he appointed the new board members that he expected them to follow a program of economy. He had selected them, he declared, because they were "practical" men who did not have extensive educational backgrounds but were committed to retrenchments and were "business experts."[59] Kelly said, in particular reference to his friend McCahey, that he was "a hard-headed business man pledged to a program of economy who will see that the people get their money's worth."[60] McCahey had "declared himself as an advocate of the strictest economies in the school system," a self-description he was shortly to prove correct.[61]

The School Cutbacks

The new school board members had been in office only a few months when they voted on July 12, 1933, to cut the school budget drastically. The previous board had been reluctant to reduce the budget and had done so only under sustained pressure from political leaders and from businessmen. The new board, however, made far more sweeping cuts without hesitation. The ten economy-minded board members made no pretense of listening to objections to their plans. At the time of the regularly scheduled July 12 meeting they held a closed-door session from which they excluded board member Helen Hefferan, who opposed the retrenchment program, and William J. Bogan, the superintendent of schools. Hefferan and Bogan waited with a large audience for several hours for the board members to return for the public portion of the meeting.[62]

When the board members did return, they quickly passed in a 20-minute meeting a list of sweeping cutbacks in the public schools. The board voted to discontinue the city's junior college, to abolish the junior high schools, to eliminate the Bureaus of Curriculum and Vocational Guidance, to abolish all vocational and home economics training from the elementary schools, and to discontinue all athletic teams and coaching. In addition, the board abolished 50 percent of the district's kindergartens, ceased funding for the school bands and orchestras, and abolished all but one of the district's continuation schools. For both the teaching staff and the principals, the cutbacks spelled special hardship. The board dismissed 1,400 teachers from the system, including all elementary school physical education teachers, and the high school teaching load was increased to seven classes a day. Elementary school principals were required to supervise two schools instead of the usual one.[63]

Board president James B. McCahey emphasized that the

cuts in the educational program were not temporary measures adopted due to crisis conditions. They were instead desirable revisions of the school program. As he explained, "After the cuts are in effect, it will be found that the effectiveness of the educational program will be increased rather than decreased."[64]

The school board elaborated further on its reasons for the cuts in a pamphlet, *Our Public Schools Must Not Close!*, that was given to 500,000 school children to take home to their parents.[65] In this defensive document, the board insisted that the only alternative to the cuts was closing the public schools. The board further maintained that the cuts only eliminated unnecessary expenses and frills that had encrusted the school program. "On the educational side," the board document declared, "investigation disclosed that support was lent to the statement that the Public School System as administered had accumulated many so-called 'fads and frills' or 'extracurricula' activities and embellishments."[66] The first such frill the board listed was the junior high schools, which the board ordered closed, with their pupils transferred to elementary schools. The board conceded that, as a result of the economy program, a large number of teachers would be "temporarily" unemployed, and it acknowledged that the salaries of all teachers would be cut as a result of shortening the school year by a month, but it asserted that "the economies resulting will create a condition which holds the only promise for financial relief."[67] The board also insinuated that only unsavory political machinations could account for the outcry that the board's actions caused. In *Our Public Schools Must Not Close!*, the board declared darkly, "Considerable agitation against this program of economy and efficiency was stirred up by certain interests, and the facts have often been wilfully or ignorantly misrepresented. Even now, for reasons which are known by many and suspected by more, agitation continues, though on a constantly diminishing scale."[68]

The school board faced a storm of opposition from the civic associations and the labor movement when the cutbacks were announced. Robert Maynard Hutchins, then president of the University of Chicago, flailed the board for initiating "a century of reaction in the schools." The board members, he wrote, "are dummies in every sense of the word. . . . But stupidity cannot be the sole explanation of their behavior. . . . They have not been making an honest effort to save money. The mayor told them what to do." Hutchins concluded, "The basis of this action is either a complete misunderstanding of the purpose of public education or a selfish determination that its purpose shall not be fulfilled, or an ignorant belief that a system that has been wrecked can still function."[69] Charles Judd accused the board of "going back to medievalism."[70]

Hutchins's language was echoed by many, but the board held fast to its ground and dismissed the outcries. The board members were reinforced because they clearly had the support of the Democratic machine in their economy program. Mayor Kelly adopted an official stance of distance from the board, but in practice encouraged the economy drive in a number of formal and informal ways. First, Kelly's school board appointees had been selected on the basis of ties to the political organization that dominated the city, so they could be expected to respond sympathetically to machine requests. Kelly had particularly close ties with board president McCahey, and the two remained friends throughout the 13 years that McCahey spent on the board. The director of the Committee on Public Expenditures, John O. Rees, in an interview conducted many years later, stressed the importance of the ideological affinity between the two men in developing a common approach: "I don't remember him [Mayor Kelly] making a statement with respect to the school system. He didn't have to. He put his board of education—he put his appointees in there. McCahey was President, and McCahey was very close to Kelly. McCahey is a pretty sharp operator, he didn't have to be told every day what to do or how to do it."[71]

Secondly, Kelly occasionally dropped his above-the-battle stance and publicly supported the school board's economy program. In August 1933 Kelly adopted a tone as dismissive of the protests as the board's own when he commented, "A constructive program of economy has been inaugurated in the schools and a microscopical examination of the criticisms of that program, some of them honest, does not bring to light one constructive suggestion for its improvement."[72] The McCahey-led school board had good grounds for believing the mayor solidly behind it, although Kelly's usual public utterances stressed that he had no influence over the board; a few days after the cutbacks were announced, for example, Kelly told reporters to ask all their questions of the school board. The board members had "been appointed to serve the best interests of the school children and the people of Chicago," Kelly said. "It is their job and their responsibility."[73]

This raises the question of why the machine wished to see funds for the Chicago public schools sharply reduced. Other government agencies were not cut back as severely; the Citizens Schools Committee* claimed that during the year of the economy program, the county government illegally kept a sum of money that was larger than the amount saved under the board's economy drive.[74] One study concluded that there was a "widespread willingness on the part of municipal and business leaders to sacrifice education before any other municipal services to the demands of retrenchment. Other municipal, even other School Board employees, never received pay cuts as large as the teachers', nor were they paid irregularly. Reductions in the Board of Education budget were always made first in the instructional fund and it took until 1947 for the teachers to be restored to pay levels equal to 1929."[75] At the same time that the school board ordered the firing of the 1,400 teachers, approximately 700 new patronage employees were hired by the city.[76] These facts led the Citizens Schools Committee to insist that the schools were being singled out; after the Sargent Committee reported that it was likely that only 75 percent of the taxes for 1930, 1931, 1932, and 1933 would ever be collected, the Citizens Schools Committee charged that it was the large taxpayers who would avoid paying. The committee went on:

*This committee, formed by representatives of more than 40 civic associations, was known as the Citizens Save Our Schools Committee until July 1934, when it changed its name to the Citizens Schools Committee. It was made up of roughly the same organizations that had participated in the Joint Committee on School Affairs that had been active during the 1920s, and it also contained many teachers.

> Why does the Sargent Committee single out the schools about which to trumpet huge deficits? According to [the Sargent Committee's] figures . . . the Board of Education deficit depends on taxes being collected only 75% instead of 90% as estimated. If this deficit materializes EVERY SINGLE COOK COUNTY GOVERNMENT FACES A HUGE DEFICIT. Why has not the Sargent Committee trumpeted the deficit of the sanitary district, or even of the city corporate fund, as well as of the schools?[77]

Harold F. Gosnell, a University of Chicago political scientist, described the machine-supported slashing of the school budget as a "mistake" in the machine's own terms. "It is an axiom of wise boss rule in the United States," he maintained, "that it is good politics to provide an efficient educational system."[78] In Gosnell's perspective, machine politicians gained from the image of providing good social services, at least to the favored sectors of the population. Under Mayor Kelly, however, the machine organization displayed a near-complete indifference to the quality of the city's educational system.

The machine's willingness to cut the school budget stemmed in part from the confidence of political leaders that the school board could be counted on to make cuts in such a way as to protect patronage wherever possible. The board dismissed 1,400 teachers, but the teachers were employees who had long demonstrated a degree of political independence that had antagonized both board members and politicians. The school board did not reduce the number of janitors, who, appointed by ward committeemen, swelled the patronage rolls of the party machine. Because the janitors served a political purpose, the Chicago school district employed proportionally more maintenance workers than did other districts. A survey team led by a Teachers College expert, George Strayer, concluded in an exhaustive study of the administration of the Chicago school system, conducted at the request of the previous board, that Chicago had at least 502 more janitors than were needed.[79] The janitors' connections with the machine gave them such influence that in Chicago many janitors received higher salaries than the school principals.

Due to the use of the schools for patronage purposes, the operating and maintenance costs of the Chicago school system were far higher than in other large cities. The Strayer survey team reported, for example, that Chicago spent 5 percent of its annual budget on maintenance while New York spent less than 3 percent.[80] The overall cost of administration in Chicago was $5.02 per pupil compared to $3.29 in New York.[81] In the area of instruction, however, Chicago spent proportionally less than did any other large city used for comparison.[82] The survey team also noted that when the school board moved to economize, it protected (in fact, substantially increased) the budget for maintenance, even while cutting back on other services.[83] Similarly, the Citizens Save Our Schools Committee in 1934 reported the results of a survey by the National Education Association of school expenditures in 65 cities over 100,000 in population. Based on the 1934 school budget, the figures showed:

	Percentage of total expenditures	
Area of expenditure	Chicago	65 other large cities
Instruction	67.3	77.5
Operation of plant	13.9	8.7
Maintenance of plant	8.0	3.8
Fixed charges	5.5	3.8

The committee acknowledged that Chicago's fixed charges in 1934 were abnormally high because of costs arising from the tax assessment situation, but nevertheless called the overall comparison "startling."[84]

The school board cut more from instructional services than from business services, in spite of the evidence of experts that the waste in the system was concentrated in the business sector of the school system. In a careful analysis, the Citizens Schools Committee concluded that under the "economy" program, the "heavy cuts were made in the schools themselves." Teachers' payrolls dropped 12 percent and instructional expenditures dropped 11 percent, while operations dropped 9 percent and the payroll for school clerks increased 3 percent.[85] The tendency of the Chicago board of education since 1924, the committee wrote, had been to spend larger and larger amounts on "the departments which supply easy political jobs and contracts, at the expense of instruction and adequate working material for teachers and pupils." The committee's general complaint was borne out by an Office of Education study conducted in 1935–1936, which showed Chicago to have the highest per pupil noninstructional costs and the lowest per pupil instructional costs of the ten largest cities in the United States.[86] By concentrating the cuts on instruction, the school board appealed to the sensibilities of economy-minded patronage politicians. The machine's most potent reward in Depression Era Chicago was jobs, and the board was careful not to restrict the supply of patronage positions within the school system. The board also moved certain categories of employees, such as lunchroom supervisors, from the educational to the business sector, thus further safeguarding the supply of patronage positions, Charles Judd charged.[87]

A second reason for the machine's willingness to sharply cut educational expenditures (at least for instructional purposes) was the close tie between the mayor and the business community. In Chicago the business elite had, in the early part of the century, concentrated its energies on narrowing the public education provided for the mass of the city's children and had not displayed enthusiasm for an expensive public school system. The Commercial Club of Chicago had fought for a dual school system with the bulk of working class youth channeled into a vocational curriculum, and business leaders had supported Superintendent McAndrew's money-saving plans for platoon schools (chapters 3 and 5). The Chicago Association of Commerce indicated a general reluctance to see the higher reaches of schooling opened on a mass scale; the association, for example, approvingly quoted President-Emeritus Arthur T. Hadley of Yale to the effect that "there is a point beyond which further taxation cripples the life of the community more than further opportunities for education help it. . . . It is as important to keep down costs as to keep up values. Higher education at the public expense should be regarded as a privilege to be earned and not as a right to be abused."[88]

In the 1930s, as the Depression took hold, Chicago business leaders again moved to the forefront of the drive to curtail public expenditures on education. The Committee on Public Expenditures gathered the city's most powerful bankers, industrialists, and merchants into a "committee of 100" whose goal was to procure retrenchments and then more retrenchments. It is noteworthy that this committee, which proclaimed the need for rooting out waste, in fact accepted the priorities of the school board in cutting the least inefficient and extravagant sector of the school system, the instructional budget. The committee's leading figure, Fred Sargent, was proud to retail the good relationship between the committee and public officials, and he never placed a strain on this relationship by attempting to reduce the inefficiencies associated with widespread political patronage. The Sargent Committee accepted the 1933 budget cuts, largely directed at instruction, and then, in 1934, pressed for what amounted to further cuts in teachers' salaries.[89] The committee opposed a plan to increase state aid to Chicago to restore some of the cuts imposed by the board of education.

Business leaders were aware that their power to dictate directly expenditure levels in the early 1930s stemmed from an unusual combination of circumstances. As the *Commercial Club Yearbook* noted, Commercial Club members had in 1932 initiated the movement that had led to the formation of the Committee on Public Expenditures and the subsequent budget cuts. The *Yearbook* warned, however, "We must bear in mind . . . that at that time money could not be had by the local governments except through private sources, and the Mayor of the city had complete political power to see that his orders were carried out."[90] At the time of the formation of the Committee on Public Expenditures, Fred Sargent had envisioned its continuation into the indefinite future. Such a committee would, he believed, play an invaluable role in reducing public expenditures because politicians were inevitably subject to public pressures that businessmen could successfully resist. "At the forefront of such a movement," he declared, "there must be men who don't care a whoop about threats or pressure; men who want no political advantage."[91] He concluded that "the problem as it extends into the future becomes one of enlisting in the public service unreachable leadership—men of sufficient stature to take charge for the people of the people's affairs." Sargent eventually abandoned this plan of maintaining the committee or a similar body as the city's financial watchdog, however, as Mayor Kelly proved to have both similar views and sufficient political power to carry out a stringent economy program. The Committee on Public Expenditures continued to influence policy for the next four years (the governor, for example, agreed that he would consider tax legislation only with the approval of the Sargent Committee), but the committee ceased to take the dominating public role that it had played in the first year of its existence.[92] In 1937 it dissolved entirely.

The evidence indicates not that Kelly felt compelled to follow the recommendations of the Sargent Committee because of its influence with the banks, but rather that he found the committee useful, while he was consolidating power, as a means of applying intense pressure to recalcitrant officials. Kelly did not have the same need for the Sargent Committee in this respect that Cermak had had, however, because Kelly's appointees controlled the board of education. The social philosophy of Cermak and Kelly was close to that of the city's businessmen, and as long as patronage sources were protected they were prepared to follow business direction in slashing educational funds. Under these circumstances, there was no need for a committee of "unreachable" businessmen; the self-made politicians and middle-level businessmen on the school board could perform the same function with less political cost. The elite members of the business world of Chicago could retire further into the background as the machine consolidated its grip.

The final reason for the machine's willingness to move against the schools was that the labor movement, which had earlier resisted efforts to restrict public education, was unprepared to offer effective resistance to the economy drives of the 1930s. There was no powerful constituency to demand that the school cutbacks be restored, and the machine was thus able to supply less in the way of social welfare benefits than was normally the case. The labor movement in the 1930s was successfully directed into pluralist demands, but, before exploring this transition in detail, it is necessary to consider the role of the one group that did strenuously resist the cutbacks, the city's liberal civic associations.

The Civic Associations
and the Fight against the Cutbacks

Four days after the board announced the budget cuts, representatives of about 40 civic associations met to create a central coordinating committee to organize a campaign against the board. The new committee, known first as the Citizens Save Our Schools Committee and later as simply the Citizens Schools Committee (CSC), included members from the Woman's City Club, the Chicago Woman's Club, the City Club of Chicago, the Chicago Bar Association, the Cook County League of Women Voters, the Conference of Jewish Women's Organizations, the Chicago and Northern District Federation of Colored Women's Clubs, and the Chicago Federation of Settlements.[93] These groups comprised a cross-section of the civic associations that made up the city's reform element, and their members had often worked in loose coalitions in the past.

The organized teachers had become somewhat estranged from the civic associations during McAndrew's superintendency because such groups as the Woman's City Club supported McAndrew's programs for platoon schools, the "Citizens' Sampling Day," and other efficiency measures.[94] The crisis of the budget cuts brought the teachers and the civic associations together again, however, and the teachers' unions supplied a good deal of the initial organizing impetus for the Citizens Schools Committee.[95] The teachers' unions formed their own organization to fight the cutbacks, but they also contributed heavily to the Citizens Schools Committee and joined it in large numbers.[96] In the earliest stages of the CSC's existence, in fact, the teachers made up the great bulk of the committee's membership; in May 1934, the committee's records indicated that teachers comprised 4,545 of the 5,159 members.[97] The teachers' unions were themselves divided. Margaret Haley's elementary school teachers' union was no longer predominant; her political prestige had suffered several damaging blows during the late 1920s and early 1930s.

Haley's support for Thompson's mayoral campaign had alienated many supporters who had admired her political independence, and her standing was further weakened by the failure of the tax reassessment campaign to produce additional revenues for the schools.[98] Further, the Federation of Women High School Teachers, the Chicago Federation of Men Teachers, and the Elementary Teachers Union were affiliated with the Chicago Federation of Labor, which gave them a sustained link with the labor movement that Margaret Haley no longer possessed. The competing teachers' groups cooperated during the initial stages of the protest movement against the cutbacks, but Margaret Haley shortly led her union out of the coalition and began a political odyssey that made her organization increasingly peripheral to the main body of teacher unionism.

The civic associations and the teachers worked together to blanket the city with material denouncing the school board. They distributed nearly two million leaflets in the first four months of the committee's existence.[99] They also organized an extensive public-speaking campaign, and by November 1933, committee members had addressed more than 125 neighborhood mass meetings.[100] The Citizens Save Our Schools Committee called a mammoth rally nine days after the board announced the cutbacks. An estimated 25,000 people jammed into the Chicago Stadium while an overflow crowd on the sidewalk outside listened to loudspeakers in what the *Federation News* described as "the most spectacular public protest meeting ever staged in Chicago."[101] The crowd heard speakers proclaim that 350,000 signatures had been gathered on a petition demanding that the board rescind the retrenchment program. Charles Merriam had tried but failed to get a businessman to address the crowd.[102] Instead, the program's main speakers were John Fitzpatrick, Mrs. Helen Hefferan, the minority member of the board, Rabbi Solomon Goldman, and Charles H. Judd.[103]

Judd's speech captured the main sentiments of Chicago's outraged liberal community. He blasted the "servile, solid majority of the Board of Education," but he reserved his harshest criticism for the politicians who had appointed the board. The board members were "mere puppets" acting on the orders of the mayor and the Sargent Committee. Judd contended that the board did not in actuality face anything like the $10 million deficit that it claimed existed; the shortening of the school year by four weeks had, by his calculations, covered the existing deficit. The board, by trumpeting the $10 million figure, was trying to frighten the city into acceptance of a futile and insincere economy program that did not even touch the main sources of waste in the school system. It also did not provide any long-range means of moving toward a fair and effective taxation system that would guarantee the schools a stable source of revenue.[104]

The committee recognized early in the campaign that the school board would be largely unresponsive to public pressure and settled in for a long-drawn battle. The committee's political program reflected the characteristic ideology of the reform groups that comprised its membership. The Citizens Schools Committee identified "political meddling in educational administration" as the main evil that had to be faced.[105] The committee sharply criticized Chicago business leaders for their role in the school cutbacks[106] but, as with Dean Judd, the main attack was reserved for "spoils politicians" who had made captives of the school board. The politicians were willing to tolerate graft in school construction and employment but refused to spend money on educational services that should, the committee argued, be the fundamental right of each child. The board was practicing false economy by making the politics-inspired cuts that it had announced on July 12 while blinking at the corruption and inefficiency of the administration of the schools.[107] The solution to the problems of the Chicago schools was to remove them from the hands of the politicians, operate them efficiently, and fund them through a reformed tax system.

The Citizens Schools Committee enunciated in stronger form the traditional perspective of the city's civic associations on the need for expert administration removed from political interference. Groups such as the City Club, the preeminent liberal political club in Chicago, consistently argued against moving to an elected school board because its members believed that this would only insure permanent political domination of the schools.[108] The education committee of the club "expressed its alarm at reports indicating that legislation [might] be introduced in the next session of the legislature to fasten upon the city the elective method of selecting the school board."[109] The committee argued, in phrases reminiscent of Ellwood Cubberley's decades before, that "the type of person most to be preferred for service on the Board should be actively engaged in professional or business work and should have wide civic interest."[110] The machine-sponsored candidates did not meet these criteria.

Dean Charles Judd developed this position to its fullest extent. Judd wrote prolifically on education, and he characteristically provided general elaborations of ideas that stemmed from the more conservative brand of progressivism, as he had done earlier with his elaboration of the role of testing in providing differentiated education for children. In his reaction against the depredations of the politically controlled board, he came out for complete control by distant, impartial experts. The very idea of lay control of education struck him as misguided:

> If communities would abolish boards of education, put experts in charge of their schools, and hold these experts accountable for what happens, we should, I feel sure, have better schools and better relations between school officers and municipal authorities than we now have. . . .
>
> Today American education is in need of highly trained, expert leadership. The problems of school administration cannot be solved without the exercise of the highest intelligence and the highest administrative skill.[111]

The intensified reaction by Judd as an individual and by the civic associations as organizations against political control of the schools stemmed not only from anger over the slashing of the school funds but also from a general disillusionment on the part of liberals with the machine administration of Chicago government. As discussed earlier, many of Chicago's most eminent reform leaders had supported Anton Cermak when he first ran for mayor. They believed that whatever the defects of Cermak's style, he would provide a more efficient administration than had Thompson and other previous Chicago mayors. They had not reckoned on the complete centralization of political power in the mayor's office, however, nor on the later divorce of local Democratic politicians from New Deal policies, even while local Democrats supported Roosevelt on the national level. Chicago reformers with New Deal connections tried to induce Roosevelt to disown the Chicago spoils politicians who ran the local party, but Roosevelt took note of Kelly's overwhelming victory over his hapless opponent in the 1935 election and moved toward closer ties with the Chicago machine.[112] Harold Ickes, James Mullenbach, and other Chicago figures who had gone to Washington to help direct the New Deal were completely frustrated in their attempts to get the Roosevelt administration to use its enormous economic leverage to bring about a shift in political control in Chicago.[113]

Merriam and Ickes, although both sophisticated political figures, had not counted on the machine's strength and its ability to centralize patronage and political control. They underestimated the power base of the machine in Chicago's immigrant communities, and they did not at first fully realize that, in the diffuse world of national Democratic party politics, Chicago's machine mayors would play an increasingly influential role. Similarly, although on a far less sophisticated level, Chicago's reformers often suggested prescriptions for the abolition of graft and political manipulation that indicated that they did not fully grasp the social base of the machine's power. Many reformers argued that education in proper citizenship would provide the long-term political remedy for self-seeking behavior such as that exhibited by spoils politicians. The public schools were important because, ideally, they could provide the necessary training in citizenship to produce a public-spirited populace that would resist the blandishments of grafters and ward bosses. Charles Judd, for example, believed that the evident defects in the governmental process could be accounted for by the failure to call upon the most highly trained and talented products of the schools. "Government," he declared, "because of its failure to enlist the promising products of the schools, is often inefficient and sometimes corrupt."[114] And Louise de Koven Bowen, a prominent liberal reformer, had argued earlier that the schools would have to take responsibility for inculcating ideals that would make young people turn a deaf ear to political grafters. She described the case of a settlement worker who tried to interest young high school graduates in reforming corrupt practices in their ward, only to be told that they would stick by the machine in the interests of getting ahead. She concluded, "If these young men had been taught in the schools something about the duties and responsibilities of citizenship, it is possible corrupt politicians would not have found it so easy to secure a following."[115]

The teachers and the Citizens Schools Committee struggled against the mayor and his appointees on the school board for the next 13 years before victory, brought by outside forces, was finally won. Even though the mayor was the frequent target of their criticism, they apparently entertained hopes that Kelly would ultimately alter his school policies. One such instance of false hope occurred in 1939. During the 1939 mayoral campaign, Kelly, evidently fearing that the school situation could be politically damaging, announced the creation of a new and distinguished committee to advise him on school board nominations. The Citizens Schools Committee and the teachers' union immediately moderated their criticisms of the mayor and the teachers declined to support his opponent. After the election, however, Kelly ignored the committee, and after several members resigned in protest it lapsed without having accomplished anything.[116] Even after six years of battling with the mayor, the reform groups had been willing to believe in his good intentions and felt disillusioned by his altered behavior after the election.

The members of the Citizens Schools Committee displayed remarkable persistence in their organizing against the school board's economy program. They won some victories as the board later quietly rescinded some of its much heralded cutbacks. Principals were returned to supervising only one school instead of two, and the school year was lengthened to 40 weeks in 1940, but the overall school situation continued to be grim from the CSC's point of view.[117] The CSC worked to extend its base and establish a more permanent organizational structure by creating ward councils across the city. The councils were designed to create a grass-roots political base through efforts to elect favorable ward committeemen, aldermen, and members of the legislature, and through the general dissemination of information in the schools.[118] By 1938, there were 15 actively functioning ward councils. The CSC annually arranged several hundred speaking engagements through its speakers bureau, and its research department, directed by Dr. Nelson B. Henry of the University of Chicago, prepared reams of reports and statistics on the schools.[119]

In the course of their prolonged campaign against the board, the civic associations succeeded in mobilizing thousands of Chicago residents to take some form of action, whether attending a meeting or rally or engaging in ward organizing. They failed, however, to make any real impact on the board or on the mayor. As Paul Douglas expressed it, the political leaders evidently did "not fear the righteous anger of the fathers and mothers of the children who are deprived of opportunities which all should have, as much as they do the pressures of large business and financial interests."[120] One reason for the relative failure of the campaign was the lack of sustained and wholehearted support from the labor movement, which had previously played an active role in demanding increased educational services.

The Labor Movement:
The Transition to Pluralist Politics

The Chicago Federation of Labor denounced the school board's economy program in scathing language but did not provide a great deal of organizational support for the Citizens Schools Committee. Further, although the campaign against the school board continued for 13 years, labor's role became increasingly passive over the course of this period. The identification of the Chicago Federation of Labor with educational issues was sufficiently strong that, in the early stages of the economy program, the labor body issued vehement denunciations of the budget cuts and organized protest rallies against the board. The Chicago Federation of Labor had not been enthusiastic about Cermak and had, in fact, endorsed Thompson; therefore, the machine-sponsored economy program was at first subject to strong attack, but the vigor of the attack weakened notably as the CFL developed a close relationship with Edward Kelly.

In 1932, the delegates to the Chicago Federation of Labor overwhelmingly passed a special resolution denouncing the Committee on Public Expenditures for its extralegal role in dictating municipal expenditures. The overt business intervention aroused strong opposition from the unionists. The C F L's resolution read in part:

> Whereas, Certain individuals have formed a so-called "Citizens' Committee" and have set themselves up as a sort of super-government and are attempting to dictate policies to the duly elected and appointed representatives of the people: and. . . .
>
> Whereas, They are the spokesmen of the bankers, publishers of large newspapers, and other financial interests which have long evaded paying their proportionate share of taxes on personal property. . . .

The C F L called on the school board (then under the control of the Thompson appointees) to resist efforts by the Sargent Committee to force cuts in expenditures. So many union members had responded to the announcement that the resolution would be presented that the meeting was packed and there was standing room only as the C F L denounced the bankers. Chicago Federation of Labor president John Fitzpatrick had not hesitated in the call to the meeting to criticize the politicians, too, for bowing to the bankers. He wrote, "The men and women we have elected to public office seem to be in fear and trembling when they hear the voice and commands of these 'interests.'" Fitzpatrick commended the board of education for not giving in to the businessmen's demand for a $33 million cut in the 1932 budget. Even the president of the Building Trades Council, which was to become a major force for conservatism in the C F L, spoke strongly against bankers' control over the elected officials; he declared in favor of the resolution, remarking that, "In place of the elected officials of our cities running the governments of our respective municipal bodies, we are faced today with these bodies being dictated to and run by the bankers of this city."[121]

A year later, Kelly had gained control of the board of education, and on July 12, 1933, the new board announced the slashing reduction of the budget. The labor federation again held the combination of bankers and politicians responsible. John Fitzpatrick spoke at the 25,000-person rally held at the Chicago Stadium nine days after the cuts were announced, and he explicitly named Mayor Kelly as one of the four chief school "wreckers." Fitzpatrick told the rally:

> The Chicago Federation of Labor proposes to publicly name those whom it deems responsible for this crime against our Public Schools.
> First, we will name Melvin A. Traylor, banker.
> Second, Public Enemy No. 1, Chairman Sargent of the "Citizens' Committee."
> Third, Sewell L. Avery of Montgomery Ward and Company.
> And last, we intend to hold Mayor Edward J. Kelly responsible until such time as this action is rescinded by the Board of Education.[122]

At this point, the organized labor movement was solidly behind the anticutback campaign, at least in terms of propagandizing against them among its membership. There were, however, potential cracks in the coalition opposing the cutbacks. An article in the CFL's newspaper revealed a possible source of strain between the labor body and the Citizens Schools Committee and other antimachine reform groups. The Citizens Schools Committee had argued that the school board was catering to the patronage politicians in not dismissing unneeded janitors and eliminating waste in the maintenance departments of the schools. This argument was not acceptable to the Chicago Federation of Labor, because it led to direct attacks on one segment of its membership, the janitors. The *Federation News* scornfully described Superintendent William J. Bogan's surprise appearance at the rally to recommend a much milder alternative to the school board's cutback scheme. Bogan had opposed the board's economy program, but the board did not bother to consult him, and the board members excluded him from their actual policymaking sessions (during the public meeting where the board quickly ratified the cutbacks, Bogan sat silently with his head in his hands).[123] At the July 21 rally, Bogan, in his own words, "forced himself upon the program" to propose a series of measures designed to reduce costs without harming instruction. He recommended in particular a reduction in the amount of money paid to the janitors. The *Federation News* denounced Bogan for making this suggestion. The newspaper described him as a "self-confessed program crasher" and said that, contrary to reports in the *Chicago Tribune,* Bogan was not well received by the audience but was roundly booed for his proposals. Specifically, the labor federation's article criticized Bogan for venturing outside his jurisdiction into the business department of the schools (which, under the Otis Law, was controlled by a separate administrator) and for suggesting "further sacrifices" for the janitors who had already, according to the *Federation News,* donated their services on many occasions to the schools during the crisis.[124]

Although seemingly a small matter, the dispute about the proper role and compensation of the janitors was indicative of more serious differences between the labor federation and the Citizens Schools Committee and other civic associations. The janitors were unionized and were members of the Chicago Federation of Labor; their union became increasingly prominent during the next two decades as the janitors became staunch supporters of the machine. The janitors' union was highly useful to the machine because the janitors, based in the large buildings of the city, could and did readily distribute campaign materials as elections neared.[125] On election day itself, the school custodians were never to be found in the schools; they were pounding the pavements in search of voters, as befitted loyal patronage employees. In the past, the city's civic associations and labor organizations had often cooperated in pressing for joint educational programs, but the coalition between the reformers and the unionists was inherently unstable because they shared a common outlook only to a limited extent. In Chicago, the alliance was capable of being broken, or at least disrupted, by issues involving either union prerogatives or conflicting views of efficiency.

The Legitimation of the Democratic Party as the Party of Labor

In 1933, the Chicago Federation of Labor called upon the local Democratic party to follow the policies set forth by

Franklin Roosevelt. The July 21 mass rally had demonstrated, the CFL said, that the local party would have to respond to people's needs: "The meeting emphasized the fact that public patience was near the breaking point and would not much longer submit to bankster domination or political gangster tactics and unless the New Deal would govern the actions of the democratic party organization in the state, to the same extent it manifested itself nationally, Illinois in general and Chicago in particular, was due for an effective political house cleaning."[126] The demand that the local party work for broad social programs became increasingly muted as the decade progressed, however, and the CFL worked out a *modus vivendi* with the machine. The development of a *modus vivendi* was made easier because, although the local party did not deviate from its tax-cutting economy measures, it increasingly sought close ties with the national New Deal and harnessed its political fortunes to Roosevelt's. Roosevelt was useful to the machine because the national New Deal provided a populist gloss to the Democratic party and helped the machine maintain its base among the poor, the unemployed, and the working class.[127] In turn, the machine helped deliver solidly Democratic majorities for national candidates; Roosevelt could not have failed to be impressed at Kelly's roughly 800,000 to 167,000 vote victory in the 1935 mayoral election, and although the machine did not roll up quite such overwhelming victories for national candidates, it guaranteed them tidy margins.

As late as 1928, Fitzpatrick had declared that he still favored the creation of a labor party, although he held no hope for the realization of this goal in the foreseeable future (see chapter 5). By the mid-1930s, however, the Roosevelt charisma was such that the Democratic party had gained greatly in legitimacy as the party of the dispossessed. Edward Nockels, secretary of the CFL, had been a labor party supporter along with Fitzpatrick, but in 1936 he wrote, in response to an inquiry from the *New Republic,* that labor would unquestionably bestow its support upon Roosevelt. He said that if there were a Farmer Labor party in the field, "it is my opinion that the support it would receive from the Organized Labor movement would be negligible." And, he continued, "I am of the opinion that if there ever was a time when Organized Labor was fully justified in giving whole-hearted support to one man, that time is now, and that man is President Roosevelt, who in my belief has given greater consideration to the interests of Organized Labor, the working man and the rank and file of our people than any other President in our history."[128]

Perhaps even more indicative of the strong swing toward Roosevelt was Lillian Herstein's transformation from an opponent of FDR into a campaign organizer for him. Herstein, a member of the teachers' union, sat on the CFL's executive board for 25 years and was noted for being on the left wing of the labor organization. In 1932, she ran for Congress on the Farmer-Labor ticket and received the endorsements of John Fitzpatrick and Victor Olander.[129] Paul Douglas, her campaign manager, had persuaded her to run by emphasizing that "the Republican and Democratic Parties were two wings of the same bird of prey."[130] Herstein did not support Roosevelt in the 1932 election because she did not see any prospect that he would introduce fundamental changes in the economic system. By 1936, however, she was the director of the speakers bureau of Labor's Non-Partisan League for Roosevelt because, as she explained, "when Roosevelt went in, he introduced a great deal of his welfare program, and all the third party people were converted to Roosevelt, even Paul Douglas."[131] When Roosevelt campaigned in Chicago in 1936, John Fitzpatrick headed a mammoth parade for him that had been organized in part by Herstein and Labor's Non-Partisan League.

The national Democratic party and the local Chicago machine reinforced each other's power. The national party provided an ideological gloss to the tax-paring, business-supported local party, and the machine provided a superbly efficient vote-getting mechanism for the national party. The alliance shut the civic reformers out of power—even those with influence in the national councils of the New Deal—and led the CFL to a close partisan identification with the Democrats and a complete abandonment of its leaders' one-time goal of an independent party.

The CFL unhesitatingly endorsed Kelly in the 1935 mayoral election in spite of his often conservative municipal policies. In response to a plea from Kelly's campaign manager for an "independent non-partisan endorsement" of Kelly from the CFL, Nockels wrote a letter describing Kelly as the "People's Friend."[132] The letter soliciting the endorsement had included a list of accomplishments of the Kelly administration which could be referred to in the requested letter of endorsement; none of the accomplishments was of a sort that would be expected to appeal to organized labor. They included the boasts that the "public schools of Chicago have been saved from bankruptcy, and the morale of its teachers, pupils and employees restored," "the budget has been balanced," and "economies have been effected in every department of the city administration, thereby increasing efficiency and service."[133] Nockels did not refer to any of these achievements in his letter of endorsement, instead declaring weakly that Kelly's actions in keeping telephone costs down were sufficient to warrant his endorsement. Kelly replied that he had read the heartening endorsement "with mingled sentiments of gratitude and humility."[134]

In the first months of the Kelly administration, the CFL had unanimously passed a resolution calling upon the mayor to appoint at least five representatives of organized labor to the school board.[135] This would be only just, the resolution stated, as the children of working people made up the vast bulk of the school population. The fact that, in the past, there was usually only one representative of organized labor on the board indicated the extent to which the union parents had been deprived of a voice in the schools. Kelly replied with dismissive courtesy and promptly appointed a board composed primarily of self-made businessmen and political cronies.[136] He did, however, appoint one union member, Charles Fry, who voted consistently with the budget-cutting majority. The CFL had a long history of interest in the public schools, and its education committee contained members with a solid knowledge of educational issues, but Fry had never distinguished himself by any particular concern for the schools or their management. He was remembered by one Citizens Schools Committee activist primarily for his statement at a board meeting that he didn't see why people made such a fuss about education; he had never had any education and he got along all right.[137]

The Citizens Schools Committee considered Fry one of the most obdurate of the board members; in 1934 Fry was the only board member to vote against returning a principal to each school instead of having them each supervise two schools. The CSC's publication remarked that Fry, who "professes to represent labor on the Board," actually took actions that were "entirely out of sympathy with the firm and fearless stand of the Chicago Federation of Labor."[138] The CFL, however, proved reluctant to censure him for his actions on the board. At a federation meeting in the summer of 1933, a motion was presented that Fry be called before the CFL executive board "to give an account of his stewardship."[139] After prolonged and heated debate, the motion was tabled.

Kelly had followed the usual machine practice of making appointments on the basis of ethnic identity and organizational affiliation. In the case of school issues, this was particularly significant, as the city's strong Catholic constituency (many of whom were working-class supporters of the Irish Catholic mayor) did not always have great sympathy for the public schools, particularly in the hard economic times of the 1930s; the Church's diocesan newspaper had endorsed the school board's economy program.[140] Through careful attention to reflecting the ethnic/religious/organizational composition of the city, party leaders were aided in maintaining policy-making control by being able to count on reflexive group pride to divert attention from substantive issues. This worked in the case of the CFL and its refusal to censure Fry in spite of the fact that the labor body took a position diametrically opposed to his. The tabling of the motion to "strongly condemn the actions of Charles Fry" and announce to the public that in no way did he represent either organized labor or the CFL on the board of education indicated also the CFL's growing political acquiescence compared to its militance on school issues in earlier decades.

Division in the Labor Movement: The Rise of the CIO

Even as forces external to the labor movement were moving the Chicago Federation of Labor into an accommodation with the increasingly powerful machine leaders, the CFL moved in a still more conservative direction in response to the challenge of the CIO. The CFL stood out among AFL-affiliated central labor bodies for its early commitment to organizing the unskilled. Fitzpatrick had made sustained and strenuous efforts to organize the workers in meatpacking and steel, efforts which collapsed due to the lack of national response. The CFL could have been expected to support the massive drive that got underway in the 1930s to organize the mass-production industries, but, after some initial positive contributions, the CFL became bitterly hostile to the CIO. The organizational split between the two union bodies had deep consequences for the shape and nature of the labor movement in Chicago and helped at least to hasten the increasing conservatism of the AFL-affiliated unions in the city.

Fitzpatrick had had good relations with the Amalgamated Clothing Workers and the International Ladies' Garment Workers Union, which had come to play increasingly important roles on the left wing of the city's labor movement, but the American Federation of Labor forced him to disaffiliate them and all other constituent unions of the CIO from the Chicago Federation of Labor. William Green, president of the AFL, sent Fitzpatrick a letter on May 28, 1937, ordering him to disaffiliate all unions that belonged to the "dual, rival" CIO.[141] Fitzpatrick reluctantly complied, severing relations with the 27 local CIO unions on June 7, 1937. He wrote to the unions involved in a tone very different from that which William Green had adopted toward the upstart organizations, concluding his letter with the regretful words, "We are exceedingly sorry that this action has become necessary, especially in view of the long years of friendship and cooperation in which we worked together, and we sincerely hope that this separation will be of short duration."[142]

The severance of the CIO unions left the CFL with a narrower membership base. As Joseph Keenan, secretary of the CFL from 1937 to 1950 put it, the departure of the CIO "just left the old staid unions like the Teamsters and the building trades and the metal trades" while the more dynamic unions committed themselves to industrial organizing as constituent elements of the CIO.[143] Not only were the unions remaining in the CFL more conservative than those outside it, but the CFL's leadership became increasingly rigid as it perceived a challenge from the CIO. Fitzpatrick's words of regret for severing ties with the CIO union were soon forgotten in bitter jurisdictional disputes with the CIO. The logic of competition between rival organizations superseded the bonds of cooperation that had made the CFL unusually responsive to industrial organizing.

The depth of the bitterness between the CIO and the Chicago Federation of Labor became evident in the events surrounding the CIO's attempts to organize the American Newspaper Guild in the city's pressrooms. The CFL had helped the Newspaper Guild organize in the period before the split in the union movement, but after the CIO broke away the AFL tried to organize its own rival craft unions in the newspaper companies.[144] When the CIO-sponsored Newspaper Guild called a strike in December 1938, the Chicago Federation of Labor opposed the strike and instructed its affiliates to cross the CIO picket lines. The strike dragged on for more than a year as the two union federations battled each other. Fitzpatrick's hostility to the CIO became so great during the course of the Guild walkout that he threw the full resources of the CFL into the attempt to break the strike. He used his connections in the union movement to secure the union label for the struck Hearst papers, the *Chicago American* and the *Herald and Examiner*.[145] He then sent a telegram proclaiming his victory in obtaining use of the label to William Green, AFL president: "The Allied Printing Trades Union Label appeared on the front pages of the *Herald and Examiner* and *Chicago American* today. The use of the union label will be of tremendous value in protecting the interests of our unions against the CIO and Communists. We deeply appreciate the service you rendered in securing the use of the label."[146]

The telegram, with its lumping of the CIO and Communists together as examples of the evils to be fought, indicates how far Fitzpatrick had gone in accepting the conservative national AFL ideology. Fitzpatrick went even further in his grim efforts to break the strike, however. In Fitzpatrick's papers, there is a handwritten draft of a telegram from him to William Randolph

Hearst calling for Hearst to use an injunction to defeat the strike. The draft of the telegram, signed by Fitzpatrick, reads, "In protecting our interests in the so-called Newspaper Guild strike we feel that the Injunction in this situation should be enforced to maintain Law and Order."[147]

In spite of its early efforts to organize the mass-production workers, the Chicago Federation of Labor either ignored or hampered the CIO's organizing drives during the 1930s. In the meatpacking industry, for example, the CIO made enormous strides in welding an extremely heterogeneous work force into an industrial union, but the CFL supported its own much weaker affiliate, the Amalgamated Meat Cutters. When AFL workers once tried to take over an area in the stockyards known as "CIO corner," where the CIO held its rallies, thousands of angry CIO supporters drove them from the area. That, declared a leading CIO activist, "was the last we saw of anybody from the Chicago Federation of Labor."[148] Ironically, this was the same industry where the CFL had initiated a national organizing drive after World War I.

There were some exceptions to the general pattern of hostility between the two federations. Fitzpatrick and Nockels had been instrumental in the organizing successes of the Amalgamated Clothing Workers and the ILGWU, and even after these two unions left the AFL, they retained an identification with them. Fitzpatrick's secretary has recalled how, when AFL central labor councils in other cities would write to the CFL asking if the ACWA label was a legitimate union label, a subtle reply would be sent saying that the clothing workers were good trade unionists without mentioning that they split from the AFL.[149] In general, however, the CFL began to exhibit intense hostility to the CIO and to extend the hostility to manifestations of left-wing activity that appeared to accompany CIO organizing. Probably the most extreme example of this hostility was the CFL reaction to the 1937 Memorial Day Massacre at the Republic Steel plant. Police had opened fire on a crowd of strikers who were demanding the right to engage in mass picketing; 10 strikers were killed and 87 wounded. The CFL declared itself uninterested because the strikers belonged to the CIO.[150]

Political Consequences of the AFL-CIO Split

By the mid-1930s, when the CIO emerged as a rival organization, the CFL had already moved toward an interest-group posture within the city's political context. The jurisdictional battles with the CIO, however, led to an ideological conflict that greatly hardened the CFL's growing conservatism. When the CFL abandoned its independent political stance in the mid-1920s, it began a process of identification with the national AFL that was hard to stop halfway. In the polarized union world of the 1930s, labor representatives had to be either AFL or CIO, and once the choice was made, the force of events created an ever widening gulf between the two.

What led the CFL, which had struggled for industrial unionism, to a position of complete identification with the national AFL? The answer is probably to be sought in the fact that the CFL represented a craft union base. The CFL's strength, as Newell has pointed out, rested on the triumvirate of the teamsters, the building service workers, and the building trades.[151] In a metropolitan setting, these unions had the bargaining power to win membership benefits and to aid other nascent organizing efforts. The teamsters controlled deliveries into the city and into specific work places; the building services workers could paralyze the city's daily life; and the building trades workers could halt construction in the city. Unions have historically found it easier to organize firms with a local market than those with a national reach, because the local firms are more vulnerable to strike pressure that will raise their costs relative to those of their competitors. The CFL, once these unions had been organized, was able to extend itself into a vast number of other trades and occupations. Its membership base was diverse and spread out across the city.

The CIO's membership was concentrated in the clothing, steel and meatpacking industries, three of the largest industries in the Chicago area. Even after its great organizing drive of the 1930s, the CIO had far fewer members in metropolitan Chicago than did the CFL. It is estimated that at the close of the 1930s the AFL unions had approximately 333,000 members to the CIO's roughly 60,000.[152]

The AFL unions remained far more politically influential in Chicago than were the CIO unions, not only because they had far more members but also because the bulk of the CFL's membership resided in the city proper while the CIO organized the outlying industrial areas. This gave the CFL added political clout in dealing with officials who were elected on a city-wide basis.

One reflection of the AFL's greater political strength in the city was the decision of the teachers' union to remain in the CFL rather than leave it to join the CIO. In 1937, the city's teachers' unions finally merged into one united organization, which succeeded in organizing nearly all of Chicago's public school teachers by 1939.[153] The national American Federation of Teachers (AFT) wavered on whether to stay in the AFL or affiliate with the CIO. At the 1937 national convention of the AFT, Lillian Herstein, long active on the left wing of Chicago's labor movement, urged that the AFT remain in the American Federation of Labor. She did not want the teachers' union to join the CIO, she said later, because "we had the unqualified support of the Illinois State Federation of Labor and the Chicago Federation of Labor" while the CIO was relatively weak locally. As she later recounted a conversation she had had with another member of the AFT committee that was considering the question of affiliation, "I said, 'You might as well look at the facts. The help that a teachers' union gets is not from the national American Federation of Labor but from the local one, because education is a local matter in America, and in many cities where you have a strong teachers' union, like Chicago and St. Paul, you don't even have a CIO council.' Even Sidney Hillman, who was one of the strong men on the CIO saw that, and he hoped that we, in a way, wouldn't [switch to the CIO]. We had no CIO council in Chicago. Who would you go to for help?"[154] She pointed out that Sidney Hillman, one of the founding figures of the CIO, recognized that the teachers were dependent on city central labor bodies for support, and that the AFL was far more powerful in such cities as Chicago. As a pragmatic matter, the teachers would gain from continued affiliation with the AFL.

It is worth noting in passing, however, that although Herstein was one of the prime advocates of continued AFL affiliation at the 1937 AFT convention, she began having increasing doubts as the AFL (and CFL) continued on a conservative course. After John Fitzpatrick refused to credential a teachers' union delegate because of his active support of the CIO-sponsored American Newspaper Guild strike, Herstein wrote to George Counts, a nationally known educator, that she was deeply disheartened. She told Counts that the matter had discouraged her very much not only because of the injustice to the individual involved, but also "because the action is indicative of a trend within the American Federation of Labor which militates against any genuine freedom of discussion and against the use of the most elemental democratic procedures. I am hoping against hope that it is a passing trend; if it is not, I would be very doubtful of the value of our affiliation."[155]

Whatever the disillusionment of some labor activists, however, the Chicago Federation of Labor retained the upper hand politically and organizationally in spite of the emergence of the CIO. The CIO unions, recognizing their relatively weak position in the Chicago metropolitan area, adapted themselves to the political realities and worked out a means of relating to the Democratic party that was essentially based on the CFL model. The CIO unions might have been expected to pursue broad welfare-state goals rather than narrower interest-group benefits, given their heterogeneous industrial base, but they early abandoned this approach in Chicago. One reason for this was that the somewhat more conservative unions in the CIO became dominant in Chicago; the steelworkers' union, which has been noted for its hierarchical, centralized pattern of control, achieved more influence in the state and city CIO than did such unions as the Amalgamated Clothing Workers or the United Electrical, Radio and Machine Workers.[156] The district director of the steelworkers, Joseph Germano, was strongly oriented toward cooperation with the city's political leaders.

In spite of some diversity among the CIO unions, however, as a group they pursued the same general political path as the CFL. They organized their members and others in support of the machine in exchange for such benefits as municipal appointments for union officials and guarantees that the police would not intervene to break strikes in the way that they had in the early 1930s. The unions recognized the importance of support from city hall, and on certain occasions they got it. Mayor Kelly, for instance, was concerned that the police actions in the Memorial Day Massacre would damage his reelection chances. The CIO unions pressured him to guarantee that the police would be better controlled in the future. Herbert March, a lawyer and former district director of the United Packinghouse Workers Union, described the union's interaction with the mayor following the shooting of the strikers:

> Mayor Kelly came out of that with none too savoury a reputation as far as the working people, the industrial workers of Chicago, were concerned. They felt that Mayor Kelly was responsible. It was his police who were out there and committed this brutal massacre, and Kelly that time is beginning to realize the impact and how deep and intense was this sentiment against him as the result of the Little Steel Massacre. He was concerned that he had to do something about this. And so when we struck the Livestock Handlers, word came to us that Kelly was interested in seeing what could be done to help resolve this situation peaceably. We said, "Well, good, if that's what you want, we appreciate your help, but in the meanwhile don't interfere with our right to picket and to carry on a lawful strike. Let's see whether you can have better behavior by the police than occurred in South Chicago."[157]

Kelly intervened directly in the Livestock Handlers' strike; when the owners declared that they would not sign a contract under any circumstances, Kelly replied that they received their water from the city of Chicago at a very favorable price, and that if they weren't more responsive, they might find that it would be cut off.[158] Kelly also acted to curb the police, and restrained police behavior in Chicago labor conflicts has often been cited since as an element of the political accommodation between organized labor and the machine.[159]

The CIO unions found that they could expect to receive some of the plums that the machine had to offer in the way of appointments to local offices. The Packinghouse Workers supported Kelly in the 1938 Democratic primary, working for him across the industrial areas of the city and guaranteeing to carry four wards for him, two in black neighborhoods and two in white. As March expressed it: "Politics, I guess, was very practical. We told them [the workers] what Kelly's role had been in the Livestock Handlers' Strike . . . and why politically this is important to see to it we have some friends in the city hall." After the four wards turned out for Kelly, the mayor approached the union officials and asked them to recommend a labor lawyer they would like to see as a judge.[160] A member of the United Electrical and Machine Workers described a similar offer from Kelly to CIO officials.[161]

The CIO unions largely joined the Chicago Federation of Labor in orienting to the machine, due to what Greenstone describes as the "particularly forbidding local political culture" of the city that inhibited expressions of welfare-state politics.[162] This orientation made the city's labor movement in general far less willing to press demands on social issues outside the immediate purview of the labor movement. The CFL had played an activist role in regard to the schools in the early decades of the 1900s, but when faced with the drastic educational cutbacks of the 1930s it responded in a largely *pro forma* manner. On April 3, 1939, John Fitzpatrick sent a telegram to an associate in New York that could serve as an epitaph for the era in which he had led the CFL on an independent political course. As Fitzpatrick summed up his political odyssey, "I was a member of the Labors Nonpartisan League to Reelect Roosevelt and we had such great success that the CIO and Communists proceeded to capture the organization which they did. I withdrew at that time and have had no part in it since. I am now a steadfast adherent to the nonpartisan program of the American Federation of Labor."[163]

The Recurrent Battle:
Vocational vs. Academic Education

Although the Chicago Federation of Labor did little to support the work of the Citizens Schools Committee during the crisis years of the 1930s, the labor body responded strongly on one occasion when it felt that its fundamental interests were threatened. Chicago's major newspapers reported that the superintendent of schools, William H. Johnson, was planning to introduce a drastic new vocational education program.[164] The old alliance of liberal professionals and labor officials that had fought the Cooley Bill was resurrected. The brief conflict over the 1937 vocational education plan is worth reviewing for what it reveals of the stability of some business, labor, and professional attitudes toward education in spite of the changed political context of the city.

William H. Johnson had been chosen as the new superintendent by the McCahey-controlled board on April 22, 1936, in spite of protests by the civic associations that the action was "precipitous."[165] The secretary of the Chicago Federation of Labor had also tried to work behind the scene to forestall his appointment.[166] The previous superintendent, William Bogan, had not taken a very active stand against the economy-oriented board, but it was obvious that he was deeply dismayed by its unwillingness to fund public education adequately.[167] Johnson displayed no such scruples. He developed a reputation for extreme subservience to the board of education in policy matters and administered the schools in such a manner as to bring accusations that he promoted teachers and principals on the basis of personal favoritism.[168] Teachers or principals who criticized him were likely to find themselves quickly demoted, and he operated an efficient spy system in the schools to report on signs of disloyalty. The Citizens Schools Committee was bitterly antagonistic to Johnson and felt that during his long tenure as superintendent the ideal of a professional, expert administrator receded so far from reality as to become a mockery.

In Johnson's first year in office, he announced a new three-point program for the elementary schools. This program called for increased emphasis on reading and on standardized tests of reading achievement, a focus on student socialization through the development of student councils and service clubs, and the initiation of cumulative records on students with information on test scores and personality characteristics.[169] At the high school level, Johnson called for increased attention to character education, which "consisted of a battery of attitude tests and trait questionnaires as well as emulative studies of great men and student-led panel discussions on character development."[170] The curriculum was narrowed to concentrate on basic subjects, which brought a charge from the Citizens Schools Committee that the underlying purpose was to save money. The committee's publication reported that "some high school principals have admitted that economy is the reason for the 'enriched' curriculum. It is possible to handle a given number of children with fewer teachers if less subjects are taught and the children are herded into large study halls several hours out of each day."[171]

In November 1937 Johnson went a step further by outlining a plan whereby 80 percent of the students would take vocational courses and only 20 percent would take courses in general academic subjects. Johnson's tentative proposal was endorsed by both board president McCahey and by Mayor Kelly.[172] Johnson had earlier given strong indications of his educational leanings when he had declared in his 1936–37 school report that "there is a tremendous swing toward the revamping of our educational structure to the end that vocational and trade objectives shall take the place largely of the traditional cultural objectives . . . it is an endeavor to cater to needs on the part of our children. It is estimated that ninety per cent of our boys and girls are faced with an economic condition which demands that they be taught skills which will fit them for some definite occupation."[173] The newspapers reported that one feature of Johnson's vocational education plan was that in the future only vocational and not academic teachers would be hired as vacancies opened up in the teaching rolls.

Both the Citizens Schools Committee and the Chicago Federation of Labor responded with instant hostility to this plan. In contrast to the earlier battle against the Cooley Bill, however, in 1937 all of the contending groups oriented their protests to the mayor's office. The secretary of the Chicago Federation of Labor, Joseph D. Keenan, reported in a letter to William Green, president of the AFL, that the CFL had made immediate representations to the mayor:

> When the newspapers came out with stories of the danger in the proposed vocational education program, etc., the Chicago Federation of Labor immediately made protest to the Mayor of Chicago and the Mayor contacted President John Fitzpatrick and asked him to appoint a committee to meet with Mr. McCahey, the President of our Board of Education, Mr. Johnson, the Superintendent of Schools, Mr. Frank Righeimer, Attorney for the School Board and Mayor Kelly in the office of the Mayor.[174]

Under the combined assault of the Chicago Federation of Labor and the Citizens Schools Committee, Johnson quickly backtracked and denied that he had ever intended an 80-20 separation of Labor responded with instant hostility to this plan. In contrast to the earlier battle against the Cooley Bill, however, in mutually agreeable vocational education program, but the discussions broke down due to the fundamentally conflicting views of the participants and their strong mutual antipathy.[175] The labor and teacher representatives objected that Johnson was entirely oriented to the needs of businessmen, a charge he implicitly acknowledged in a much later interview when he declared that, in practice, businessmen were the only people equipped to determine the type of training required.[176] Other groups might interfere with the schools, but they lacked the knowledge to discuss the educational program.

Johnson ultimately abandoned his vocational education program, as the Commercial Club had been forced to abandon the Cooley Bill. The Citizens Schools Committee and the organized labor movement had united more effectively than they had during their mobilization against the cutbacks.

Outside Pressure Ends
the Machine–Board of Education Alliance

The Citizens Schools Committee continued its attacks on McCahey and Johnson and their narrow, utilitarian view of education throughout the war years, but with the support of the machine the two school officials remained firmly entrenched. The administration of the Chicago schools became an increasing scandal, however, as teachers continued to complain that promotion was based on subservience to Johnson. They and others charged that the superintendent made a personal profit through the sale of textbooks and that he only passed those candidates for a principal's exam who had paid for a class from him on school administration.[177]

In 1943, the teachers and the reform associations turned to outside groups in the hope that effective pressure could be brought to bear upon the city to clean up its school system. The Chicago Division of the Illinois State Teachers Association asked the parent National Education Association to undertake an investigation of the Chicago schools. In response, the NEA abandoned its policy of ignoring Chicago's long-running school crisis, and its Commission for the Defense of Democracy through Education began a thorough study of the Chicago situation.[178] The NEA issued its 70-page report in May 1945; the report detailed the many charges against Superintendent Johnson and denounced the interference of board president McCahey in the administration of the schools. The report recommended that the tripartite administrative system set up under the 1917 Otis Law, with the superintendent, business manager, and attorney having equal power in their own spheres of influence, be ended because the dilution of executive authority resulted in the board president gaining undue control. The NEA followed up its report by expelling Superintendent Johnson from membership in the association for unprofessional conduct.

The mayor, school board, and city council all shrugged off the NEA investigation, with the machine-controlled city council issuing a report in response that praised the Chicago schools.[179] The city council pointed out that the Chicago schools retained their accreditation in spite of the charges leveled against them. This proved a dangerous line of defense, however; as early as 1934, the secretary of the North Central Association of Schools and Colleges had told members of the Citizens Schools Committee that Chicago was in danger of losing its high school accreditation.[180] On March 30, 1946, the North Central Association made good its early threat and warned the Chicago schools that unless major reforms were made within the next year, accreditation would be withdrawn. The threat of disaccreditation of the entire school system of the nation's second largest city brought a massive groundswell of opposition to Kelly, McCahey, Johnson, and all those associated with the 13-year program of budget cutting and political manipulation of the schools.

Kelly's political support began to erode as the newspapers carried huge headlines about the threat to the schools. His position had already been weakened because of the election of a factional opponent, Henry Horner, as governor. The decline of New Deal funds also harmed the workings of the patronage machine. The Democratic organization retained enormous power but faced the need for making tactical concessions to maintain itself in light of the outcries over the school crisis. Kelly did not respond to the North Central Association's demand that administrative responsibility be centered in the superintendent, but he did appoint an advisory committee in response to the association's requirement that a politically independent board of education be installed.

The committee, made up of the presidents of Chicago-area universities and named the Heald Committee after its chairman, Henry Heald, the president of the Illinois Institute of Technology, proved far more vigorous than Kelly had evidently expected. He had promised in advance that he would accept its recommendations, and the committee members "needled the mayor into extensions of the sphere that this committee was to cover. He kept being forced to admit that he would accept advice from them."[181] On June 17, 1946, the committee reported that its three chief recommendations were that Johnson should resign as superintendent, the mayor should create a permanent representative commission to make nominations for the school board, and that the old Kelly appointees on the school board should be removed.

The committee report had an immediate impact. Superintendent Johnson resigned on the day the report was made public (he was given a less prestigious but high-paying job in the school system). Several board members resigned but most refused, and Mayor Kelly was reluctant to remove them.[182] Kelly's political problems mounted until they reached the point where it appeared that for him to run again would be damaging for the organization. On December 19, 1946, Kelly announced that he would not run for reelection in the spring of 1947. The Democrats slated a businessman, Martin Kennelly, who had had little direct connection with Chicago politics, as the new mayoral candidate. His above-the-battle image was useful for the besieged Democrats.[183]

James McCahey resigned as board president when Kelly announced that he would not run for reelection, and the Citizens School Committee responded to the dual announcements by saying "Siamese twins to the end!"[184] McCahey's departure, although greatly welcomed by the civic associations and many others weary of Chicago's school scandals, still did not solve the fundamental problem of the relationship of the board president to the superintendent. The North Central Association and the Heald Committee had both demanded that the tripartite administrative system mandated by the Otis Law be ended so that the school board president could not act as unofficial coordinator for the school system. Only in this way, they believed, would it be possible for the Chicago school district to be administered in a professional and nonpolitical manner. The shift to a unitary administrative system required action by the state legislature, however, and, ironically, it was the Chicago Federation of Labor that lobbied against the change and for a time stymied passage of the requisite bill. The CFL ignored the recommendations of the Chicago Teachers Union, which strongly favored passage of the bill, and, at the behest of the school janitors and engineers among its membership, opposed restructuring the school system. To the anger of the teachers, the executive board of the CFL authorized lobbying against the bill without informing the teachers' union delegates. The move demonstrated that the Chicago Teachers Union, although one of the largest locals in the CFL, lacked political clout compared to the building service workers and that the CFL leadership was no longer willing to defer to the teachers on education-related questions. The janitors and engineers had profited from the tripartite system, which gave considerable autonomy to the business division. The Illinois State Federation of Labor wanted to work for the bill to restructure the schools but felt that it could not oppose the wishes of its Chicago affiliate.[185]

The bill appeared to be headed for defeat because of the opposition of the CFL and of many Chicago legislators for whom the janitors served as precinct captains. Victor Olander, secretary-treasurer of the Illinois State Federation of Labor, who had had a lifelong interest in education and had been deeply involved in legislative measures on the schools, eventually arranged a compromise with the cooperation of the mayor. Olander met with representatives of the janitors in Mayor Kennelly's office, and they agreed that if the school system attorney remained autonomous, they would support the bill. This was a relatively minor amendment, as the board attorney was not a particularly important figure and the key task was to merge the educational and business functions of the school system under one head. With the acquiescence of the politically important janitors, the CFL then supported the bill and it passed in the state legislature.

The 1940s closed with the superintendency of Herold G. Hunt, a noncontroversial administrator who sought good working relations with both the teachers' unions and with the civic reform associations. The Citizens Schools Committee, local parent-teacher associations, and the teachers' unions responded joyfully to his assumption of the superintendency in August 1947.[186] *Chicago's Schools* remarked that a "refreshed atmosphere" pervaded the school district offices and that a new "spirit of democracy" was in the air.[187] The Citizens Schools Committee and other progressive groups ceased trying to mobilize outside pressure in favor of working from the inside, concentrating on developing a close relationship with the superintendent. In keeping with the progressives' basic preference for working administratively rather than politically, *Chicago's Schools* summed up the change in the committee's approach with the arrival of the new superintendent: "For its first ten years the Committee fought, with some successes, a Fabian fight against the spoils system in the schools. For five years thereafter it took the field aggressively to uproot the spoilsmen. Then, having achieved a new administration of the schools, it devoted itself to constructive support of that administration."[188] The teacher's unions, engaged in an initial push for collective bargaining rights, also moved into a position of basic political support for the superintendent, in spite of differences between them. When Hunt retired in 1953, it briefly appeared that the jarring political battles that had characterized school politics in the city for the preceding fifty years had abated. The school desegregation crises of the 1960s and the financial crises of the 1980s put an end to the illusion of peace, but in the new controversies the labor movement did not play the same type of crusading role that it had earlier in Chicago's history.

Conclusions:
The Transition to Pluralist Bargaining

The CFL's reluctance to support the administrative reform bill because it could damage the interests of the janitors reflects a swing toward a pluralist bargaining emphasis. The labor federation had couched its opposition to earlier school policies in terms of a class outlook on the role of schooling. The outlook became less evident as the Chicago Federation of Labor (and the CIO unions) entered into a close political alliance with the party officials who controlled the basic political decisions of the city. It should be stressed, however, that the CFL and the city's labor movement as a whole consistently opposed the school economy program; they did not *favor* the school reductions (as there is strong evidence that the leading businessmen of the city did), but they did not aggressively fight them. In a pluralist bargaining system, each group has the best chance of winning demands centered on the immediate interests of its members.[189] The CFL and CIO unions increasingly followed a policy of pressing the machine for such benefits as political appointments of union members, favorable city wage scales, adoption of labor-intensive works programs that increased employment opportunities, and city restraint in dealing with strikes. These demands could be fulfilled within the context of a system that rigidly limited the possibilities of winning broader demands.

The immediate and intense labor reaction to public reports of Superintendent Johnson's proposal for a school system overwhelmingly geared toward vocational education demonstrated that there were limits beyond which the school board (and, indirectly, the mayor) could not go without generating opposition too widely based and deeply felt to be readily placated. The mayor attempted to set up a series of negotiating sessions between labor figures and the superintendent to work out a compromise vocational education program. The negotiating sessions collapsed because the differences between the two sides involved fundamental questions about the content of schooling. The Chicago labor movement accepted, with protest, a school system that suffered enormous financial cutbacks, but the labor organizations would not accept a school system that would have denied even the possibility of educational equality. The defeat of the Cooley Bill 20 years earlier had demonstrated that a broad social consensus existed among all but certain elements of the business community that the schools should be unified and should basically offer a common curriculum. Individuals with very different ideologies could unite around this point and were willing to bitterly contest efforts to turn the Chicago public schools into a giant trade school. The superintendent's dropping of the proposal and later attempts to deny that he had ever intended to implement the plan indicated awareness of the strength and depth of the opposition.

There was a final important respect in which the organized labor movement's mode of relating to educational issues changed during the 1930s. During the first decades of the century the teachers' union had played a critical role in helping to orient the central labor federation toward school issues and providing the expertise needed for sustained involvement. The close working relationship between Margaret Haley and John Fitzpatrick had been based on a common ideology and a willingness to cooperate on a broad range of issues to alter the political framework of the city. This alliance had greatly increased the impact of both groups in dealing with educational issues. The very success of the alliance, however, made opposition elements in the city very anxious to split the groups, and the Loeb Rule was designed to sever the teachers from the rest of the organized labor movement. Out of a belief that the teachers could continue to work with the C F L even though not formally affiliated, both Fitzpatrick and Haley evidently viewed the enforced split as not particularly damaging. In practice, however, Haley followed an increasingly erratic course, and her Chicago Teachers' Federation began to lose influence compared to the initially smaller groups such as the Federation of Women High School Teachers, which remained affiliated with the C F L.

During the 1930s, the C F L-affiliated teachers' unions united and formed a 7,000-member unit, the Chicago Teachers Union. (The Chicago Teachers' Federation remained outside the C T U and became increasingly conservative and organizationally irrelevant.) The new union was sufficiently large that it could have played a significant role in the C F L, but it was challenged on questions of school system organization by the rising janitors' union. The janitors were more politically influential because of their ties to the machine, and the C F L leadership increasingly heeded them over the teachers. In this sense, the teachers, even after they had achieved a large measure of unity and formed a significant bloc within the C F L, had lost their particular access to the labor movement. Their claims to special interest and expertise had to be weighed against the interests of the janitors and other workers as the C F L adopted pluralistic criteria for determining social policy. The teachers valued the connection to the city's labor movement, as was indicated by their decision to stay in the A F L rather than join the C I O. They could not count, however, on the C F L's support in the same way that the teachers had counted on it just before and after World War I.

In contrast to the labor movement, the liberal professionals who operated through Chicago's civic associations experienced no particular change in political direction during the 1930s. They had long believed that Chicago's schools should be administered by specially trained, professionally qualified experts who would keep the schools free of political influence. They were, however, forced to work politically during the 1930s in a way that they did not like to do. As Cohen points out in his study of educational progressives in New York City, they almost always preferred to work through established administrative structures rather than through mobilizing mass pressure.[190] They thoroughly distrusted the electorate and politicians. Chicago's progressives were similar in this respect, but their complete shutout from influence with school officials during the 1930s left them with no alternative but to join the teachers in crusading for more money for the schools and a change in educational policies.

During the administration of Superintendent McAndrew, it had briefly appeared that the progressives had attained their goal of a scientifically minded superintendent who would run the schools on an expert basis. McAndrew's dismissal, however, proved to be only the beginning of a long period during which the schools were made patronage instruments for the machine and the superintendent became merely a figurehead. The civic associations generally considered the machine to be the key enemy because patronage, influence buying, and the accompanying corruption struck the liberal activists as the antithesis of the impartial, expert direction that they sought. The reform leaders also attacked Chicago's businessmen for the degradation of the schools because they had worked so openly and aggressively to slash the educational budget during the 1930s. The sentiments of many of the reform leaders on this point were expressed by Mrs. Walter F. Heineman, a minority school board member who opposed McCahey and his associates on the board, and who had her political base in the reform community. Mrs. Heineman told a City Club forum in April 1944 that the city could not expect any improvement in its schools until the machine ceased its intervention in school matters. The report of the meeting said, however, that she "saw another equally sinister influence—an element which for eleven years had exerted pressure on the school board for 'cheaper and poorer education.'" That element, she told the City Club, was big business, which was primarily interested in lowering taxes.[191]

Business leaders in Chicago had, in fact, succeeded in working out a political arrangement with the Democratic party machine. During Anton Cermak's brief administration, business committees such as the Committee on Public Expenditures acted directly to secure slashing budget cuts. When Kelly came to office, however, the business leaders were able to allow the committees to wither away as Kelly took on the task of reducing expenditures for social services. As mayor, Kelly pursued policies in regard to the schools that were very much in accord with the thrust of business positions as expressed over the years by such groups as the Commercial Club and the Chicago Association of Commerce. Kelly's close friend and hand-picked school board president, James B. McCahey, wielded enormous influence as he worked to cut the amount of money spent on schools and sought to narrow the curriculum. In Chicago, where the alliance with the machine held the labor movement in check, the business community had the political means to slash the school budget and restrict public education.

7 | CONCLUSIONS: CONFLICTS OVER SCHOOLING

THE REVISIONIST WRITERS created intensified interest in the history of public education because they advanced a notion of the expansion of schooling that ran directly counter to the conventional view: education was not expanded in response to popular demand and it was not intended to serve as a democratizing institution. They argued that members of social elites, either upper class or capitalist, depending on the particular theorist, pushed schooling on a reluctant working-class population that was sullenly suspicious of their motives but unwilling or unable to take concerted action to challenge the proposed mode of schooling. In its specifics, the revisionist interpretation does not correspond to the facts of educational development in Chicago. Far from resisting schooling, the labor movement fought for the expansion of public education. Local and state labor organizations argued for better funding of the schools, for higher school-leaving ages, and for the development of a broad curriculum for working-class students. Although the labor movement varied in the breadth of its orientation toward the schools, labor representatives emphasized the importance of public schooling for a more equitable society. Further, businessmen were often reluctant to promote increased schooling. They wanted children effectively trained in job-related skills, but they supported proposals that were intended to limit working-class education in both amount and scope. Clearly, expanded education did not pose any essential challenges to the stability of the capitalist order, but it could potentially lead to a gap between expectations and reality that could heighten discontent. In addition, businessmen were highly cost conscious and were reluctant to see education or other social services expand because of the resulting tax burden.

What are the implications of the fact that the Chicago pattern differs from the one that, if the revisionist theory has general significance, we would have expected to find? Identifying who supported the schools and why is crucial to the revisionists' analysis because it is their views on these points that strikingly distinguish them from the earlier, more orthodox historians of education. Katz's book, *The Irony of Early School Reform,* was original and provocative because of his assertion that "one dynamic of educational controversy was the attempt of social leaders to impose innovation upon a reluctant working class."[1] In this perspective, industrialists and their intellectual spokespeople actively promoted public schooling in order to develop a tractable labor force. Working people are described as being at best indifferent and at worst hostile to the expansion of the school system. This perspective is similar to that elaborated by "corporate liberal" historians since the 1960s. The revisionists and the corporate liberal theorists describe the upper class as holding decisive power on a practical but, more importantly, also an ideological level. Working-class restiveness served only to spur the intensified development of agencies of social control, such as the public schools. Only in this very limited sense do the revisionists describe the schools as being the products of popular struggles. The schools were not a goal of the working class, in their view, but an outcome of social disruption, however undirected that opposition might have been.

The Chicago experience indicates the working out of a very different process of historical change on several levels. On the first level, the conflicts over the control and content of schooling demonstrate that working-class groups were able to generate an ideology that was in significant respects counter to that held by the dominant elements in the society. The method of the revisionist authors in approaching history makes it difficult to understand the political consciousness of working-class organizations because such authors disregard the study of collective forms of political protest. They ignore both the workingmen's political parties of the late 1820s and 1830s in New England and the later development of trade unions. While the labor movement is far from being synonymous with the "working class," being too often distant or divorced from working-class life, it remains the key expression of working-class politics in the United States.

In Western Europe, labor parties express, in some measure, working-class political goals; in the United States, in the absence of such a party the labor movement has thus far assumed this function, with greater or lesser militancy and political involvement, depending on the context and the pressure from below. It is historically unwarranted to *assume* that the working class developed no collective consciousness.

It is important to understand individual acts of resistance to schools and other institutions by working-class youth; we need to know more about how the schools actually functioned. But we also have to credit the organized labor movement with some political significance. The often authoritarian nature of schooling was doubtless apparent to countless working-class youth in the crowded classrooms of the Chicago public schools in the early 1900s; the history of conflict over the schools reveals that it was also apparent to labor activists. Ironically, the representatives of the Chicago Federation of Labor often rivaled the later revisionist writers in their condemnation of the inequalities and class biases of the school system. They did not withdraw from school controversies or abandon support of the schools, however, but threw their political resources into battles over changing the content and direction of the public schools. The labor movement was both far more sophisticated than the revisionists have given it credit for and far more willing to engage in battle than has ever emerged in revisionist writings.

Was Chicago exceptional in this regard? It may have been exceptional in that both business and labor groups presented their ideas with sophistication and clarity and battles were often overt; the educational perspectives of all groups in the city developed in years of controversy. Yet even in the Northeast where religious and ethnic conflicts between Yankee employers and Catholic workers led to tangled school controversies, there is strong evidence of early commitment to public schools by workers. In the late 1820s and during the 1830s, workingmen's political parties sprang up in dozens of cities in New York, New Jersey, Delaware, Massachusetts, Connecticut, New Hampshire, Maine, and Vermont. The programs of the parties were remarkably similar, being broadly modeled after the program of the

Philadelphia Working Men. This program "included, above all, a call for a free, tax-supported school system" to provide working-class children with an education without the taint of charity.[2] Historians have argued at length over how much workingmen's parties actually helped to power the drive for public schools; whatever the outcome of that debate, examination of the workingmen's programs leaves no doubt of their support for free and expanded schools.

While every city has a very particular local history, Chicago did offer an opportunity for studying the labor movement in varying political contexts because the emergence of the Democratic party machine in the 1930s led to such marked changes in the city's political life. The labor movement continued to support the schools even after becoming linked to the machine. It continued to argue for greater school funding and it continued to oppose attempts or threatened attempts to narrow the curriculum in a vocational direction. The labor movement's educational policies lost their breadth and impact, however, as, after the 1930s, a range of class issues in regard to schooling became submerged. This occurred because of changes in the way the labor movement related to the dominant political powers of the city. This leads to the hypothesis that the full development of a counter-ideology on the part of working-class institutions requires political independence; where this is lacking, there will be constraints on the types of issues addressed and the freedom with which they are considered. In other cities where the labor movement has exhibited the kind of political independence that first characterized the Chicago Federation of Labor, it might be expected that specific conflicts with a class bearing could be traced over many aspects of the city's life. Where the labor movement is more firmly incorporated into the established political structure, it would be likely still to adhere to traditional liberal values in regard to schooling, but to view them in a narrower framework and to cease to place priority on fighting for social issues.

On a second level, the Chicago experience points to the one-sidedness of the revisionists' stress on the ability of the upper class to shape social institutions unilaterally. Not only did the

Chicago Federation of Labor enunciate a different educational ideology from that propounded by businessmen in the city, but the labor organization was able to take, in some specific historical circumstances, effective action to support its educational demands. The outcome of struggles was not always a foregone conclusion: the successful mobilization against the Cooley Bill and the platoon schools proposed by Superintendent McAndrew were examples of labor victories. They were limited and partial victories, as the labor movement at no time possessed the strength to win implementation of its own view of schooling. They do demonstrate, however, that even the most powerful of Chicago's businessmen were not able to mold the schools or other public institutions to their dictates; rather, they were forced to take into account the possibility of determined working-class resistance, a resistance based on an awareness of the class implications of different policies. The history of educational development in Chicago is a history of struggle, compromise, and resistance, not of simple elite domination.

A third point of difference with the revisionist authors concerns the impact of education itself on people's consciousness. The revisionist analysis is frequently deterministic in assuming that expanded schooling is necessarily effective in fostering elite control; from the capitalists' perspective, increased schooling is at least more problematic than this. Businessmen in Chicago acted in ways that show they were aware of the potential double-edged character of increased schooling. They supported the development of a highly stratified school system that would not have led to the overeducation of the children of the working-class population; they tried to limit both the amount and type of schooling that working-class children received. Through the Cooley Bill, they sought to give working-class children, except those with particular and demonstrated academic talent, vocational training. Even this training was to be of a highly limited sort for most of the vocational students. Cooley explained that it would be for six hours a week for students in the continuation schools. The stress on moral rather than academic education could also serve as a powerful rationale for limiting the actual education received by the majority of working-class children.

The labor movement recognized, and argued, that moral education was often a synonym for very little education. During the Depression, a period of general social turbulence, businessmen responded not by increasing education, with its presumed socializing power, but by taking the opportunity to make massive cutbacks in public expenditures. It is hard to find a pattern of business eagerness for increased education, but there is a pattern of business efforts to control and orient the nature of the education provided in such a way that most children did not receive education beyond that which would be necessary for their likely station in life.

The revisionist authors often argue that employers favored the expansion of schools because of the social control functions of schooling; skills training is assumed to be secondary. In Chicago, however, the records of the business clubs show that businessmen were anxious that schools produce employees with adequate job skills. It is true that the level of education required by factory workers for satisfactory job performance was minimal, but other types of employees, especially those involved in commercial operations, needed certain levels of math and verbal skills to perform competently. In the business view, however, there was little point to providing students who would not need such skills with extensive academic training. Liberal education held the potential of making students more demanding, more critical, more aware of social inequalities and of possible solutions; raising students' expectations could carry a social risk in the long run, and it was also unquestionably expensive in the short run. Highly stratified school systems, with different tracks and social purposes, and with different costs per student, could help to solve the problem of creating employees who were educated to the requisite level without undue risk or expense. The frequency and passion with which labor and business groups clashed over educational issues in the early 1900s arose from fundamentally divergent views on the scope of education to be made available for working-class children. Labor groups argued that working-class children should receive a broad liberal education, and business leaders promoted much more limited, cheap and hierarchical forms of schooling.

Public education is a highly expensive form of socialization, and businessmen, as major taxpayers, had an incentive to try to limit educational costs. During the Depression, Chicago experienced what were probably the most severe cutbacks in the country, but business groups in other cities also moved against the schools.[3] The United States Chamber of Commerce elaborated a retrenchment program that seemed "to have set the pattern for the economy measures advocated by many local taxpayers' associations."[4] The Chamber of Commerce program called for retrenchments in 20 areas of educational services; it recommended that supervisors be transferred to classrooms, that the curriculum be simplified, that the school day be shortened by one hour, that class sizes be increased and the school year shortened, that kindergartens be discontinued, that fees be imposed on high school students, that the high school program be shortened from four years to three, and that teachers' salaries be reduced while their classroom hours were increased.[5]

The Chicago experience was more extreme than in most cities, in part perhaps because in Chicago the emergence of the machine allowed for social service cutbacks with relative political impunity for business. Across the country, however, businessmen demonstrated a desire to cut back on the schools during a period when, because of lack of jobs, more students were staying in school. This appears to demonstrate that businessmen valued their tax monies as much as they valued the potential socializing effects of schooling.

On a fourth level, some of the revisionist writers have argued that middle-class civic reformers such as Jane Addams in reality had an ideology that reinforced business dominance of the schools. This is not necessarily the view of all the revisionist authors, but few have closely analyzed the particular political role played by such reformers. The history of the Chicago schools indicates that the city's middle-class liberals were energetic in defining and publicizing school issues; their ideological belief in efficiency and rational direction led them to value education greatly as a means of training youth for citizenship and work. They deplored the corrupt administration of the Chicago schools, which not only wasted money and violated elementary standards of honesty but resulted in a lowering of school quality. The civic reformers could significantly aid the labor movement in fighting for its educational objectives, as when they provided publicity and organizational support during the campaign against the Cooley Bill. The two groups in coalition could be a major force in city politics, and Margaret Haley based some of her early hopes for social reform on their continued cooperation. The 1930s demonstrated that the civic reformers could not usually win struggles on their own. In spite of great effort, they failed to wrest the school board from machine control.

While in some respects the middle-class reformers shared an ideology similar to that of business leaders, in other respects they differed from them in ways that had practical importance for the shaping of the school system in Chicago. They held a distinctive perspective—valuing both efficiency and democratic procedures in somewhat uneasy combination—that did not allow them to identify fully with either labor or business positions on many school-related issues. They also differed among themselves, as exemplified by the 1907 split between Charles Merriam and Raymond Robins over the city charter question, with one favoring the charter for its organizational advantages and the other rejecting it because of its undemocratic features.

The reformers' distinctive stance was reflected in their specific positions. They rejected the business drive to narrow the school system; they did, however, identify with the goal of tracking students and of creating a differentiated curriculum for students of differing abilities. They tried and failed to mediate the conflicts over the Cooley Bill. The labor movement was likely to find but little support when it appeared to be contravening the principles of rationality and efficiency. This occurred, for example, during the superintendencies of Cooley and McAndrew, when civic reformers were far more supportive of the efficiency-oriented superintendents than of the embattled labor movement. George Herbert Mead, chair of the City Club's education committee, captured this ambivalence of the middle-class progressives. In 1907 he called the Chicago Teachers' Federation "irresponsible," but he also said that it was necessary given the conditions that the teachers faced.[6] Similarly, school administrators, such as Ella

Flagg Young, with ties to the civic reformers, could find themselves playing an ambivalent role, often facing political problems as they tried to find a middle ground in polarized situations.

It is, finally, important to consider how the analysis presented here differs from that of Diane Ravitch and others who identify with the "democratic liberal," or, as I would call it, pluralist tradition in American politics. Ravitch describes a series of successes in her critique of the revisionists; American society adapts to the demands of different groups, making erratic and perhaps too slow but overall progress toward the goal of a more democratic and humane society.[7] In this perspective, the idea of social class has no place. Historical actors neither view issues in class terms nor is there meaningful collective organization along class lines.

I believe that it is difficult to explain the consistency and depth of controversy over the Chicago schools without reference to class terms. In the early 1900s, the effect of class was open, while in other decades class considerations more often worked themselves out just beneath the surface of the official political life of the city. In Chicago the participants in the struggles over the schools often described them in class terms. Those who used class terms included Ella Flagg Young, superintendent of the Chicago schools from 1909 to 1915, who declared that she thought that businessmen in Chicago initially turned against the teachers because of "class antagonism"; she was herself accused of stirring up class prejudice by the *Chicago Daily News* when she criticized the Cooley Bill on the grounds that it would condemn some children to the industrial class. Charles H. Judd, a political moderate, argued in the 1930s that businessmen wanted to wreck a school system of the common people. And the Chicago Federation of Labor argued that businessmen wanted workers to learn only simple skills of reading, writing, and computing that would fit them for work but not much more. Even those who were on the more conservative wing of the labor movement, such as Victor Olander, explicitly mobilized opposition to various school reorganization plans on the grounds that they represented attempts at class domination. Working-class children would become the victims of those who wished to use the schools to secure their own political and economic advantage. In the politically divided world of Chicago in the early 1900s, class was not a foreign category to those active in the political arena. People from many different points along the political spectrum considered it to be the element that fueled the recurring school controversies.

More fundamentally, the view of reforms developed here differs from that of writers in the pluralist tradition. Reforms as analyzed here are not primarily viewed as waystations along the road toward a more perfect society. They are, rather, the products of a continuing, sometimes open, sometimes submerged, political struggle where gains can often be important but are also only partial and subject to revocation. The pluralist writers elevate these partial reforms to major victories in the development of a beneficent society; the revisionists deny their significance on any level. I would argue that the schools remained class biased and dominated from the top; that the labor movement, even at its most politically conscious and most militant, never had the strength to impose its own vision of schooling. This does not mean that gains did not occur, but that social movements grow through a process of partial victories and losses that themselves sometimes spur further conflict. It is one-sided to see the schools only as oppressive and elitist institutions. It is also, in this perspective, one-sided to see them only as institutions that are steadily, if incrementally, evolving toward being more truly democratic.

This study demonstrates the need to take seriously the idea that it is not only retrospectively that people understand their circumstances. With all the limitations of the political consciousness of the Chicago labor movement—and it was limited in many crucial respects—it was a movement that also understood and acted upon its own worked-out political and educational ideas. It is not sufficient to assume the existence of a social system without major cracks or fault lines, where socialization from above is so complete that those below do not even grasp, except on the most elemental level, their own oppression. While not romanticizing social struggles, researchers should consider the potentially contradictory quality of institutions such as the public schools and should try to specify the varying historical conditions that give rise to passivity or resistance.

What are the broader implications of what was found in Chicago? This study represents an attempt to consider the playing out of class controversies around a concrete social issue over a long time period. In the United States, authors with a class perspective frequently write at a high level of abstraction. They write of the role of capitalists, of the state, of class consciousness; it is often extremely difficult to know how to connect these abstractions with the mundane working out of politics on a local or national level. In this study, I have tried to demonstrate that there are in fact vital linkages between the abstractions of these writers and the realities of day-to-day political struggles. "Chicago business leaders" may not correspond exactly with our notion of "capitalists"; certainly "the labor movement" does not correspond in a one-to-one fashion with "working class." Yet in Chicago, these actors did in fact relate to issues in class terms, even when the issues themselves were removed from those larger economic and political questions most powerfully associated in people's minds with class questions. Without a sense of how concrete controversies translate into the abstract analyses frequently employed, both our understanding of the workings of the capitalist system and the advancement of political theory will remain limited.

NOTES

THE FOLLOWING ABBREVIATIONS are used in the notes:

CAC   Chicago Association of Commerce

CAC Bulletin   *Chicago Association of Commerce Bulletin*

CBE   Chicago Board of Education

CFL   Chicago Federation of Labor

CTF   Chicago Teachers' Federation

CTF Bulletin   *Chicago Teachers' Federation Bulletin*

CTSBJ   *Chicago Teacher and School Board Journal*

ISFL   Illinois State Federation of Labor

1

1. *New Majority*, December 29, 1923, p. 4.

2. Michael B. Katz, *Class, Bureaucracy and Schools: The Illusion of Educational Change in America*, 2nd ed. (New York: Praeger, 1975), p. xv.

3. See, for example: Joel H. Spring, *The Sorting Machine: National Educational Policy Since 1945* (New York: David McKay, 1976).

4. See, for example: Martin Carnoy, "Introduction," in Martin Carnoy, ed., *Schooling in a Corporate Society: The Political Economy of Education in America* (New York: McKay, 1972), pp. 1–19; Joel H. Spring, *Education and the Rise of the Corporate State* (Boston: Beacon Press, 1972); Samuel Bowles, "Unequal Education and the Reproduction of the Social Division of Labor," in Carnoy, *Schooling in a Corporate Society*, pp. 38–66; Samuel Bowles and Herbert Gintis, *Schooling in Capitalist America: Educational Reform and the Contradictions of Economic Life* (New York: Basic Books, 1976); Alexander J. Field, "Educational Reform and Manufacturing Development in Mid-Nineteenth Century Massachusetts" (Ph.D. diss., University of California at Berkeley, 1974); Clarence J. Karier, Paul C. Violas, and Joel H. Spring, *Roots of Crisis: American Education in the Twentieth Century* (Chicago: Rand-McNally, 1973).

Alexander J. Field, an economic historian, occupies a distinctive place in the list of educational writers, as in many ways he does not share the revisionists' overall perspective on the society. His work parallels theirs only in certain respects; he clearly has been strongly influenced by the revisionists' stress on the socializing functions of schooling. He believes that the expansion of schooling in mid-nineteenth-century Massachusetts can best be explained as arising from a "perceived need on the part of manufacturers and professionals for a universal agency of socialization which would insure a self-disciplined, deferential, orderly, punctual, and honest citizenry and labor force which would work well in manufacturing or bureaucratic units characterized by administrative hierarchies, and in nonworking hours go about business in an orderly fashion in an increasingly interdependent social order" ("Educational Reform," p. ii–iii). He also believes that manufacturers, with support from professionals, provided the driving force behind the expansion of the schools. Because his work shares these key features with the revisionists', and because he explicitly identifies his analysis with that of such corporate liberal theorists as Gabriel Kolko, it is useful to consider his work within the same framework as that of the revisionist writers, bearing in mind the lack of radical thrust behind his analysis.

5. See, for example: David B. Tyack, *The One Best System: A History of American Urban Education* (Cambridge: Harvard University Press, 1974); Marvin Lazerson, *Origins of the Urban School: Public Education in Massachusetts, 1870–1915* (Harvard University Press, 1971).

6. See, for example: Frank Tracy Carlton, *Economic Influences upon Educational Progress in the United States, 1820–1850*, University of Wisconsin Bulletin, No. 221, Economics and Political Science Series, Vol. 4, No. 1 (Madison, Wis., 1908); John R. Commons et al., *History of Labour in the United States*, vol. 1 (New York: Macmillan, 1921); and John R. Commons et al., eds., *A Documentary History of American Industrial Society*, vol. 5 (New York: Russell and Russell, 1958).

7. See, for example: Arthur M. Schlesinger, Sr., *New Viewpoints in American History* (New York: Macmillan, 1961 [1st ed. 1922]); Mary R. Beard, *A Short History of the American Labor Movement* (New York: Harcourt, Brace and Howe, 1920). For a critical discussion of the labor education thesis, see Jay M. Pawa, "Workingmen and Free Schools in the Nineteenth Century: A Comment on the Labor-Education Thesis," *History of Education Quarterly* 11 (Fall 1971): 287–302.

8. See, for example: Lawrence A. Cremin, *The Transformation of the School: Progressivism in American Education, 1876–1957* (New York: Knopf, 1961); Bernard Bailyn, *Education in the Forming of American Society: Needs and Opportunities for Study* (New York: Vintage, 1960). For a useful analysis of changing currents in the sociology of education, see Philip Wexler, *The Sociology of Education: Beyond Equality* (Indianapolis: Bobbs-Merrill, 1976).

9. See, for example: Colin Greer, *The Great School Legend: A Re-*

visionist Interpretation of American Public Education (New York: Basic Books, 1972).

10. Michael B. Katz, *The Irony of Early School Reform: Educational Innovation in Mid-Nineteenth Century Massachusetts* (Boston: Beacon Press, 1968), p. 86.

11. Bowles, *"Unequal Education,"* p. 44.

12. Carnoy, "Introduction," p. 3.

13. Katz, *Irony of Reform*, p. 22.

14. Ibid., p. 214.

15. See, for example: David W. Eakins, "The Development of Corporate Liberal Policy Research in the United States, 1885–1965" (Ph.D. diss., University of Wisconsin, Madison, 1966); Gabriel Kolko, *The Triumph of Conservatism: A Reinterpretation of American History, 1900–1916* (Chicago: Quadrangle, 1967); Ronald Radosh, *American Labor and United States Foreign Policy* (New York: Random House, 1969); James Weinstein, *The Corporate Ideal in the Liberal State, 1900–1918* (Boston: Beacon Press, 1968).

16. Katz, *Irony of Reform*, p. 214.

17. Kolko, *Triumph of Conservatism*, pp. 4–5.

18. See, for example: Ralph Miliband, "The Capitalist State—Reply to Nicos Poulantzas," *New Left Review* 59 (January–February 1970): 53–60; Nicos Poulantzas, "The Problem of the Capitalist State," *New Left Review* 58 (November–December 1969): 67–78, and "The Capitalist State: A Reply to Miliband and Laclau," *New Left Review* 95 (January–February 1976): 63–83.

19. Kolko, "The Decline of American Radicalism in the Twentieth Century," in Milton Mankoff, ed., *The Poverty of Progress: The Political Economy of American Social Problems* (New York: Holt, Rinehart and Winston, 1972), p. 463.

20. Bowles and Gintis, *Schooling*, p. 37.

21. Hobsbawm, "Class Consciousness in History," in Istvan Meszaros, ed., *Aspects of History and Class Consciousness* (London: Routledge and Kegan Paul, 1971), p. 15.

2

1. J. David Greenstone, *Labor in American Politics* (New York: Vintage Press, 1970), p. 92.

2. Alex Gottfried, *Boss Cermak of Chicago: A Study of Political Leadership* (Seattle: University of Washington Press, 1962), pp. 353–354.

3. U.S. Department of the Interior, Census Office, *Report on the Population of the United States at the Eleventh Census: 1890* (Washington, D.C.: Government Printing Office, 1895), part 1, p. 370.

4. U.S. Department of Commerce, Bureau of the Census, *1970 Census of the Population*, vol. 1, part 15 (Washington, D.C.: Government Printing Office, 1973), "Illinois," pp. 15–20.

5. Paul Pike Pullen, "Population Movements in the Chicago Metropolitan Area from 1900 to the Present" (M.A. thesis, Northwestern University, 1942), p. 90.

6. Gene Delon Jones, "The Local Political Significance of New Deal Relief Legislation in Chicago: 1933–1940" (Ph.D. diss., Northwestern University, 1970), p. 10.

7. Barbara Warne Newell, *Chicago and the Labor Movement: Metropolitan Unionism in the 1930's* (Urbana, Ill.: University of Illinois Press, 1961), pp. 230, 236.

8. Jones, "New Deal Relief," p. 10.

9. Ibid., p. 10.

10. Charles E. Merriam, *Chicago: A More Intimate View of Urban Politics* (New York: Macmillan, 1929), p. 97.

11. Ibid., p. 142. John M. Allswang, *A House for All Peoples: Ethnic Politics in Chicago, 1890–1936* (Lexington, Ky.: University Press of Kentucky, 1971), pp. 33, 87–88.

12. Allswang, *A House for All Peoples*, p. 23.

13. Merriam, *Chicago*, pp. 90–91.

14. "The Kelly-Nash Political Machine," *Fortune* 14 (August 1936): 52.

15. Newell, *Chicago and the Labor Movement*, p. 232.

16. Ibid., p. 210.

17. George S. Counts, *School and Society in Chicago* (New York: Harcourt Brace, 1928), p. 165.

18. Jeremy Brecher, *Strike!* (San Francisco: Straight Arrow Books, 1972). See, for example, pp. 44–47 and pp. 92–93.

19. Ibid., pp. 44–47.

20. Emmett Dedmon, "A Short History of the Commercial Club" (speech delivered at Commercial Club on occasion of its 600th meeting, September 25, 1968), p. 11.

21. *Chicago Dispatch*, quoted in Eugene Staley, *History of the Illinois State Federation of Labor* (Chicago: University of Chicago Press, 1930), p. 128.

22. Bessie Louise Pierce, *A History of Chicago*: vol. 2, *From Town to City, 1848–1871* (New York: Knopf, 1940), p. 187.

23. Newell, *Chicago and the Labor Movement*, p. 12.

24. Ibid., p. 20.

25. Ibid., p. 23.

26. Ibid., pp. 80–81.

27. John Howard Keiser, "John Fitzpatrick and Progressive Union-

ism, 1915–1925" (Ph.D. diss., Northwestern University, 1965); *Chicago Daily News*, September 28, 1946, p. 5.

28. Keiser, "John Fitzpatrick."

29. John Fitzpatrick, Stenographic report of speech delivered at meeting of Chicago Federation of Men Teachers, Federation of Women High School Teachers, and the Elementary Teachers Union, March 2, 1928, Chicago Teachers' Federation Papers, Chicago Historical Society.

30. Jacob Potofsky, Interview conducted by Elizabeth Balanoff, August 4, 1970, transcript in Roosevelt University Oral History Project, Roosevelt University Library, Chicago.

31. Frank Rosenblum, Interview conducted by Elizabeth Balanoff, August 14, 1970, transcript in Roosevelt University Oral History Project, Roosevelt University Library, Chicago.

32. Lillian Herstein, Interview conducted by Elizabeth Balanoff, October 26, 1970, transcript in Roosevelt University Oral History Project, Roosevelt University Library, Chicago.

33. Newell, *Chicago and the Labor Movement*, pp. 61–62.

34. Robert R. R. Brooks, *As Steel Goes: Unionism in a Basic Industry* (New Haven, Conn.: Yale University Press, 1940), pp. 40–41.

35. Newell, *Chicago and the Labor Movement*, p. 153.

36. Ibid., pp. 155–156.

37. Brooks, *As Steel Goes*, p. 35.

38. Newell, *Chicago and the Labor Movement*, pp. 119–120.

39. Brooks, *As Steel Goes*, pp. 40–41.

40. Keiser, "John Fitzpatrick," p. v.

41. Catharine Goggin, "The Chicago Teachers' Federation," *CTSBJ* 1 (May 1899): 257–259.

42. Ibid., p. 258.

43. "City Items," *CTSBJ* 1 (February 1899):89; CTF, *Report, Showing Results of Fifteen Years of Organization, to the Teachers of Chicago*, (1908):4–5, Chicago Teachers' Federation Papers, Chicago Historical Society.

44. George Creel, "Why Chicago's Teachers Unionized," *Harper's Weekly* 60 (June 19, 1915):598–600.

45. William R. Chenery, "Adulterated Education," *New Republic* 4 (October 23, 1915):304–306.

46. Herrick, *Chicago Schools*, pp. 104–105.

47. CTF, "Fifteen Years of Organization," pp. 16–17.

48. Margaret A. Haley, "Autobiography" (Seattle, Wash., December 27, 1911–February 13, 1912), p. 8, Chicago Teachers' Federation Papers, Chicago Historical Society (typescript); Creel, "Why Chicago's Teachers Unionized."

49. Haley, "Autobiography," p. 6.

50. "Teachers and Labor Unions," *CTF Bulletin* 2 (January 30, 1903):4.

51. Margaret A. Haley, "Catharine Goggin," *Margaret A. Haley's Bulletin* 2 (January 27, 1916):3.

52. CTF, "Fifteen Years of Organization," p. 16.

53. Creel, "Why Chicago's Teachers Unionized," p. 600.

54. George S. Counts, *School and Society in Chicago* (New York: Harcourt, Brace, 1928), p. 165.

55. Keiser, "John Fitzpatrick," p. 78; for early signs of the tension between the CFL and the AFL, see the Minutes of the December 19, 1915, CFL Meeting, pp. 17–28. John Fitzpatrick Papers, Chicago Historical Society.

56. Ibid., pp. 96–97.

57. Ibid., pp. 98–99.

58. Greenstone, *Labor in American Politics*, p. 30.

59. Harry Bird Sell, "The American Federation of Labor and the Labor Party Movement of 1918–1920" (M.A. thesis, University of Chicago, 1922), p. 73.

60. CFL, "Independent Labor Party Platform: Endorsed Unanimously by The Chicago Federation of Labor at the Regular Meeting, November 17, 1918," Chicago Teachers' Federation Papers, Chicago Historical Society.

61. Ibid., p. 2.

62. Nathan Fine, *Labor and Farmer Parties in the United States, 1828–1928* (New York: Rand School of Social Science, 1928), p. 381.

63. Ibid., p. 383.

64. Ibid., p. 379.

65. Robert M. Buck, quoted in ibid., pp. 385–386.

66. *New Majority*, March 27, 1920, p. 2; see also Samuel Gompers, "Should a Labor Party be Formed?" in Charles M. Rehmus and Doris B. McLaughlin, eds., *Labor and American Politics: A Book of Readings* (Ann Arbor: University of Michigan Press, 1967), pp. 103–107.

67. *New Majority*, March 27, 1920, p. 2.

68. Sell, "American Federation of Labor," pp. 66–67.

69. Ibid., p. 72.

70. Margaret A. Haley and Agnes Nestor, Leaflet for the Labor Party of Cook County, January 22, 1919, Chicago Teachers' Federation Papers, Chicago Historical Society.

71. Sell, "American Federation of Labor," p. 83.

72. "Description of John Fitzpatrick Papers" [Introduction and Guide to the Papers], John Fitzpatrick Papers, Chicago Historical Society (typescript).

73. *New Majority*, April 5, 1919.

74. Sell, "American Federation of Labor," p. 86.

75. Herstein, interview transcript, p. 60.

76. Ibid., p. 64.

77. James Weinstein, *The Decline of Socialism in America, 1912–1925* (New York: Vintage Press, 1967), pp. 282–283.

78. Herstein, interview transcript, p. 63.

79. *New Majority*, July 14, 1923, p. 2.

80. Ibid., July 21, 1923, p. 5.

81. Herstein, interview transcript, p. 67.

82. Fine, *Labor and Farmer Parties*, p. 390.

83. Weinstein, *Decline of Socialism*, pp. 285–286; Fine, *Labor and Farmer Parties*, p. 386.

84. Keiser, "John Fitzpatrick," pp. 146–147.

85. Ibid., p. 145.

86. Ibid., pp. 146–147.

87. Fine, *Labor and Farmer Parties*, p. 412.

88. Weinstein, *Decline of Socialism*, p. 324.

89. Keiser, "John Fitzpatrick," p. 147.

90. Weinstein, *Decline of Socialism*, p. 324.

91. *New Majority*, July 26, 1924, p. 4.

92. Keiser, "John Fitzpatrick," p. 182.

93. Ibid., pp. 180–181.

1. CFL, *A Report on Public School Fads. An Investigation Made by the Legislative Committee of the Chicago Federation of Labor*, 1902, p. 6.

2. Ibid.

3. Mary J. Herrick, *The Chicago Schools: A Social and Political History* (Beverly Hills, Calif.: Sage Publications, 1971), pp. 59, 75.

4. Emmett Dedmon, "A Short History of the Commercial Club" (speech delivered at Commercial Club on occasion of its 600th meeting, September 25, 1968), p. 10.

5. Herrick, *Chicago Schools*, p. 59.

6. Dedmon, "Commercial Club," p. 10.

7. Ibid.

8. Stephen D. London, "Business and the Chicago Public School System, 1890–1966" Ph.D. diss., University of Chicago, 1968), p. 63.

9. Wayne Andrews, *Battle for Chicago* (New York: Harcourt, Brace, 1946), p. 6.

10. Merchants' Club of Chicago, "Commercial High Schools," (introduction and transcript of discussion held on February 9, 1901), *Minutes of 1900–1901*, p. 99.

11. Jeremiah W. Jencks, "Remarks on Commercial High Schools" (address delivered at meeting of Merchants' Club of Chicago, February 9, 1901), *Merchants' Club Minutes of 1900–1901*, pp. 99–100.

12. Ibid., p. 106.

13. Ibid., p. 104.

14. Ibid., p. 110.

15. Ibid., pp. 113–114.

16. Edwin Gilbert Cooley, "Remarks on Commercial High Schools" (address delivered at meeting of Merchants' Club of Chicago, February 9, 1901), *Merchants' Club Minutes of 1900–1901*, p. 118.

17. Ibid., pp. 120, 117.

18. Ibid., p. 117.

19. Merchants' Club, "Commercial High Schools," p. 114.

20. Hannah Belle Clark, *The Public Schools of Chicago: A Sociological Study* (Chicago: University of Chicago Press, 1897), p. 77.

21. John M. Beck, "Chicago Newspapers and the Public Schools, 1890–1920" (Ph.D. diss., University of Chicago, 1953), p. 207.

22. Clark, *Public Schools*, pp. 72–73.

23. Beck, "Newspapers and Schools," p. 296.

24. Clark, *Public Schools*, pp. 77–78.

25. Beck, "Newspapers and Schools," p. 208.

26. Herrick, *Chicago Schools*, p. 73.

27. *Chicago Tribune*, March 14, 1893, p. 4.

28. John G. Shedd, "Remarks on Commercial High Schools" (address delivered at meeting of Merchants' Club of Chicago, February 9, 1901), *Merchants' Club Minutes of 1900–1901*, p. 125.

29. Herrick, *Chicago Schools*, p.73.

30. C F L, *Report on Fads*, p. 1.

31. Ibid., p. 2.

32. Ibid.

33. Ibid., p. 3.

34. Ibid.

35. Ibid., p. 4.

36. Ibid., pp. 4–5.

37. Ibid., p. 5.

38. Ibid., p. 7.

39. Ibid.

40. Ibid., p. 6.

41. Ibid., p. 8.

42. Herrick, *Chicago Schools*, p. 119.

43. C F L, *Report on Fads*, p. 6.

44. Herrick, *Chicago Schools*, p. 118. Robert A. Nottenburg, "The Relationship of Organized Labor to Public School Legislation in Ill-

inois, 1880–1948" (Ph.D. diss., University of Chicago, 1950), p. 234.

45. Forrest Crissey, *The Making of an American School-Teacher* (Chicago: C. M. Barnes, 1906), pp. 45–47.

46. Edwin G. Cooley to William Rainey Harper, October 18, 1901, Presidents' Papers, Special Collections, University of Chicago Library.

47. Merchants' Club, "Commercial High Schools," p. 114.

48. Commercial Club of Chicago, *Yearbook, 1911–1912*, p. 277.

49. London, "Business and the School System," pp. 40, 63.

50. Ibid., p. 61.

51. CAC, *Industrial and Commercial Education in Relation to Conditions in the City of Chicago: Report of a Preliminary Survey by Committee on Industrial and Commercial Education of the CAC*, December 1909, p. 4.

52. Ibid., p. 7.

53. Ibid., p. 3.

54. City Club of Chicago, *A Report on Vocational Training in Chicago and in Other Cities*, 1912, pp. 44, 46.

55. Commercial Club of Chicago, *Yearbook, 1911–1912*, p. 15; Edwin G. Cooley, *Vocational Education in Europe* (report prepared for the Commercial Club, 1912).

56. Commercial Club of Chicago, *Yearbook, 1912–1913*, p. 154.

57. Edwin G. Cooley, *Public School Education in Morals*, Address delivered before Principals' Association, September 8, 1906 (Chicago: Normal School Press, 1906).

58. Ibid., p. 16.

59. Ibid., p. 13.

60. Ibid., p. 5.

61. Ibid., p. 4.

62. Ibid., p. 5.

63. Ibid., pp. 5–6.

64. Commercial Club of Chicago, *Vocational Schools for Illinois* (report prepared by Commercial Club, n.d.) p. 1, Chicago Historical Society.

65. Ibid., p. 2.

66. Theodore W. Robinson, *The Need of Industrial Education in Our Public Schools* (pamphlet version, prepared for Commercial Club of Chicago, of address delivered before the National Education Association, Boston, July 6, 1910) p. 9, Chicago Historical Society.

67. Ibid.

68. Theodore W. Robinson, "The Need of Vocational Education" (report of address delivered at American Steel Institute meeting, Chicago, October 24, 1913), p. 7, Victor Olander Papers, Chicago Historical Society.

69. Ibid., p. 7.

70. Ibid., p. 16.

71. Commercial Club of Chicago, *Yearbook, 1911–1912*, pp. 298–299.

72. Ibid., p. 298.

73. Edwin G. Cooley, *The Need for Vocational Schools in the United States* (pamphlet prepared for publication by Commercial Club of Chicago, 1914), p. 1, Chicago Historical Society.

74. Ibid., p. 3.

75. Ibid., p. 1.

76. Commercial Club of Chicago, *Yearbook, 1910–1911*, pp. 16–17.

77. Ibid., p. 17.

78. Ibid., p. 18.

79. Georg Kerchensteiner, *Education for Citizenship*, trans. A. J. Pressland (Chicago: Rand-McNally [under auspices of Commercial Club], 1911), pp. 23–24.

80. Robinson, "Need of Vocational Education," p. 10.

81. Kerchensteiner, *Education*, pp. 23–24.

82. Ibid., p. 55.

83. Ibid., p. 24.

84. Cooley, "Education in Morals," p. 6; Kerchensteiner, *Education*, pp. 98–99.

85. "Dr. Kerchensteiner Praises American Educational System,"*National Association of Corporation Schools Bulletin* 1 (August 1914):3–4.

86. Commercial Club, *Yearbook, 1912–1913*, p. 22.

87. H. E. Miles, "What I am Trying to Do," *World's Work* 26 (October 1913):667.

88. Ibid., pp. 669, 672.

89. Kerchensteiner, *Education*, p. 127; Miles, "What I am Trying to Do," pp. 671–672.

90. H. E. Miles, "How Shall the Obligation to Provide Industrial Education be Met: The Obligation of the Employer," *Proceedings of the Fifth Annual Meeting of the National Society for the Promotion of Industrial Education*, Bulletin no. 15, 1911, p. 33.

91. Commercial Club of Chicago, *Yearbook, 1914–1915*, p. 275.

92. Ibid., p. 278.

93. Ibid., p. 274.

94. Cooley, "Need for Vocational Schools," p. 6.

95. Miles, "Obligation," p. 33.

96. Chicago Federation of Labor, Minutes of Meeting of June 15, 1913, pp. 7–8. John Fitzpatrick Papers, Chicago Historical Society.

97. ISFL, "Report of the Committee on Vocational Education of the Illinois State Federation of Labor," *Thirty-Second Annual Proceedings* (1914), p. 46.

98. Ibid.

99. Ibid., p. 47.

100. Ibid.

101. See, for example: Harry Braverman, *Labor and Monopoly Capital: The Degradation of Work in the Twentieth Century* (New York: Monthly Review Press, 1974); Stanley Aronowitz, *False Promises: The Shaping of Working-Class Consciousness* (New York: McGraw-Hill, 1973); David F. Noble, *America by Design: Science, Technology and the Rise of Corporate Capitalism* (New York: Knopf, 1977).

102. ISFL, "Vocational Education," p. 49; Chicago Federation of Labor, Minutes of Meeting of June 15, 1913, pp. 7–8. John Fitzpatrick Papers, Chicago Historical Society.

103. ISFL, "Vocational Education," p. 49.

104. *New Majority*, October 27, 1923, p. 1.

105. Ibid., December 29, 1923, p. 4.

106. ISFL, "Vocational Education," pp. 52, 53.

107. John Walker, "President's Report; Cooley Measure," *Thirty-Third Annual Proceedings of the Illinois State Federation of Labor* (1915):73.

108. Ibid.

109. *City Club Bulletin* 1 (April 24, 1907):121.

110. City Club of Chicago, *Report on Vocational Training*.

111. Beck, "Newspapers and Schools," p. 280.

112. Frank M. Leavitt, "Needed Laws for Vocational Plan," *Chicago Tribune*, December 22, 1912, p. 6.

113. George H. Mead, "Gives Plan for Trade Schools; Prof. G. H. Mead Compares City Club Scheme with the Cooley Measure," *Chicago Tribune*, December 16, 1912, p. 4.

114. "A Report of the Public Education Committee of the City Club of Chicago," *City Club Bulletin* 5 (December 4, 1912):374.

115. Ibid., p. 375.

116. Ibid., p. 376.

117. Charles H. Judd, "Argues against Dual School Plan," *Chicago Tribune*, December 21, 1912, p. 6.

118. Ella Adams Moore, "Trade Training Need Emphasized," *Chicago Tribune*, December 25, 1912, p. 8.

119. John Dewey, "Some Dangers in the Present Movement for Industrial Education," *Child Labor Bulletin* 1 (February 1913): 69–74, and "Splitting up the School System."

120. Edwin G. Cooley, *In Reply to Dr. John Dewey's 'Some Dangers in the Present Movement for Industrial Education'* (pamphlet probably printed by Commercial Club, n.d. [(1913)]), Chicago Historical Society.

121. Commercial Club of Chicago, *Yearbook, 1913–1914*, p. 16.

122. Ibid., pp. 16–17.

123. Commercial Club of Chicago, *Yearbook, 1914–1915*, p. 252.

124. Ibid., p. 254.

125. Ibid., p. 255.

126. Walker, "President's Report," pp. 72–74.

127. ISFL, *Weekly Newsletter*, May 8, 1915.

128. Commercial Club of Chicago, *Yearbook, 1918–1919*, pp. 364–365.

129. CTF, Stenographic "Report of Special Meeting of the CTF" (minutes of the Overflow Meeting, Playhouse Theater, Chicago, May 8, 1924), p. 8, Chicago Teachers' Federation Papers, Chicago Historical Society.

130. Commercial Club of Chicago, *Yearbook, 1918–1919*, p. 367.

131. Ibid.

132. Francis G. Blair, "The Smith-Hughes Act in Illinois," *Chicago Schools Journal* 1 (September 1918):8–10.

1. Samuel Haber, *Efficiency and Uplift: Scientific Management in the Progressive Era, 1890–1920* (Chicago: University of Chicago Press, 1964).

2. "The Educational Commission and Its Report," *CTSBJ* 1 (January 1899):19.

3. Robert Louis Reid, "The Professionalization of Public School Teachers: The Chicago Experience, 1895–1920" (Ph.D. diss., Northwestern University, 1968), p. 46.

4. "Educational Commission," p. 20.

5. Educational Commission of the City of Chicago, *Report of the . . . Appointed by the Mayor, Hon. Carter H. Harrison. William R. Harper, Chairman* (Chicago: R. R. Donnelly, 1899), p. xiii.

6. Ibid., pp. xiii–xiv.

7. Ibid., p. xiii.

8. James J. Storrow, "Remarks of Mr. James J. Storrow, of Boston, Mass., Before the Merchants' Club of Chicago, Saturday, December 8th, at the Auditorium," in Merchants' Club, *Public Schools and Their Administration* (Chicago: Merchants' Club, 1906), p. 35.

9. David B. Tyack, *The One Best System: A History of American Urban Education* (Cambridge: Harvard University Press, 1974), p. 127.

10. Horace S. Tarbell, quoted in "Educational Commission," footnote 19, pp. 41–42.

11. Samuel P. Hays, "The Politics of Reform in Municipal Government in the Progressive Era," *Pacific Northwest Quarterly* 55 (October 1964):157–169.

12. Educational Commission, *Report*, p. xiv.

13. "Chicago Schools: February Meetings of the Chicago Teachers' Associations," *CTSBJ* 1 (March 1899):138–139.

14. "Editorial: The Chicago Teachers' Federation," *CTSBJ* 1 (May 1899):254.

15. Catharine Goggin, "The Report of the Educational Commission," *CTSBJ* 1 (February 1899):85.

16. Educational Commission, *Report*, p. 60.

17. "Chicago Schools," p. 140.

18. Educational Commission, *Report*, p. xiv.

19. "City Items," *CTSBJ* 1 (February 1899), pp. 87–88.

20. Educational Commission, *Report*, pp. 60, 78–80.

21. Ibid., p. xv.

22. Ibid., p. 174.

23. Ibid., p. 177.

24. Ibid., p. 178.

25. Reid, "Professionalization," p. 57.

26. Margaret A. Haley, "Autobiography" (Seattle, Wash., December 29, 1911–February 13, 1912), p. 216, Chicago Teachers' Federation Papers, Chicago Historical Society (typescript).

27. Ibid., p. 265.

28. Edwin G. Cooley to William Rainey Harper, May 31, 1901, Presidents' Papers, Special Collections, University of Chicago Library; William Rainey Harper to E. Benjamin Andrews, July 22, 1898, December 15, 1898, and December 19, 1898, all in Presidents' Papers, Special Collections, University of Chicago Library.

29. *American Socialist*, September 11, 1915, p. 2.

30. "Mayor Harrison's Attitude toward the Educational Commission Bill," *CTSBJ* 1 (February 1899):107–108.

31. Chester C. Dodge, *Reminiscences of a Schoolmaster* (Chicago: Ralph Fletcher Seymour, 1941), p. 71.

32. William Rainey Harper to E. Benjamin Andrews, June 16, 1898, Presidents' Papers, Special Collections, University of Chicago Library.

33. "Chicago Schools"; "School Board Department: Superintendent Andrews on the Proposed Changes in School Board Organization," *CTSBJ* 1 (May 1899): 244–245; "Chicago Schools: Superintendent Andrews and the Teachers," *CTSBJ* 1 (March 1899):149.

34. E. Benjamin Andrews, "Practical Topics Connected with the Principalship" (address delivered before the meeting of the Chicago Principals, October 8, 1898).

35. Ibid.

36. Charles D. Lowry, "Genesis of a School System" (paper read before the Chicago Literary Club, February 28, 1944), Newberry Library.

37. "Chicago Schools: Superintendent Andrews and the Chicago School Board," *CTSBJ* 1 (January 1899):27.

38. Dodge, *Reminiscences*, p. 72.

39. "Mrs. Young's Resignation," *CTSBJ* 1 (June 1899):306.

40. E. Benjamin Andrews, *The Public School System as an Instrumentality in Social Advance* (address delivered before the Chicago and Cook County High School Association, 1895), p. 7.

41. Ibid., pp. 13–14.

42. Harper to Andrews, July 22, 1898, and December 15, 1898.

43. E. Benjamin Andrews to William Rainey Harper, December 16, 1898, Presidents' Papers, Special Collections, University of Chicago Library.

44. E. Benjamin Andrews to William Rainey Harper, n.d. (1898?), Presidents' Papers, Special Collections, University of Chicago Library.

45. Tyack, *One Best System*, p. 169.

46. Daniel Levine, *Varieties of Reform Thought* (Madison, Wis.: State Historical Society of Wisconsin, 1964), p. 57; Ralph Easley, *The Work of the Civic Federation* (report of the Secretary read at the fifth annual meeting of the Civic Federation of Chicago, April 26, 1899), pp. 14–15, Chicago Historical Society.

47. Tyack, *One Best System*, pp. 169, 175.

48. Andrew S. Draper, *Common School Problems of Chicago* (address delivered at a citizens' meeting under the auspices of the Education Commission of One Hundred of the Civic Federation of Chicago, December 1, 1900), p. 30.

49. Reid, "Professionalization," pp. 85–86.

50. Ibid.

51. Margaret A. Haley, "Comments on New Educational Bill," *CTF Bulletin* 2 (January 16, 1903):1; "Comments on New Educational Bill [continued from last issue]," *CTF Bulletin* 2 (January 23, 1903):1; "The New Educational Bills: Further Comments," *CTF Bulletin* 2 (January 30, 1903):1.

52. Louis F. Post, "Comments on New Educational Bill," *CTF Bulletin* 2 (February 6, 1903):2.

53. Ibid., p. 1.

54. Truman C. Bigham, "The Chicago Federation of Labor" (M.A. thesis, University of Chicago, 1925), pp. 107–108.

55. CTF, *Report, Showing Results of Fifteen Years of Organization, to the Teachers of Chicago*, 1908, pp. 6, 16, Chicago Teachers' Federation Papers, Chicago Historical Society.

56. Charles E. Merriam, "Home Rule Features of the New City Charter," *City Club Bulletin* 1 (June 19, 1907):148; Charles E. Merriam, "The Charter Situation: What Next?," *City Club Bulletin* 1 (October 23, 1907):212.

57. Harold L. Ickes, "Political Features of the Proposed City Charter," *City Club Bulletin* 1 (July 10, 1907):167–172.

58. Theodore W. Robinson, "Remarks of Theodore W. Robinson, Chairman Public School Committee, Before the Merchants' Club, on Saturday, December 8th, at the Auditorium," in Merchants' Club, *Public Schools and Their Administration* (Chicago: Merchants' Club, 1906), p. 6.

59. Nicholas Murray Butler, "Remarks of Dr. Butler, President of Columbia University, Before the Merchants' Club on Saturday, December 8th, at the Auditorium," in Merchants' Club, *Public Schools and Their Administration* (Chicago: Merchants' Club, 1906), p. 45.

60. Ibid., pp. 50, 40.

61. Reid, "Professionalization," pp. 137–138.

62. *Chicago Record-Herald*, July 22, 1907, p. 3.

63. "Resolutions Adopted by Chicago Federation of Labor at Mass Meeting on School Situation, December 2, 1906," *CTF Bulletin* 6 (December 7, 1906):1.

64. *Chicago Record-Herald*, July 22, 1907, p. 3.

65. "Ways and Means Session: Association's Largest Committee Hears Discussion Enlightening on Functions and Merits of Charter," *CAC Bulletin* 3 (August 23, 1907):2–3.

66. Ibid., p. 1.

67. Merriam, "Home Rule," pp. 148–152.

68. Ickes, "Proposed City Charter," p. 172.

69. Raymond Robins, "The Charter Situation: What Next?," *City Club Bulletin* 1 (October 23, 1907):217.

70. Nicholas Michels, "The Charter Situation: What Next?," *City Club Bulletin* 1 (October 23, 1907):215.

71. Ibid., p. 216.

72. Merriam, "The Charter Situation," p. 212.

73. Reid, "Professionalization," pp. 138–139.

74. Truman A. DeWeese, "Two Years' Progress in the Chicago Public Schools," *Educational Review* 24 (November 1902):325.

75. Dodge, *Reminiscences*, p. 72; Lowry, "Genesis of a School System," p. 3.

76. DeWeese, "Two Years' Progress"; Dodge, *Reminiscences*, pp. 73–75; Lowry, "Genesis of a School System," p. 11.

77. Lowry, "Genesis of a School System," p. 10; DeWeese, "Two Years' Progress," p. 336.

78. DeWeese, "Two Years' Progress," pp. 326–328.

79. Forrest Crissey, *The Making of an American School-Teacher* (Chicago: C. M. Barnes, 1906), p. 50; Lowry, "Genesis of a School System," pp. 6–7.

80. DeWeese, "Two Years' Progress," p. 328.

81. Lowry, "Genesis of a School System," p. 6.

82. DeWeese, "Two Years' Progress," p. 328.

83. Mary J. Herrick, *The Chicago Schools: A Social and Political History* (Beverly Hills, Calif: Sage Publications, 1971), pp. 109–110.

84. Cited in Lowry, "Genesis of a School System," p. 8.

85. Crissey, *Making of [a] School-Teacher*, p. 61; CTF, *Fifteen Years of Organization*; George Herbert Mead, "The Educational Situation in the Chicago Public Schools," *City Club Bulletin* 1 (May 8, 1907):134.

86. Lowry, "Genesis of a School System," p. 13.

87. Herrick, *Chicago Schools*, p. 110; William R. Chenery, "Adulterated Education," *New Republic* 4 (October 23, 1915):304–306.

88. Haley, "Autobiography," p. 145.

89. Ibid., p. 8; see also: "Worth While Opinions on Teachers in Labor Unions: Jane Addams on Teachers Affiliating with Federation of Labor, November 8, 1902," *Margaret A. Haley's Bulletin* 1 (October 21, 1915):10.

90. Haley, "Autobiography," p. 183.

91. Ibid., pp. 165–166.

92. Jane Addams, *Twenty Years at Hull-House* (New York: Macmillan, 1910), p. 335.

93. Ibid., p. 335.

94. Ibid., p. 333.

95. Ibid., p. 335.

96. Ibid., p. 329.

97. Ibid., pp. 330–331.

98. Ibid., p. 335.

99. Ibid., p. 336.

100. Herrick, *Chicago Schools*, p. 110.

101. Haley, "Autobiography," pp. 181, 183.

102. CBE, *Special Report on the Promotional Examination and Secret Marketing of Teachers* (report of the Sub-Committee of the School Management Committee of the Board of Education, 1906), p. 20.

103. Herrick, *Chicago Schools*, p. 110; Haley, "Autobiography," p. 221.

104. Lowry, "Genesis of a School System," p. 13.

105. Addams, *Twenty Years*, p. 337.

106. Lowry, "Genesis of a School System," p. 14.

107. "A Business Administration," *CAC Bulletin* 2 (April 26, 1907):10.

108. Herrick, *Chicago Schools*, p. 111.

109. Addams, *Twenty Years*, p. 336.

110. Lowry, "Genesis of a School System," p. 15.

111. Haley, "Autobiography," p. 240.

112. Rosemary V. Donatelli, "The Contributions of Ella Flagg Young

to the Educational Enterprise" (Ph.D. diss., University of Chicago, 1971), pp. 279–280.

113. *Chicago Tribune*, June 17, 1909, p. 1.

114. Herrick, *Chicago Schools*, p. 111.

115. "Tribute to Mrs. Young," *Chicago Schools Journal* 4 (December 1921): 121.

116. "Ella Flagg Young [Editorial]," *Chicago Schools Journal* 1 (October 1918):4–5.

117. "City Items," pp. 87–88.

118. Joan K. Smith, *Ella Flagg Young: Portrait of a Leader* (Ames, Iowa: Educational Studies Press and the Iowa State University Research Foundation, 1979), p. 123.

119. Ella Flagg Young, *Isolation in the School*, Contributions to Education, no. 1 (Chicago: University of Chicago Press, 1901).

120. Cited in John T. McManis, *Ella Flagg Young and a Half-Century of the Chicago Public Schools* (Chicago: McClurg, 1916), pp. 120–121.

121. "Ella Flagg Young," pp. 4–5.

122. "Mrs. Young's Resignation," pp. 305–306.

123. E. B. Andrews to Rainey, n.d.

124. McManis, *Ella Flagg Young*, p. 96.

125. "Ella Flagg Young," pp. 4–5.

126. Donatelli, "Ella Flagg Young," pp. 284–285.

127. Ibid., pp. 285–288.

128. Ella Flagg Young, "The Educational Progress of Two Years," *Addresses and Proceedings of the National Education Association* 45 (1907):383.

129. Elementary Teachers' General Council, *Report* No. 12, pp. 195–196, University of Chicago Library.

130. Cited in McManis, *Ella Flagg Young*, p. 158.

131. Elementary Teachers' General Council, *Report* No. 12, p. 196.

132. CTF, Stenographic "Report of Special Meeting of the CTF" (minutes of the Overflow Meeting, Playhouse Theater, Chicago, May 8, 1924), p. 18, Chicago Teachers' Federation Papers, Chicago Historical Society.

133. McManis, *Ella Flagg Young*, p. 163.

134. Donatelli, "Ella Flagg Young," p. 359–360; Smith, *Ella Flagg Young*, p. 214.

135. "Report of the Committee on Vocational Education of the Illinois State Federation of Labor," *Thirty-Second Annual Proceedings of the Illinois State Federation of Labor* (1914):45–54.

136. Cited in John M. Beck, "Chicago Newspapers and the Public Schools, 1890–1920" (Ph.D. diss., University of Chicago, 1953), p. 289.

137. Smith, *Ella Flagg Young*, p. 186.

138. CTF, *Fifteen Years of Organization*, p. 3.

139. Smith, *Ella Flagg Young*, p. 188.

140. Ibid., p. 193.

141. Ibid., p. 188.

142. Margaret A. Haley, "Forty Fighting Years," 1935, p. 524, Chicago Teachers' Federation Papers, Chicago Historical Society (typescript).

143. Jacob Loeb, "The Business Man and the Public Service," *Addresses and Proceedings of the National Education Association* 54 (1916): 351–355.

144. Ella Flagg Young, "A Reply [to Jacob Loeb]," *Addresses and Proceedings of the National Education Association* 54 (1916):357–358, 359.

145. Smith, *Ella Flagg Young*, p. 187.

146. Ibid., p. 201; Margaret A. Haley to Mayor William E. Dever, in "City Council Takes No Action on Appointees to School Board," *Margaret Haley's Bulletin*, December 31, 1926, p. 139.

147. Haley, "City Council Takes No Action," p. 139.

148. Smith, *Ella Flagg Young*, p. 196.

149. Ibid., p. 198.

150. Ibid., p. 202.

151. Ibid., pp. 205–206.

152. "Ella Flagg Young," pp. 4–5.

153. McManis, *Ella Flagg Young*, p. 168.

154. "Anti-Organization Rule Adopted Sept. 1, 1915, and Pledge," *Margaret A. Haley's Bulletin*, September 23, 1915, p. 2.

155. *Chicago Herald*, September 2, 1915, as cited in *Margaret A. Haley's Bulletin*, September 23, 1915, p. 4.

156. CFL, "Verbatim Report of a Meeting Held under the Auspices of the Chicago Federation of Labor, as a public protest against the action taken on September 1, by the Board of Education of Chicago, in adopting the rule which compels the teachers to relinquish their membership in said Federation, or suffer discharge from their positions," September 8, 1915, Chicago Teachers' Federation Papers, Chicago Historical Society.

157. Herrick, *Chicago Schools*, p. 123.

158. *American Socialist*, September 11, 1915, p. 1.

159. "A Critical Situation," *Margaret A. Haley's Bulletin*, October 21, 1915, p. 7 [reprinted from *American Teacher*].

160. E. N. Nockels to Alderman Robert M. Buck, October 1, 1915, Robert M. Buck Papers, Chicago Historical Society; also see Chicago Federation of Labor, Minutes of Meeting of September 5, 1915, pp. 6–11 and the Minutes of the Meeting of October 17, 1915, p. 7. John Fitzpatrick Papers, Chicago Historical Society.

161. International Brotherhood of Teamsters and Chauffeurs Joint Council Number 25, Leaflet signed by T. F. Neary, secretary (resolution on Loeb Rule adopted at September 14, 1915, Joint Council Meeting), Robert M. Buck Papers, Chicago Historical Society.

162. ISFL, "Report of the Committee on Schools," *Thirty-Fourth Annual Proceedings of the Illinois State Federation of Labor*, October 16, 1916, pp. 4–5.

163. "Adoption of the Anti-Organization Rule," *Margaret A. Haley's Bulletin*, September 23, 1915, p. 4.

164. Chenery, "Adulterated Education."

165. Herrick, *Chicago Schools*, p. 121.

166. Samuel M. Hastings to Mayor William Hale Thompson, September 9, 1915, Chicago Teachers' Federation Papers, Chicago Historical Society.

167. Victor A. Olander to Secretaries, Local Unions and Central Bodies, State of Illinois, reprinted in *Margaret A. Haley's Bulletin*, October 21, 1915, p. 9.

168. *Chicago Tribune*, October 4, 1915.

169. *Chicago Herald*, October 5, 1915.

170. Jacob Loeb, "Statement to Newspapers . . . in Re. Chicago Teachers' Federation," April 10, 1916, p. 4, Chicago Teachers' Federation Papers, Chicago Historical Society.

171. Ibid.

172. Dodge, *Reminiscences*, p. 38.

173. "The Business Man in Office," *New Republic* 7 (July 15, 1916): 267.

174. Mary E. McDowell to board of education, with attachment, June 12, 1916, Chicago Teachers' Federation Papers, Chicago Historical Society; George Herbert Mead to board of education in behalf of the City Club of Chicago, June 13, 1916, Chicago Teachers' Federation Papers, Chicago Historical Society.

175. CTF, Stenographic "Report of a Public Demonstration Held at the Auditorium on Saturday, June 17, 1916, called to remonstrate against the action of the Board of Education in passing the rule providing for the re-election of teachers every year," Chicago Teachers' Federation Papers, Chicago Historical Society.

176. Reid, "Professionalization," p. 183.

177. Alfred H. Kelly, "A History of the Illinois Manufacturers' Association" (Ph.D. diss., University of Chicago, 1938), p. 21.

178. Ibid.

179. Herrick, *Chicago Schools*, p. 126.

180. Reid, "Professionalization," p. 185.

181. Carl Scholz to Harry Judson, November 20, 1916, Presidents' Papers, Special Collections, University of Chicago Library.

182. Harry Judson to Carl Scholz, March 1, 1917, Presidents' Papers, Special Collections, University of Chicago Library; Carl Scholz to Harry Judson, March 3, 1917, Presidents' Papers, Special Collections, University of Chicago Library.

183. "Otis Law Has Never Had a Fair Trial, Says Shannon," *City Club Bulletin* 21 (February 27, 1928):1.

184. Public Education Association of Chicago, Bulletin No. 1, n.d., p. 4.

185. Ibid., p. 6.

186. Public Education Association of Chicago, Bulletin No. 3, March 9, 1916, p. 5.

187. Ibid., p. 7.

188. Herrick, *Chicago Schools*, p. 135.

189. Dodge, *Reminiscences*, p. 86.

190. Reid, "Professionalization," p. 191.

191. For a comparison of the three bills, see Public Education Association of Chicago, Bulletin No. 2, March 3, 1917 [1916].

192. Reid, "Professionalization," p. 194.

193. *Chicago Tribune*, May 23, 1917, pp. 1–2.

194. Reid, "Professionalization," p. 196; for statement of Loeb's views on how businessmen should control government, see Loeb, "The Businessman and Public Service," *Addresses and Proceedings of the National Education Association* 54 (1916):351–355.

195. "Report of Commission on Superintendent," *Chicago Schools Journal* 1 (March 1919):22.

196. John L. Lovett to Julius Rosenwald, April 27, 1917, Julius Rosenwald Papers, Special Collections, University of Chicago Library.

197. *Chicago Tribune*, May 23, 1917, p. 2.

198. James Minnick to W. C. Graves, May 23, 1917, Julius Rosenwald Papers, Special Collections, University of Chicago Library.

199. Ibid.

200. Charles E. Merriam, *Chicago: A More Intimate View of Urban Politics* (New York: Macmillan, 1929), p. 194.

201. Douglas Sutherland, *Fifty Years on the Civic Front* (Chicago: Civic Federation of Chicago, 1943), p. 35.

202. Wallace Heckman to Julius Rosenwald, February 3, 1925, Julius Rosenwald Papers, Special Collections, University of Chicago Library.

203. Herrick, *Chicago Schools*, p. 139.

204. Lillian Herstein, Interview conducted by Elizabeth Balanoff, October 26, 1970, transcript in Roosevelt University Oral History Project, p. 86, Roosevelt University Library, Chicago.

205. Haley, "City Council Takes No Action," p. 126.

206. Herrick, *Chicago Schools*, p. 135.

207. Herstein, interview transcript, p. 86.

208. Agnes B. Closehy, "The Province of the Labor Union in the Schools," *Joint Bulletin of Chicago Federation of Men Teachers, Federation of Women High School Teachers, Elementary Teachers Union*, October 1928, p. 10.

209. CTF, Stenographic "Report of Minutes of the Regular Meeting of the CTF" (held in Corinthian Hall, the Capitol Building, Chicago, January 12, 1924) pp. 139–145, Chicago Teachers' Federation Papers, Chicago Historical Society.

210. CTF, Stenographic "Report of the Silver Jubilee Luncheon: Given by the CTF in honor of the 25th Anniversary of its entry into the now-historic tax campaign on Janury 20, 1900 by Miss Catharine Goggin and Margaret A. Haley" (held at the Morrison Hotel, Chicago, January 12, 1924), pp. 139–145, Chicago Teachers' Federation Papers, cago Historical Society; Stenographic "Report of Special Meeting of the Chicago Teachers' Federation" (held at the Studebaker Theater, Chicago, September 11, 1925), p. 35, Chicago Teachers' Federation Papers, Chicago Historical Society.

211. CTF, Stenographic "Report of Special Meeting of the CTF" (held at Commandery Hall, Capitol Building, Chicago, February 18, 1927), pp. 40–41, Chicago Teachers' Federation Papers, Chicago Historical Society; see also CTF, "Report on Meeting held on September 11, 1925."

212. Mead, "Educational Situation in Chicago," p. 135.

1. Mary J. Herrick, *The Chicago Schools: A Social and Political History* (Beverly Hills, Calif.: Sage Publications, 1971), p. 142.

2. Municipal Voters' League, *Twenty-Seventh Annual Report* (Chicago, 1923), p. 9.

3. Herrick, *Chicago Schools*, p. 142.

4. William McAndrew to Charles H. Judd, April 12, 1927, C. H. Judd Papers, Special Collections, University of Chicago Library.

5. *New York Times*, June 29, 1937, p. 21.

6. McAndrew to Judd, April 12, 1927.

7. Ibid., William McAndrew to Charles H. Judd, January 29, 1930, C. H. Judd Papers, Special Collections, University of Chicago Library.

8. William McAndrew, "The Principal," *Chicago Schools Journal* 7 (November 1924):81–85.

9. William McAndrew, "What Public Schools are For," *Woman's City Club Bulletin* 15 (February 1926):197–200.

10. McAndrew to Judd, January 29, 1930.

11. George S. Counts, *School and Society in Chicago* (New York: Harcourt, Brace, 1928), pp. 71–72.

12. Wallace Heckman to Julius Rosenwald, February 3, 1925, Rosenwald Papers, Special Collections, University of Chicago Library.

13. Margaret A. Haley, "Autobiography" (Seattle, Wash., December 29, 1911–February 13, 1912), p. 220, Chicago Teachers' Federation Papers, Chicago Historical Society (typescript).

14. Counts, *School and Society*, p. 70.

15. McAndrew to Judd, April 12, 1927.

16. Ibid.

17. CBE, *Annual Report of the Superintendent of Schools* (Chicago: Department of Education, 1926), pp. 55–56, 81.

18. Counts, *School and Society*, p. 81.

19. See, for example: Samuel Bowles and Herbert Gintis, *Schooling in Capitalist America: Educational Reform and the Contradictions of Economic Life* (New York: Basic Books, 1976); Joel H. Spring, *Education and the Rise of the Corporate State* (Boston, Beacon Press, 1972); David B. Tyack, *The One Best System: A History of American Urban Education* (Cambridge, Harvard University Press, 1974).

20. McAndrew, "The Principal," CBE, *Annual Report* (1926), pp. 16–17.

21. Abraham Flexner and Frank P. Bachman, *The Gary Schools: A General Account* (New York: General Education Board, 1918).

22. John Dewey and Evelyn Dewey, *Schools of Tomorrow* (New York: Dutton, 1962 [first ed. 1915]).

23. Randolph S. Bourne, *The Gary Schools* (Boston: Houghton Mifflin, 1916).

24. Flexner and Bachman, *Gary Schools*; Bourne, *Gary Schools*; George D. Strayer and Frank P. Bachman, *The Gary Public Schools: Organization and Administration* (New York: General Education Board, 1918).

25. *Weekly News Letter*, July 26, 1924, pp. 2–3. Victor A. Olander, "'Work' in Work-Study-Play Plan is Discussed at Convention; Victor Olander in Address before A. F. of L. Seeks Platoonists' Meaning," *Margaret Haley's Bulletin*, November 16, 1925, p. 83; "Victor Olander Discusses Two Educational Questions; Platoon and Junior High Schools considered in Second Installment of Address," *Margaret Haley's Bulletin*, November 30, 1925, p. 103; Victor A. Olander, "Intelligence Tests Akin to Hindu Caste System, Says Olander: Chicago Speaker Tells Labor Convention of Dangers," *Margaret Haley's Bulletin*, December 16, 1925, p. 123.

26. Olander, "'Work'," "Two Educational Questions," and "Intelligence Tests"; CTF, Stenographic "Report of Minutes of the Regular

Meeting of the CTF" (held in Corinthian Hall, the Capitol Building, Chicago, January 12, 1924), p. 52, Chicago Teachers' Federation Papers, Chicago Historical Society. For text of CFL resolution criticizing platoon schools, see: "Labor Protests Confirmation of Dr. Schmidt and Mrs. Hefferan," *Margaret Haley's Bulletin*, January 17, 1927, pp. 151–152.

27. Flexner and Bachman, *Gary Schools*, p. 43.

28. Elementary Teachers' General Council, *Report* No. 11 (March 1924), p. 159.

29. Ibid., p. 160.

30. Ibid., p. 157.

31. Elementary Teachers' General Council, "Supplement to Report No. 12," (September 1924), p. 216.

32. See Victor A. Olander's comments, CTF, Stenographic "Report of Minutes of Special Meeting of the CTF" (minutes of the overflow meeting, Playhouse Theater, Chicago, May 8, 1924), p. 19, Chicago Teachers' Federation Papers, Chicago Historical Society.

33. Haley, "Autobiography," p. 220.

34. Elementary Teachers' General Council, *Report* No. 13 (May 1925), p. 296.

35. Ibid., p. 288.

36. Reprinted in ibid., p. vi.

37. James Mullenbach, "Councils Furnished Intelligent Contact between Teachers and Administration," *Margaret Haley's Bulletin*, April 15, 1927, pp. 227–228.

38. Peter A. Mortenson, "Report of the Superintendent of Schools," *Chicago Schools Journal* 5 (October 1922):62.

39. Elementary Teachers' General Council, *Report* No. 13 (May 1925), p. 287.

40. Ibid.

41. Sol Cohen, *Progressives and Urban School Reform: The Public Education Association of New York City, 1895–1954* (New York: Teachers College Press, 1963), p. 224.

42. CBE, "Proposal to Establish Junior High Schools in the City of Chicago" (report by the Educational Commission appointed by the board of education, December 12, 1923), Chicago Historical Society; Joseph F. Gonnelly, "Development of the Junior High School in Chicago," *Chicago Schools Journal* 12 (October 1929):46–51.

43. "Labor Protests," pp. 151–152; "Organized Labor Assails Mayor's Nominees; John Fitzpatrick tells Schools' Committee of Labor's Treatment by Mrs. Hefferan," *Margaret Haley's Bulletin*, February 15, 1927, p. 165.

44. CBE, "Proposal to Establish Junior High Schools," p. 8.

45. Ibid, p. 11.

46. *New Majority*, May 31, 1924, p. 1.

47. Ibid.

48. See McAndrew's comments as reported in Elementary Teachers' General Council, *Report* No. 11, p. 160.

49. Elementary Teachers' General Council, "Supplement," pp. 237–239.

50. See Victor A. Olander to Reuben S. Ebert, February 12, 1926, Victor Olander Papers, Chicago Historical Society, for an example of die-hard opposition to the junior high schools. For an illustration of the slowly changing labor attitudes toward the schools, see William T. McCoy, "Giving the Junior High a Chance" (transcript of radio talk), *Joint Bulletin of Chicago Federation of Men Teachers, Federation of Women High School Teachers, Elementary Teachers Union* 14 (October 1928):14–15.

51. *New Majority*, April 26, 1924, p. 4.

52. Elementary Teachers' General Council, *Report* No. 2 (December 1921), pp. 2–3.

53. See, for example, Denton L. Geyer, "Can We Depend upon the Results of Group Intelligence Tests?," *Chicago Schools Journal* 4 (February 1922):203–210; Arthur O. Rape, "What Mental Tests Mean to the Class-Room Teacher," *Chicago Schools Journal* 7 (September 1924): 18–19; E. E. Keener, "Homogeneous Classification of Junior High School Pupils," *Chicago Schools Journal* 9 (October 1926):51–54.

54. *New Majority*, April 26, 1924, p. 4.

55. *Weekly News Letter*, July 26, 1924, p. 1.

56. *New Majority*, December 29, 1923, p. 4.

57. *New Majority*, October 21, 1922, p. 4.

58. Ibid.

59. *Federation News*, October 11, 1924, p. 1.

60. Ibid.

61. *New Majority*, July 1, 1922, p. 4.

62. *Weekly News Letter*, July 26, 1924, p. 1.

63. CTF, "Report of Meeting of January 12, 1924," p. 63.

64. Counts, *School and Society*, p. 200.

65. Herrick, *Chicago Schools*, p. 153.

66. William McAndrew to William Bogan, February 25, 1926 (copy sent to Charles H. Judd), C. H. Judd Papers, Special Collections, University of Chicago Library.

67. Chicago Principals' Club, *The Chicago Public Schools: How They Teach Healthful Living and Help the Physically Handicapped* (Chicago: Row, Peterson, 1925).

68. McAndrew, "The Principal," pp. 83–84; Herrick, *Chicago Schools*, p. 156.

69. William McAndrew, "Speaking of This and That: Democracy,

Appearances, Personalities, Professional Pride, Being Respectable," *Chicago Schools Journal* 8 (September 1925):4.

70. *Chicago Daily Journal*, April 18, 1927, reprinted in "Superintendent Lets the Cat out of the Bag; From the News Columns," *Margaret Haley's Bulletin*, May 15, 1927, pp. 246, 255.

71. Margaret A. Haley, "What's Wrong in our Schools; Veteran Teacher Gives Views," *Chicago Daily News*, January 7, 1928.

72. "Association of Commerce Representatives Visit Schools: Superintendent of Schools Extends Invitation," *Margaret Haley's Weekly Bulletin*, June 25, 1925, p. 74.

73. CBE, *Annual Report* (1926), p. 29.

74. William McAndrew, "Speaking of This and That," *Chicago Schools Journal* 8 (December 1925):121–124; "Arithmetic Outside and Inside," *Chicago Schools Journal* 9 (October 1926):41–44.

75. McAndrew, "The Principal," p. 83.

76. "McAndrew's Regime was what Sherman Called War," *Margaret Haley's Bulletin*, December 15, 1927, pp. 82–83.

77. William McAndrew to Charles H. Judd, May 20, 1926, C. H. Judd Papers, Special Collections, University of Chicago Library.

78. CBE, *Citizens' Sampling Day: Chicago Public Schools* (held at Fullerton Hall Art Institute, Chicago, January 23, 1926).

79. William McAndrew to John Fitzpatrick, printed in the *Federation News*, June 12, 1926, p. 1.

80. *Federation News*, June 12, 1926, p. 1.

81. Ibid.

82. CTF, Stenographic "Report of Regular Meeting of the CTF" (held at Corinthian Hall, Chicago, June 12, 1926), pp. 32–33, Chicago Teachers' Federation Papers, Chicago Historical Society.

83. Counts, *School and Society*, p. 227.

84. Robert Louis Reid, "The Professionalization of Public School Teachers: The Chicago Experience, 1895–1920" (Ph.D. diss., Northwestern University, 1968), pp. 82–83.

85. Herrick, *Chicago Schools*, pp. 149–150.

86. Ibid., p. 166.

87. *New Majority*, December 29, 1923, p. 1.

88. Ibid., November 3, 1923, p. 1.

89. Chicago Bureau of Public Efficiency, *Proposed Tax Increase for School Buildings—Vote No* (Chicago, 1923), Chicago Historical Society.

90. *New York Times*, November 4, 1927, p. 23; Counts, *School and Society*, p. 227; for a listing of the organizations involved in the Joint Committee, see Joint Committee on Public School Affairs, *Educational Extension and Community Centers; Recommendation and Report, Based*

on a Survey of 76 Chicago Schools, January 16, 1924, Chicago Historical Society.

91. CTF, Stenographic "Report of a Public Demonstration Held at the Auditorium on Saturday, June 17, 1916, called to remonstrate against the action of the Board of Education in passing the rule providing for the re-election of teachers every year," pp. 19–24, Chicago Teachers' Federation Papers, Chicago Historical Society.

92. Charles H. Judd, "Modern Trends in American Public Education" (transcript of radio talk given December 4, 1925), C. H. Judd Papers, Special Collections, University of Chicago Library, p. 9.

93. Ibid., pp. 12, 13.

94. Margaret A. Haley, "Why Teachers Should Organize," *Addresses and Proceedings of the National Education Association* 43 (1904):150.

95. Ibid., p. 151.

96. "Council Hearings on School Board Nominees. Alderman Oscar F. Nelson," *Margaret Haley's Bulletin*, March 15, 1927, p. 189. Nelson said of Hefferan, "Her ability is what makes her dangerous."

97. McAndrew to Judd, April 12, 1927.

98. "Labor Protests," p. 151.

99. "Organized Labor," pp. 165, 173; on Hefferan's support of McAndrew, see her obituary in the *Chicago Tribune*, December 26, 1941.

100. Elementary Teachers' General Council, *Report* No. 13 (May 1925), p. 297.

101. Margaret A. Haley, "From the Masthead by the Lookout," *Margaret Haley's Bulletin*, November 16, 1925, pp. 84–86.

102. "Labor Protests," pp. 151–152.

103. Harold F. Gosnell, *Machine Politics: Chicago Model*, 2nd ed. (Chicago: University of Chicago Press, 1968); Alex Gottfried, *Boss Cermak of Chicago: A Study of Political Leadership* (Seattle: University of Washington Press, 1962).

104. Gottfried, *Boss Cermak*, pp. 135, 151.

105. *New Majority*, May 17, 1924, p. 1.

106. *Federation News*, October 18, 1924, pp. 6–7.

107. Herrick, *Chicago Schools*, p. 166.

108. Ibid., p. 167; Lloyd Wendt and Herman Kogan, *Big Bill of Chicago* (Indianapolis: Bobbs-Merrill, 1953), p. 257; *Federation News*, April 9, 1927, p. 1.

109. Herrick, *Chicago Schools*, footnote 12, p. 417.

110. John Fitzpatrick, Stenographic "Report of Speech Delivered at Meeting of Chicago Federation Of Men Teachers, Federation of Women High School Teachers, and the Elementary Teachers' Union," March 2, 1928, p. 34, Chicago Teachers' Federation Papers, Chicago Historical Society.

111. Ibid., pp. 35–36, 36.

112. Gottfried, *Boss Cermak*, p. 151.

113. William H. Stuart, *The Twenty Incredible Years* (Chicago: M. A. Donohue, 1935), p. 296.

114. Herrick, *Chicago Schools*, p. 166.

115. *Chicago Daily Journal*, April 18, 1927, reprinted in "Superintendent Lets the Cat out of the Bag."

116. *New York Times*, October 27, 1927, p. 28.

117. Ibid.

118. Ibid., p. 1.

119. Ibid., October 1, 1927, p. 18.

120. McAndrew to Judd, April 12, 1927.

121. Wendt and Kogan, *Big Bill of Chicago*, p. 284.

122. Broome to Charles H. Judd, September 2, 1927, C. H. Judd Papers, Special Collections, University of Chicago Library.

123. Ira T. Chapman to Charles H. Judd, August 31, 1927, C. H. Judd Papers, Special Collections, University of Chicago Library.

124. *New York Times*, October 21, 1927, p. 3.

125. Ibid., November 4, 1927, p. 23.

126. William McAndrew to Charles H. Judd, June 14, 1927, C. H. Judd Papers, Special Collections, University of Chicago Library.

127. M. A. McCherney to Edgar Greenebaum, January 24, 1928, Julius Rosenwald Papers, Special Collections, University of Chicago Library.

128. *New York Times*, June 29, 1937, p. 21.

129. McAndrew to Judd, January 29, 1930.

130. Even sympathetic politicians deplored McAndrew's abrasive style. In an effort to convince McAndrew of the need to be more diplomatic in dealing with teachers and board members, Mayor Dever arranged for him to meet with Charles Merriam. Merriam failed to convince him to change his style, however, as the superintendent scorned such suggestions; he had a job to do and would do it as he saw fit. See Wendt and Kogan, *Big Bill of Chicago*, p. 236.

131. See, for example: Paul C. Violas, "Jane Addams and the New Liberalism," in Clarence J. Karier, Paul Violas, and Joel H. Spring, *Roots of Crisis: American Education in the Twentieth Century* (Chicago: Rand McNally, 1973), pp. 66–83.

132. See, for example: James Weinstein, *The Corporate Ideal in the Liberal State, 1900–1918* (Boston: Beacon Press, 1968).

6 1. Barbara Newell, *Chicago and the Labor Movement: Metropolitan Unionism in the 1930's* (Urbana, Ill.: University of Illinois Press, 1961), p. 32.

2. John Fitzpatrick, Telegram to Allied Printing Trades Council, In-

dianapolis, March 3, 1939, John Fitzpatrick Papers, Chicago Historical Society; John Fitzpatrick to William Green, March 14, 1939, John Fitzpatrick Papers, Chicago Historical Society; John Fitzpatrick, Draft telegram to William Randolph Hearst, March 27, 1939, John Fitzpatrick Papers, Chicago Historical Society; Herbert March, Interview conducted by Elizabeth Balanoff, November 16, 1970, transcript in Roosevelt University Oral History Project, Roosevelt University Library, Chicago.

3. J. David Greenstone, *Labor in American Politics* (New York: Vintage Press, 1970).

4. Ibid., p. 107.

5. Ibid., p. 37; Gene Delon Jones, "The Local Political Significance of New Deal Relief Legislation in Chicago: 1933–1940" (Ph.D. diss., Northwestern University, 1970), pp. 9–10.

6. Alex Gottfried, *Boss Cermak of Chicago: A Study of Political Leadership* (Seattle: University of Washington Press, 1962), p. 345.

7. J. David Greenstone and Paul E. Peterson, *Race and Authority in Urban Politics: Community Participation and the War on Poverty* (New York: Russell Sage, 1973).

8. Jones, "New Deal Relief," p. 10.

9. Harold F. Gosnell, *Machine Politics: Chicago Model*, 2nd ed. (Chicago: University of Chicago Press, 1968), p. 149.

10. Gottfried, *Boss Cermak*, p. 197.

11. Ibid., pp. 53–54.

12. Ibid., p. 166.

13. Gosnell, *Machine Politics*, p. 9; Gottfried, *Boss Cermak*, pp. 197–198.

14. Gosnell, *Machine Politics*, p. 13.

15. Gottfried, *Boss Cermak*, p. 210.

16. Gosnell, *Machine Politics*, p. 13.

17. Gottfried, *Boss Cermak*, p. 210.

18. Ibid., pp. 215–216; Jones, "New Deal Relief," p. 5.

19. *New York Times*, July 24, 1931, p. 1.

20. Gosnell, *Machine Politics*, p. 14.

21. *Federation News*, March 18, 1933, p. 4.

22. Newell, *Chicago and the Labor Movement*, p. 33.

23. Gottfried, *Boss Cermak*, p. 241.

24. Newell, *Chicago and the Labor Movement*, p. 34.

25. Gottfried, *Boss Cermak*, p. 257.

26. Jones, "New Deal Relief," p. 27.

27. Ibid., pp. 17–18.

28. Gottfried, *Boss Cermak*, p. 247.

29. Jones, "New Deal Relief," p. 19.

30. John K. Norton, "Financing the Schools," in George D. Strayer

et al., *Report of the Survey of the Schools of Chicago, Illinois*, vol. 1 (New York: Teachers College Press, 1932), p. 195.

31. "The Kelly-Nash Political Machine," *Fortune* 14 (August 1936): 114.

32. Ibid., p. 126.

33. William H. Stuart, *The Twenty Incredible Years* (Chicago: M. A. Donohue, 1935), p. 473.

34. Mary J. Herrick, *The Chicago Schools: A Social and Political History* (Beverly Hills, Calif.: Sage Publications, 1971), p. 187; "Spasmodic Diary of a Chicago School-Teacher," *Atlantic Monthly* 152 (November 1933):513–526.

35. Gottfried, *Boss Cermak*, p. 210.

36. Stephen D. London, "Business and the Chicago Public School System, 1890–1966" (Ph.D. diss., University of Chicago, 1968), pp. 87–89.

37. Quoted in Penny Joan Lipkin, "Payless Paydays: The Financial Crisis of the Chicago Board of Education, 1930–1934," (M. A. thesis, Columbia University, 1967), pp. 10–11.

38. Herrick, *Chicago Schools*, pp. 199–200.

39. *Chicago Tribune*, March 15, 1932, p. 3.

40. Fred W. Sargent, "The Taxpayer Takes Charge," *Saturday Evening Post*, January 14, 1933, pp. 21, 78.

41. Ibid., p. 21.

42. Ibid., p. 74.

43. Ibid., p. 80.

44. William W. Wattenberg, *On the Educational Front: The Reactions of Teachers' Associations in New York and Chicago* (New York: Columbia University Press, 1936), pp. 33–34.

45. Chicago Principals' Club, Report in letter form on findings of a club committee on investigation of Sargent Committee, approved December 2, 1932, Citizens School Committee Papers, Chicago Historical Society; Charles B. Stillman, "Chicago, a Key Situation," *American Teacher* 17 (October 1932):19.

46. Chicago Principals' Club, Report.

47. London, "Business and the School System," p. 97.

48. See Charles B. Stillman, "Financial Fascism," *American Teacher* 17 (April 1933):10–11; "Spasmodic Diary."

49. Herrick, *Chicago Schools*, p. 199.

50. Cited in "Speaking of Laps," *American Teacher* 17 (February 1933):19.

51. *Chicago Tribune*, July 26, 1932, p. 1.

52. Ibid.

53. Ibid., January 18, 1933, p. 11.

54. Gosnell, *Machine Politics*, pp. 15–16.

55. Ibid., p. 13.

56. Hazlett, "Crisis in School Government," p. 35.

57. Wattenberg, *On the Educational Front*, p. 35.

58. Elizabeth Murray, "The Chicago Board of Education," chapter 3 in Robert J. Havighurst, Robert L. McCaul, Elizabeth L. Murray et al., "Education and Society in Metropolitan Chicago: Studies in the Sociology and History of Urban Educaton" (manuscript, n.d.), p. 6.

59. Hazlett, "Crisis in School Government," p. 54.

60. Murray, "Chicago Board of Education," p. 5.

61. *Chicago Tribune*, May 25, 1933, p. 1.

62. Margaret Campbell Hancock, Interview conducted by Elizabeth Murray, n.d., transcript in possession of Robert J. Havighurst, University of Chicago; *Chicago Tribune*, July 13, 1933, pp. 1–2.

63. Martin Levit, "The Chicago Citizens Schools Committee: A Study of a Pressure Group" (M.A. thesis, University of Chicago, 1947); "The Net Savings of the 'Economy' Program in Chicago Schools," *Chicago's Schools* 1 (October 1934):4; Citizens Save Our Schools Committee, Leaflet dated August 19, 1933, Citizens School Committee Papers, Chicago Historical Society; *Chicago Tribune*, July 13, 1933, p. 2.

64. *Chicago Tribune*, July 13, 1933, p. 2.

65. CBE, *Our Public Schools Must Not Close!*, Chicago, 1933.

66. Ibid., p. 5.

67. Ibid., pp. 14–15.

68. Ibid., p. 3.

69. Robert Maynard Hutchins, "Who Ordered Cuts in Schools?" Leaflet distributed by Citizens Schools Committee, reprinted from the *Chicago Herald and Examiner*, July 16, 1933. Citizens School Committee Papers, Chicago Historical Society.

70. *Chicago Tribune*, July 13, 1933, p. 2.

71. London, "Business and the School System," p. 116.

72. Cited in Hazlett, "Crisis in School Government," p. 71.

73. *Chicago Tribune*, July 16, 1933, p. 7.

74. "Net Savings," p. 4.

75. Lipkin, "Payless Paydays," p. 56.

76. London, "Business and the School System," pp. 117–118.

77. Citizens Save Our Schools Committee, Leaflet dated August 21, 1933, Citizens School Committee Papers, Chicago Historical Society.

78. Gosnell, *Machine Politics*, p. 17.

79. Norton, "Financing the Schools," p. 232.

80. Ibid., p. 174.

81. Ibid., p. 181.

82. Ibid., p. 149.

83. Ibid., p. 205.

84. Citizens Save Our Schools Committee, Leaflet dated April 14, 1934, Citizens School Committee Papers, Chicago Historical Society.

85. "Net Savings," p. 4.

86. Herrick, *Chicago Schools*, p. 228.

87. *Chicago Herald and Examiner*, July 22, 1933, p. 6.

88. "Association on Costs of Public Education; There is a Point Where Further Taxation Cripples Community Life more than Further Educational Opportunities Help It," *Chicago Commerce* 19 (July 1923:39.

89. Herrick, *Chicago Schools*, p. 218.

90. Commercial Club of Chicago, *Yearbook, 1938–1939*, pp. 255–256.

91. Sargent, "Taxpayer Takes Charge," p. 74.

92. London, "Business and the School System," p. 113.

93. [Groups endorsing legislative program], *Chicago's Schools* 1 (December 1934):1; Levit, "Citizens Schools Committee," p. 18; *Chicago Tribune*, August 1, 1933, p. 13.

94. George S. Counts, *School and Society in Chicago* (New York: Harcourt, Brace, 1928), p. 227.

95. Levit, "Citizens Schools Committee," p. 18.

96. Hancock, interview transcript, p. 57.

97. Levit, "Citizens Schools Committee," p. 18.

98. Herrick, *Chicago Schools*, p. 238.

99. Hancock, interview transcript, p. 22.

100. Levit, "Citizens Schools Committee," p. 23.

101. *Federation News*, July 29, 1933, p. 3.

102. Herrick, *Chicago Schools*, p. 211.

103. *Federation News*, July 29, 1933, p. 3.

104. *Chicago Herald and Examiner*, July 22, 1933, p. 6.

105. "A New Attempt at the Political Control of Public School Teachers," *Chicago's Schools* 1 (December 1934):2.

106. Citizens Save Our Schools Committee, Leaflet dated August 21, 1933; see also William T. McCoy, "'Smoke,'" *American Teacher* 17 (February 1933):13–14, for strong criticism of businessmen by a labor figure.

107. Citizens Save Our Schools Committee, "The 1934 School Budget" (leaflet dated April 7, 1934), Citizens School Committee Papers, Chicago Historical Society.

108. "Concur in Education Proposals," *City Club Bulletin* 39 (June 24, 1946):2.

109. "Invite School Board Resignations," *City Club Bulletin* 39 (December 16, 1946):1.

110. "Increased School Board Effectiveness," *City Club Bulletin* 40 (November 10, 1947):1.

111. Charles H. Judd, "New Problems in Citizenship Training," *Elementary School Journal* 33 (May 1933):660, 666.

112. Jones, "New Deal Relief," p. 234.

113. Harold L. Ickes, *The Secret Diary of Harold L. Ickes* (New York: Simon and Schuster, 1954), 1:272, 275, 463; 2:561.

114. Judd, "Citizenship Training," p. 661.

115. Louise de Koven Bowen, "Teach School Children Citizenship!," *Woman's City Club Bulletin* 10 (March 1922):7.

116. Hazlett, "Crisis in School Government," p. 218.

117. "The Principals are Back," *Chicago's Schools* 1 (October 1934):2; Hazlett, "Crisis in School Government," p. 83.

118. "S.O.S. Plan and Platform for Ward Organization," *Chicago's Schools* 1 (August 1934):3.

119. Mabel P. Simpson [Executive Secretary], "Program and Accomplishments for 1935: Annual Report of the Citizens School Committee," *Chicago's Schools* 2 (January 1936):3–4.

120. Cited in Lipkin, "Payless Paydays," p. 55.

121. *Federation News*, March 12, 1932, p. 1; see also the denunciation of the Sargent Committee by Victor Olander as a "volunteer, extralegal, self-styled Citizens' Committee" that had usurped the legitimate functions of the board of education; Victor Olander to Board of Education [of Chicago], January 13, 1933. Victor Olander Papers, Special Collections, University of Illinois Library at Chicago Circle Campus.

122. Ibid., July 29, 1933, p. 1.

123. *Chicago Tribune*, July 13, 1933, p. 1.

124. *Federation News*, March 12, 1932, p. 1. For further statements on the need to protect the janitors, see the comments of William McFetridge, president of the Building Service Employees Union and one of the most powerful leaders in the CFL, as quoted in the *Chicago Tribune*, July 26, 1932, p. 2.

125. Mary J. Herrick, Interview conducted by author, Chicago, February 23, 1976. See Herrick, *Chicago Schools*, p. 253.

126. *Federation News*, July 29, 1933, p. 1.

127. Greenstone, *Labor in American Politics*; Jones, "New Deal Relief."

128. Edward N. Nockels to Bruce Bliven, March 20, 1936, John Fitzpatrick Papers, Chicago Historical Society; Lillian Herstein, Interview conducted by Elizabeth Balanoff, October 26, 1970, transcript in Roosevelt University Oral History Research Project, Chicago, pp. 269–271; Letter of endorsement from Reuben G. Soderstrom [president of the Illinois State Federation of Labor] and Victor Olander to James Mullenbach, Harry G. Gideonse, and Mrs. W. A. Roberts, Chairmen, Non-Partisan Committee for Lillian Herstein for Congress, October 28, 1932.

Victor Olander Papers, Special Collections, University of Illinois Library at the Chicago Circle Campus.

129. Lillian Herstein, Interview conducted by Elizabeth Balanoff, October 26, 1970, pp. 269–271, transcript in Roosevelt University Oral History Research Project, Roosevelt University Library, Chicago.

130. "Autobiographical Data, Lillian Herstein," typewritten statement in Lillian Herstein Papers (n.d.), Chicago Historical Society.

131. Herstein, interview transcript, p. 275.

132. Edward N. Nockels to Edward Kelly, March 23, 1935, copy in John Fitzpatrick Papers, Chicago Historical Society.

133. Irwin Walker to Edward N. Nockels, March 19, 1935, John Fitzpatrick Papers, Chicago Historical Society.

134. Edward Kelly to Edward N. Nockels, March 28, 1935, John Fitzpatrick Papers, Chicago Historical Society.

135. C F L, Resolution calling on Mayor Edward Kelly to appoint labor members to school board, May 8, 1933, copy in John Fitzpatrick Papers, Chicago Historical Society.

136. Edward Kelly to John Fitzpatrick, May 10, 1933, John Fitzpatrick Papers, Chicago Historical Society.

137. Hancock, interview transcript, p. 37.

138. "Principals are Back," p. 2.

139. *Federation News*, July 22, 1933, p. 5; see also *Chicago Tribune*, July 13, 1933, p. 8, and July 17, 1933, p. 4.

140. Hazlett, "Crisis in School Government," pp. 226–228; Gosnell, *Machine Politics*, p. 17; see also James W. Sanders, "The Education of Chicago Catholics: A Social History" (Ph.D. diss., University of Chicago, 1970).

141. William Green to John Fitzpatrick, May 28, 1937, John Fitzpatrick Papers, Chicago Historical Society.

142. *Federation News*, June 12, 1937, p. 11.

143. Joseph D. Keenan, Interview conducted by Joanna Skivens, August 8, 1970, p. 22, transcript in Roosevelt University Oral History Project, Roosevelt University Library, Chicago.

144. Newell, *Chicago and the Labor Movement*, pp. 186–193.

145. Fitzpatrick, telegram to Allied Printing Trades Council.

146. Fitzpatrick to Green.

147. Fitzpatrick, draft telegram to Hearst.

148. March, interview transcript, p. 93.

149. Molly Levitas, Interview conducted by Elizabeth Balanoff, July 24, 1970, p. 143, 149, transcript in Roosevelt University Oral History Project, Roosevelt University Library, Chicago.

150. Newell, *Chicago and the Labor Movement*, pp. 137, 185.

151. Ibid., p. 210.

152. Ibid., p. 205.

153. Herrick, *Chicago Schools*, p. 243; Newell, *Chicago and the Labor Movement*, p. 202.

154. Herstein, interview transcript, pp. 156, 88.

155. Lillian Herstein to George S. Counts, January 23, 1941, Lillian Herstein Papers, Chicago Historical Society.

156. George Patterson, Interview conducted by Ed Sadlowski, December 1970, transcript in Roosevelt University Oral History Project, Roosevelt University Library, Chicago; Earnest DeMaio, Interview conducted by Morris Vogel, November 16, 1970, transcript in Roosevelt University Oral History Project, Roosevelt University Library, Chicago.

157. March, interview transcript, p. 73.

158. Ibid., pp. 76–77.

159. Greenstone, *Labor in American Politics*, p. 195.

160. March, interview transcript, pp. 94, 95.

161. DeMaio, interview transcript, pp. 74–75.

162. Greenstone, *Labor in American Politics*, p. 107.

163. John Fitzpatrick, Telegram to Max Zaritsky, April 3, 1939, John Fitzpatrick Papers, Chicago Historical Society.

164. *Chicago Daily News*, November 10, 1937, p. 1.

165. "Reaping the Whirlwind," *Chicago's Schools* 3 (June 1937):1.

166. Edward N. Nockels, Telegram to Magaret A. Haley, n.d. [1936], John Fitzpatrick Papers, Chicago Historical Society.

167. William Bogan, "Public Cooperation in School Policies," *Addresses and Proceedings of the National Education Association* 67 (1929):148–154; William Bogan, "The Danger to Free Public Education," *American Teacher* 17 (February 1933):7–8.

168. "Reaping the Whirlwind," p. 1; National Education Association, *Certain Personnel Practices in the Chicago Public Schools. Report of an Investigation by the National Commission for the Defense of Democracy through Education of the NEA* (Washington, D.C.: National Education Association Defense Commission, 1945).

169. Chicago Board of Education, *Annual Report of the Superintendent of Schools, 1937–1938*, Chicago, p. 18. Also see Hazlett, "Crisis in School Government," pp. 124–125.

170. Hazlett, "Crisis in School Government," p. 127; *Annual Report of the Superintendent, 1937–1938*, pp. 172–174, 184–185.

171. "Three Majors—or Four?," *Chicago's Schools* 5 (October 1938):3.

172. Herrick, *Chicago Schools*, p. 229.

173. Chicago Board of Education, *Annual Report of the Superintendent of Schools, 1936–1937*, Chicago, p. 265.

174. Joseph D. Keenan to William Green, March 10, 1938. Copy of letter in John Fitzpatrick Papers, Chicago Historical Society.

175. Hazlett, "Crisis in School Government," p. 136. On the mayor's role in setting up the meetings between Superintendent Johnson and the labor representatives, see "Public Schools Safeguarded: Cause for Alarm Removed," an undated and unsigned labor federation press release in the Victor Olander Papers, Special Collections, University of Illinois Library at the Chicago Circle Campus.

176. Cited in ibid., pp. 136–137.

177. NEA, *Personnel Practices.*

178. Herrick, *Chicago Schools*, p. 271.

179. Ibid., p. 273.

180. "Chicago Citizens Enter the Permanent Phases of Organization for Schools," *Chicago's Schools* 1 (November 1934):2.

181. Hancock, interview transcript, p. 30.

182. Hazlett, "Crisis in School Government," p. 291.

183. Gosnell, *Machine Politics*, p. 225.

184. Hazlett, "Crisis in School Government," p. 291.

185. *Federation News*, January 18, 1947, p. 2; *Federation News*, April 12, 1947, pp. 2–3; Letter from the International Union of Operating Engineers to Reuben G. Soderstrom [president of the Ill. State Fed. of Labor], March 25, 1947 in Victor Olander Papers, Special Collections, Library of the University of Illinois at the Chicago Circle Campus; *Chicago Sun*, April 23, 1947; Herrick, *Chicago Schools*, p. 278.

186. Kay H. Kamin, "A History of the Hunt Administration of the Chicago Public Schools, 1947–1953" (Ph.D. diss., University of Chicago, 1970), p. 38.

187. "Looking Forward," *Chicago's Schools* 14 (September 1947):2.

188. "The CSC, Its Scope and Activities," *Chicago's Schools* 18 (June 1952):1.

189. Robert Alford, "Paradigms of Relations between State and Society," pp. 145–160, in Leon N. Lindberg, Robert Alford, Colin Crouch and Claus Offe, *Stress and Contradiction in Modern Capitalism: Public Policy and the Theory of the State* (Lexington, Mass.: Lexington Books, 1975); Greenstone, *Labor in American Politics.*

190. Sol Cohen, *Progressives and Urban School Reform: The Public Education Association of New York City, 1895–1954* (New York: Teachers College Press, 1963), p. 226.

191. "Reviews Chicago School Record," *City Club Bulletin* 37 (April 10, 1944):1.

7

1. Michael B. Katz, *The Irony of Early School Reform: Innovation in Mid-Nineteenth Century Massachusetts* (Boston: Beacon Press, 1968), p. 86.

2. Edward Pessen, "The Working Men's Parties of the 1820's and '30's," in Charles M. Rehmus and Doris B. McLaughlin, eds., *Labor and American Politics: A Book of Readings* (Ann Arbor, Mich.: University of Michigan Press, 1967), p. 46.

3. John Dewey, "The Crisis in Education," *American Teacher* 17 (April 1933):5–9.

4. William W. Wattenberg, *On the Educational Front: The Reactions of Teachers' Associations in New York and Chicago* (New York: Columbia University Press, 1936), p. 20.

5. "Who Are Your Friends? Two Programs—Choose," *American Teacher* 17 (April 1933):16.

6. George Herbert Mead, "The Educational Situation in the Chicago Public Schools," *City Club Bulletin* 1 (May 1907):135.

7. Diane Ravitch, *The Revisionists Revised: A Critique of the Radical Attack on the Schools* (New York: Basic Books, 1978).

REFERENCES

ADDAMS, JANE. *Twenty Years at Hull-House.* New York: Macmillan, 1910.

"Adoption of the Anti-Organization Rule." *Margaret A. Haley's Bulletin,* September 23, 1915, pp. 3–5.

Alford, Robert. "Paradigms of Relations between State and Society." In *Stress and Contradiction in Modern Capitalism: Public Policy and the Theory of the State,* Leon N. Lindberg, Robert Alford, Colin Crouch, and Claus Offe, pp. 145–160. Lexington, Mass.: Lexington Books, 1975.

Allswang, John M. *A House for All Peoples: Ethnic Politics in Chicago, 1890–1936.* Lexington, Ky.: University Press of Kentucky, 1971.

Andrews, E. Benjamin. *The Public School System as an Instrumentality In Social Advance: Address Delivered before the Chicago and Cook County High School Association.* Chicago: David Oliphant, printer, 1895.

——. "Practical Topics Connected with the Principalship." Address delivered before the meeting of the Chicago principals, Chicago, October 8, 1898.

Andrews, Wayne. *Battle for Chicago.* New York: Harcourt, Brace, 1946.

"Anti-Organization Rule Adopted Sept. 1, 1915, and Pledge." *Margaret A. Haley's Bulletin,* September 23, 1915, p. 2.

Aronowitz, Stanley. *False Promises: The Shaping of American Working Class Consciousness.* New York: McGraw-Hill, 1973.

"Association of Commerce Representatives Visit Schools; Superintendent of Schools Extends Invitation." *Margaret Haley's Weekly Bulletin,* June 25, 1925, p. 74.

Bailyn, Bernard. *Education in the Forming of American Society: Needs and Opportunities for Study.* New York: Vintage, 1960.

Beard, Mary R. *A Short History of the American Labor Movement.* New York: Harcourt, Brace and Howe, 1920.

Beck, John M. "Chicago Newspapers and the Public Schools, 1890–1920." Ph.D. dissertation, University of Chicago, 1953.

Beverly, Leon. Interview conducted by Elizabeth Butters, December 6, 1970. Transcript in Roosevelt University Oral History Project, Roosevelt University Library, Chicago.

Bigham, Truman C. "The Chicago Federation of Labor." M.A. thesis, University of Chicago, 1925.

Blair, Francis G. "The Smith-Hughes Act in Illinois." *Chicago Schools Journal* 1 (September 1918): 8–10.

Bogan, William J. "Public Cooperation in School Policies." *Addresses and Proceedings of the National Education Association* 67 (1929):148–154.

———. "The Danger to Free Public Education." *American Teacher* 17 (February 1933):7–8.

Bourne, Randolph S. *The Gary Schools*. Boston: Houghton Mifflin, 1916.

Bowen, Louise de Koven. "Teach School Children Citizenship!" *Woman's City Club Bulletin* 10 (March 1922):7.

Bowles, Samuel. "Unequal Education and the Reproduction of the Social Division of Labor." In *Schooling in a Corporate Society: The Political Economy of Education in America*, edited by Martin Carnoy, pp. 38–66. New York: McKay, 1972.

Bowles, Samuel, and Gintis, Herbert. *Schooling in Capitalist America: Educational Reform and the Contradictions of Economic Life*. New York: Basic Books, 1976.

Braverman, Harry. *Labor and Monopoly Capital: The Degradation of Work in the Twentieth Century*. New York: Monthly Review Press, 1974.

Brecher, Jeremy. *Strike!* San Francisco: Straight Arrow Books, 1972.

Brooks, Robert R. R. *As Steel Goes: Unionism in a Basic Industry*. New Haven: Yale University Press, 1940.

"The Business Man in Office." *New Republic* 7 (July 15, 1916):267–268.

Butler, Nicholas Murray. "Remarks of Dr. Butler, President of Columbia University, before the Merchants' Club on Saturday, December 8th, at the Auditorium." In Merchants' Club, *Public Schools and Their Administration*, pp. 39–51. Chicago: Merchants' Club, 1906.

Callahan, Raymond E. *Education and the Cult of Efficiency: A Study of the Social Forces That Have Shaped the Administration of the Public Schools*. Chicago: University of Chicago Press, 1962.

Carlton, Frank Tracy. *Economic Influences upon Educational Progress in the United States, 1820–1850*. University of Wisconsin Bulletin no. 221, Economics and Political Science Series, vol. 4, no. 1. Madison, Wisc., 1908.

Carnoy, Martin. "Introduction." In *Schooling in a Corporate Society: The Political Economy of Education in America*, edited by Martin Carnoy, pp. 1–19. New York: McKay, 1972.

Chenery, William R. "Adulterated Education." *New Republic* 4 (October 23, 1915):304–306.

Chicago Association of Commerce. "A Business Administration." *Chicago Association of Commerce Bulletin* 2 (April 26, 1907):10.

———. "Ways and Means Session; Association's Largest Committee

Hears Discussion Enlightening on Functions and Merits of Charter." *Chicago Association of Commerce Bulletin* 3 (August 23, 1907):1–3.

———. *Industrial and Commercial Education in Relation to Conditions in the City of Chicago: Report of a Preliminary Survey by the Committee on Industrial and Commercial Education of the Chicago Association of Commerce.* Chicago, December 1909.

———. "Association on Costs of Public Education; There is a Point Where Further Taxation Cripples Community Life More than Further Educational Opportunities Help It." *Chicago Commerce* 19 (July 14, 1923):9–10, 39.

Chicago Association of Commerce and the Civic Federation. *Report on the Administrative Organization and Business Procedures of the Board of Education of the City of Chicago.* By Administrative Survey Commission, Aubrey H. Mellinger, Chairman. Chicago, April 1943.

Chicago Board of Education. *Special Report on the Promotional Examination and Secret Marking of Teachers.* Report of the Sub-Committee of the School Management Committee of the Board of Education, Louis F. Post, Chairman. Chicago, 1906.

———. *Proceedings of the Chicago Board of Education, 1908–1909.*

———. "Proposal to Establish Junior High Schools in the City of Chicago." Report by the Educational Commission, Appointed by the Board of Education, Chicago, December 12, 1923. Chicago Historical Society.

———. *Annual Report of the Superintendent of Schools, 1923–24.*

———. "Citizens' Sampling Day: Chicago Public Schools." Fullerton Hall Art Institute, Chicago, January 23, 1926. C. H. Judd Papers, Special Collections, University of Chicago Library.

———. *Annual Report of the Superintendent of Schools, 1925–26.*

———. *Our Public Schools Must Not Close!* Chicago, 1933.

———. *Annual Report of the Superintendent of Schools, 1936–37.*

———. *Annual Report of the Superintendent of Schools, 1937–38.*

———. *The Chicago Public Schools in Wartime, 1941–42.* Chicago: Department of Education.

———. *Annual Report of the Superintendent of Schools, 1951–52.*

Chicago Bureau of Public Efficiency. *Proposed Tax Increase for School Buildings—Vote No.* Chicago, 1923.

———. *Chicago School Finances, 1915–1925.* Chicago, December 1927.

Chicago. Robert M. Buck Papers, Chicago Historical Society.

———. Chicago Teachers' Federation Papers.

———. Chicago Teachers Union Papers.

———. Citizens School Committee Papers.

———. John Fitzpatrick Papers.

———. Lillian Herstein Papers.

————. Victor Olander Papers.

"Chicago Citizens Enter the Permanent Phases of Organization for Schools." *Chicago's Schools* 1 (November 1934):2.

Chicago Daily Journal, April 18, 1927. Article reprinted in "Superintendent Lets the Cat out of the Bag: From the News Columns," *Margaret Haley's Bulletin*, May 15, 1927, pp. 246, 255.

Chicago Federation of Labor. *A Report on Public School Fads. An Investigation Made by the Legislative Committee of the Chicago Federation of Labor.* Chicago: Chicago Federation of Labor, 1902.

————. "Verbatim Report of a Meeting Held under the Auspices of the Chicago Federation of Labor, as a Public Protest against the Action Taken on September 1, by the Board of Education of Chicago, in Adopting the Rule which Compels the Teachers to Relinquish Their Membership in Said Federation, or Suffer Discharge from Their Positions." Meeting held at Auditorium, Chicago, September 8, 1915. Chicago Teachers' Federation Papers, Chicago Historical Society.

"Chicago Notes." *Chicago Teacher and School Board Journal* 1 (April 1899):186.

Chicago Principals' Club. *The Chicago Public Schools: How They Teach Healthful Living and Help the Physically Handicapped.* Chicago: Row, Peterson, 1925.

Chicago Public School League. *Better Schools for Chicago.* Chicago, 1916.

————. *How the Public Schools Are Manacled.* Chicago, 1917.

"Chicago Schools: February Meetings of the Chicago Teachers' Associations." *Chicago Teacher and School Board Journal* 1 (March 1899): 138–140.

"Chicago Schools: Superintendent Andrews and the Chicago School Board." *Chicago Teacher and School Board Journal* 1 (January 1899):27.

"Chicago Schools: Superintendent Andrews and the Teachers." *Chicago Teacher and School Board Journal* 1 (March 1899): 149.

Chicago Teachers' Federation. *Report, Showing Results of Fifteen Years of Organization, to the Teachers of Chicago.* Chicago, 1908. Chicago Teachers' Federation Papers, Chicago Historical Society.

————. Stenographic "Report of a Public Demonstration Held at the Auditorium on Saturday, June 17, 1916, Called to Remonstrate against the Action of the Board of Education in Passing the Rule Providing for the Re-election of Teachers Every Year." Chicago Teachers' Federation Papers, Chicago Historical Society.

————. Stenographic "Report of Minutes of Regular Meeting of the Chicago Teachers' Federation." Meeting held at Corinthian Hall, the Capitol Building, Chicago, January 12, 1924. Chicago Teachers' Federation Papers, Chicago Historical Society.

———. Stenographic "Report of Special Meeting of the Chicago Teachers' Federation: Minutes of the Overflow Meeting, Playhouse Theater, Chicago." May 8, 1924. Chicago Teachers' Federation Papers, Chicago Historical Society.

———. Stenographic "Report of the Silver Jubilee Luncheon: Given by the Chicago Teachers' Federation in Honor of the 25th Anniversary of Its Entry into the Now-Historic Tax Campaign on January 20, 1900 by Miss Catharine Goggin and Margaret A. Haley." Luncheon held at the Morrison Hotel, Chicago, January 24, 1925. Chicago Teachers' Federation Papers, Chicago Historical Society.

———. Stenographic "Report of Special Meeting of the Chicago Teachers' Federation." Meeting held at Studebaker Theater, Chicago, September 11, 1925. Chicago Teachers' Federation Papers, Chicago Historical Society.

———. Stenographic "Report of Regular Meeting of the Chicago Teachers' Federation." Meeting held at Corinthian Hall, Chicago, June 12, 1926. Chicago Teachers' Federation Papers, Chicago Historical Society.

———. Stenographic "Report of Special Meeting of the Chicago Teachers' Federation." Meeting held at Commandery Hall, Capitol Building, Chicago, February 18, 1927. Chicago Teachers' Federation Papers, Chicago Historical Society.

Chicago. University of Chicago. Department of Special Collections. Charles H. Judd Papers.

———. Presidents' Papers.

———. Julius Rosenwald Papers.

City Club Bulletin 1 (April 24, 1907):121.

City Club of Chicago. *A Report on Vocational Training in Chicago and in Other Cities*. Chicago: City Club of Chicago, 1912.

"City Council Takes No Action on Appointees to School Board; Mayor Says He did not Know Dr. Schmidt Supported Loeb Policies." *Margaret Haley's Bulletin*, December 31, 1926, pp. 126, 127, 139.

"City Items." *Chicago Teacher and School Board Journal* 1 (February 1899):87–89.

Clark, Hannah Belle. *The Public Schools of Chicago: A Sociological Study*. Chicago: University of Chicago Press, 1897.

Closehy, Agnes B. "The Province of the Labor Union in the Schools." *Joint Bulletin of Chicago Federation of Men Teachers, Federation of Women High School Teachers, Elementary Teachers Union* (October 1928):1, 10, 11.

Cohen, Sol. *Progressives and Urban School Reform: The Public Education Association of New York City, 1895–1954*. New York: Teachers College Press, 1963.

Commercial Club of Chicago. *Yearbooks 1910–1911, 1911–1912, 1912–*

1913, 1913–1914, 1914–1915, 1918–1919, 1938–1939. Chicago: Commercial Club of Chicago, 1911, 1912, 1913, 1915, 1919, 1939.

——. *Vocational Schools for Illinois.* Chicago: Commercial Club of Chicago, n.d.

Commons, John Rogers, Saposs, David J., Sumner, Helen L., Mittelman, E. G., Hoagland, H. E., Andrews, John B., and Perlman, Selig. *History of Labour in the United States.* 4 vols. Vol. 1. New York: Macmillan, 1921.

Commons, John Rogers, Phillips, Ulrich B., Gilmore, Eugene A., Sumner, Helen L., and Andrews, John B., eds. *A Documentary History of American Industrial Society.* 10 vols. Vol. 5. New York: Russell and Russell, 1910.

"Concur in Education Proposals." *City Club Bulletin* 39 (June 24, 1946):2.

Cooley, Edwin Gilbert. *In Reply to Dr. John Dewey's 'Some Dangers in the Present Movement for Industrial Education.'* Chicago: Commercial Club of Chicago [?], n.d. [1913?].

——. Remarks on "Commercial High Schools." In Merchants' Club of Chicago, "Commercial High Schools" (addresses delivered at meeting of February 9, 1901) in *Season of 1900–1901,* pp. 115–124. Chicago: Merchants' Club of Chicago, 1901.

——. *Public School Education in Morals.* Address delivered before the Principals' Association, Chicago, September 8, 1906. Chicago: Normal School Press, 1906.

——. *Vocational Education in Europe.* Chicago: Commercial Club of Chicago, 1912.

——. *The Need for Vocational Schools in the United States.* Chicago: Commercial Club of Chicago, 1914.

"Council Hearings on School Board Nominees. Alderman Oscar F. Nelson." *Margaret Haley's Bulletin,* March 15, 1927, p. 189.

Counts, George S. *School and Society in Chicago.* New York: Harcourt, Brace, 1928.

Creel, George. "Why Chicago's Teachers Unionized." *Harper's Weekly* 60 (June 19, 1915):598–600.

Cremin, Lawrence A. *The Transformation of the School: Progressivism in American Education, 1876–1957.* New York: Knopf, 1961.

——. "Foreword." In *Economic Influences upon Educational Progress in the United States, 1820–1850,* by Frank Tracy Carlton, pp. ix-xviii. New York: Teachers College Press, 1965.

Crissey, Forrest. *The Making of an American School-Teacher.* Chicago: C. M. Barnes, 1906.

"A Critical Situation." [Reprinted from *American Teacher.*] *Margaret A. Haley's Bulletin,* October 21, 1915, p. 7.

Cronin, Joseph M. *The Control of Urban Schools: Perspective on the Power of Educational Reformers.* New York: The Free Press, 1973.

"The CSC, Its Scope and Activities." *Chicago's Schools* 18 (June 1952):1.

Cubberley, Ellwood Patterson. *Public School Administration.* Boston: Houghton Mifflin, 1916.

Curoe, Philip R. V. *Educational Attitudes and Policies of Organized Labor in the United States.* New York: Teachers College Press, 1926.

Dedmon, Emmett, "A Short History of the Commercial Club." Speech delivered at the 600th meeting of the Commercial Club of Chicago, September 25, 1968.

DeMaio, Earnest. Interview conducted by Morris Vogel, November 16, 1970. Transcript in Roosevelt University Oral History Project, Roosevelt University Library, Chicago.

DeWeese, Truman A. "Two Years' Progress in the Chicago Public Schools." *Educational Review* 24 (November 1902):325–337.

Dewey, John. "Some Dangers in the Present Movement for Industrial Education." *Child Labor Bulletin* 1 (February 1913):69–74.

———. "Splitting up the School System." *New Republic* 2 (April 17, 1915):283–284.

———. "Education vs. Trade-Training—Dr. Dewey's Reply." *New Republic* 2 (May 15, 1915):42–43.

———. "The Crisis in Education." *American Teacher* 17 (April 1933): 5–9.

Dewey, John, and Dewey, Evelyn. *Schools of Tomorrow.* New York: Dutton, 1962 (first published 1915).

"Dr. Kerchensteiner Praises American Educational System." *National Association of Corporation Schools Bulletin* 1 (August 1914):3–4.

Dodge, Chester C. *Reminiscences of a Schoolmaster.* Chicago: Ralph Fletcher Seymour, 1941.

Donatelli, Rosemary V. "The Contributions of Ella Flagg Young to the Educational Enterprise." Ph.D. dissertation, University of Chicago, 1971.

Draper, Andrew S. *Common School Problems of Chicago.* Pamphlet version of address delivered at a citizens' meeting under the auspices of the Education Commission of One Hundred of the Civic Federation of Chicago, Chicago, December 1, 1900. Chicago Historical Society.

Eakins, David W. "The Development of Corporate Liberal Policy Research in the United States, 1885–1965." Ph.D. dissertation, University of Wisconsin, Madison, 1966.

Easley, Ralph W. "The Work of the Civic Federation." Report of the secretary, read at the Fifth Annual Meeting of the Civic Federation of Chicago, Chicago, April 26, 1899.

"Editorial: The Chicago Teachers' Federation." *Chicago Teacher and School Board Journal* 1 (May 1899):254.

"The Educational Commission and Its Report." *Chicago Teacher and School Board Journal* 1 (January 1899):19–21.

Educational Commission of the City of Chicago. *Report of the Educational Commission of the City of Chicago, Appointed by the Mayor, Hon. Carter H. Harrison.* Chicago: R. R. Donnelly, 1899.

Elementary Teachers' General Council. *Reports.* With a Supplement on the history of teachers' councils in Chicago. October 1921 to May 1925.

"Ella Flagg Young [editorial]." *Chicago Schools Journal* 1 (October 1918):4–5.

Field, Alexander J. "Educational Reform and Manufacturing Development in Mid-Nineteenth Century Massachusetts." Ph.D. dissertation, University of California, Berkeley, 1974.

Fine, Nathan. *Labor and Farmer Parties in the United States, 1828–1928.* New York: Rand School of Social Science, 1928.

Flexner, Abraham, and Bachman, Frank P. *The Gary Schools: A General Account.* New York: General Education Board, 1918.

Forthal, Sonya. *Cogwheels of Democracy: A Study of the Precinct Captain.* New York: William-Frederick Press, 1946.

Geyer, Denton L. "Can We Depend upon the Results of Group Intelligence Tests?" *Chicago Schools Journal* 4 (February 1922):203–210.

Goggin, Catharine. "The Report of the Educational Commission." *Chicago Teacher and School Board Journal* 1 (February 1899):84–85.

————. "The Chicago Teachers' Federation." *Chicago Teacher and School Board Journal* 1 (May 1899):257–259.

Gompers, Samuel. "Should a Labor Party be Formed?" In *Labor and American Politics: A Book of Readings*, edited by Charles M. Rehmus and Doris B. McLaughlin, pp. 103–107. Ann Arbor: University of Michigan Press, 1967.

Gonnelly, Joseph F. "Development of the Junior High in Chicago." *Chicago Schools Journal* 12 (October 1929):46–51.

Gosnell, Harold F. *Machine Politics: Chicago Model.* 2nd. ed. Postscript by author. Chicago: University of Chicago Press, 1968.

Gottfried, Alex. *Boss Cermak of Chicago: A Study of Political Leadership.* Seattle: University of Washington Press, 1962.

Greenstone, J. David. *Labor in American Politics.* New York: Vintage Press, 1970.

Greenstone, J. David, and Peterson, Paul E. *Race and Authority in Urban Politics: Community Participation and the War on Poverty.* New York: Russell Sage Foundation, 1973.

Greer, Colin. *The Great School Legend: A Revisionist Interpretation of American Public Education.* New York: Basic Books, 1972.

[Groups endorsing legislative program.] *Chicago's Schools* 1 (December 1934):1

Haber, Samuel. *Efficiency and Uplift: Scientific Management in the Progressive Era, 1890–1920.* Chicago: University of Chicago Press, 1964.

Haley, Margaret A. "Comments on New Educational Bill." *Chicago Teachers' Federation Bulletin* 1 (January 16, 1903):1.

————. "Comments on New Educational Bill [continued from previous issue]." *Chicago Teachers' Federation Bulletin* 2 (January 23, 1903):1.

————. "The New Educational Bills: Further Comments." *Chicago Teachers' Federation Bulletin* 2 (January 30, 1903):1.

————. "Why Teachers Should Organize." *Addresses and Proceedings of the National Education Association* 43 (1904):145–152.

————. "Autobiography." Seattle, Wash., December 27, 1911–February 13, 1912. Chicago Teachers' Federation Papers. Chicago Historical Society. (Typescript.)

————. "Alderman Kennedy's Four Points." *Margaret A. Haley's Bulletin*, October 21, 1915, p. 6.

————. "Catharine Goggin." *Margaret Haley's Bulletin*, January 27, 1916, pp. 2–3.

————. "From the Masthead by the Lookout." *Margaret Haley's Bulletin*, November 16, 1925, pp. 84–86.

————. Letter from Haley to Mayor William E. Dever, in "City Council Takes No Action on Appointees to School Board." *Margaret Haley's Bulletin*, December 31, 1926, p. 126.

————. "What's Wrong in Our Schools; Veteran Teacher Gives Views." *Chicago Daily News*, January 7, 1928.

————. "Forty Fighting Years." 1935. Chicago Teachers' Federation Papers, Chicago Historical Society. (Typescript.)

Hancock, Margaret Campbell. Interview conducted by Elizabeth Murray. n.d. Transcript in possession of Robert J. Havighurst, Department of Education, University of Chicago.

Hays, Samuel P. "The Politics of Reform in Municipal Government in the Progressive Era." *Pacific Northwest Quarterly* 55 (October 1964): 157–169.

Hazlett, James Stephen. "Crisis in School Government: An Administrative History of the Chicago Public Schools, 1933–1947." Ph.D. dissertation, University of Chicago, 1968.

Hefferan, Helen [Mrs. William S.]. "The Present Status of the Continuation School Laws." *Woman's City Club Bulletin* 10 (September 1921):9.

Herrick, Mary J. *The Chicago Schools: A Social and Political History.* Beverly Hills, Calif.: Sage Publications, 1971.

————. Interview with author, Chicago, February 23, 1976.

Herstein, Lillian. Interview conducted by Elizabeth Balanoff, Chicago, October 26, 1970. Transcript in Roosevelt University Oral History Project, Roosevelt University Library, Chicago.

Hobsbawm, Eric J. "Class Consciousness in History." In *Aspects of History and Class Consciousness*, edited by Istvan Meszaros, pp. 5–21. London: Routledge and Kegan Paul, 1971.

Howe, Irving, and Widick, B. J. *The UAW and Walter Reuther*. New York: Random House, 1949.

Ickes, Harold L. "Political Features of the Proposed City Charter." *City Club Bulletin* 1 (July 10, 1907):167–172.

———. *The Secret Diary of Harold L. Ickes*. Vols. 1 and 2. New York: Simon and Schuster, 1954.

Illinois State Federation of Labor. "Report of the Committee on Vocational Education to the Illinois State Federation of Labor." *Thirty-Second Annual Proceedings of the Illinois State Federation of Labor* (1914):45–54.

———. "Report of the Committee on Schools." *Thirty-Fourth Annual Proceedings of the Illinois State Federation of Labor* (1916).

———. "Labor Analyses Public School Policy." *Weekly News Letter*, July 26, 1924, p. 1.

"Increased School Board Effectiveness." *City Club Bulletin* 40 (November 10, 1947):1.

"Invite School Board Resignations." *City Club Bulletin* 39 (December 16, 1946):1.

Jackson, Sidney L. *America's Struggle for Free Schools: Social Tension and Education in New England and New York: 1827–42*.

Jencks, Jeremiah W. "Remarks on 'Commercial High Schools.'" In Merchants' Club of Chicago, *"Commercial High Schools"* (addresses delivered at meeting of February 9, 1901) in *Season of 1900–1901*, pp. 99–114. Chicago: Merchants' Club of Chicago, 1901.

Joint Committee on Public School Affairs. "Educational Extension and Community Centers: Recommendation and Report, Based on a Survey of 76 Chicago Schools." Chicago, January 16, 1924. Chicago Historical Society.

Jones, Gene Delon. "The Local Political Significance of New Deal Relief Legislation in Chicago: 1933–1940." Ph.D. dissertation, Northwestern University, 1970.

Judd, Charles H. "Argues against Dual School Plan." *Chicago Tribune*, December 21, 1912, p. 6.

———. "New Problems in Citizenship Training." *Elementary School Journal* 33 (May 1933):656–668.

Kamin, Kay H. "A History of the Hunt Administration of the Chicago Public Schools, 1947–1953." Ph.D. dissertation, University of Chicago, 1970.

Karier, Clarence J., Violas, Paul C., and Spring, Joel. *Roots of Crisis: American Education in the Twentieth Century*. Chicago: Rand-Mc-Nally, 1973.

Katz, Michael B. *The Irony of Early School Reform: Educational Innovation in Mid-Nineteenth Century Massachusetts*. Boston: Beacon Press, 1968.

―――. *Class, Bureaucracy and Schools: The Illusion of Educational Change in America*. New York: Praeger, 1971, 1975.

Keenan, Joseph D. Interview conducted by Joanna Skivens, Chicago, August 8, 1970. Transcript in Roosevelt University Oral History Project, Roosevelt University Library, Chicago.

Keener, E. E. "Homogeneous Classification of Junior High School Pupils." *Chicago Schools Journal* 9 (October 1926):51–54.

Keiser, John Howard. "John Fitzpatrick and Progressive Unionism, 1915–1925." Ph.D. dissertation, Northwestern University, 1965.

Kelly, Alfred H. "A History of the Illinois Manufacturers' Association." Ph.D. dissertation, University of Chicago, 1938.

"The Kelly-Nash Political Machine." *Fortune* 14 (August 1936):47.

Kerchensteiner, Georg. *Education for Citizenship*. Translated by A. J. Pressland. Published under the auspices of the Commercial Club of Chicago. Chicago: Rand-McNally, 1911.

Kolko, Gabriel. *The Triumph of Conservatism: A Reinterpretation of American History, 1900–1916*. Chicago: Quadrangle, 1967.

―――. "The Decline of American Radicalism in the Twentieth Century." In *The Poverty of Progress: The Political Economy of American Social Problems*, edited by Milton Mankoff, pp. 457–470. New York: Holt, Rinehart and Winston, 1972.

"Labor Protests Confirmation of Dr. Schmidt and Mrs. Hefferan." *Margaret Haley's Bulletin*, January 17, 1927, pp. 151–152.

"Labor Refuses to Endorse McAndrew Salary Schedule; Men's Federation Appeals in Vain; Fitzpatrick Assails McAndrew." *Margaret Haley's Bulletin*, May 15, 1927, p. 245.

Lazerson, Marvin. *Origins of the Urban School: Public Education in Massachusetts, 1870–1915*. Cambridge: Harvard University Press, 1971.

Leavitt, Frank M. "Needed Laws for Vocational Plan." *Chicago Tribune*, December 22, 1912, p. 6.

Levine, Daniel. *Varieties of Reform Thought*. Madison, Wis.: State Historical Society of Wisconsin, 1964.

Levit, Martin. "The Chicago Citizens School Committee: A Study of a Pressure Group." M.A. thesis, University of Chicago, 1947.

Levitas, Molly. Interview conducted by Elizabeth Balanoff, Chicago, July 24, 1970. Transcript in Roosevelt University Oral History Project, Roosevelt University Library, Chicago.

Lipkin, Penny Joan. "Payless Paydays: The Financial Crisis of the Chicago Board of Education, 1930–1934." M.A. thesis, Columbia University, 1967.

Loeb, Jacob M. "Statement to Newspapers by Jacob M. Loeb in Re. Chicago Teachers' Federation," April 10, 1916. Chicago Teachers' Federation Papers, Chicago Historical Society.

———. "The Business Man and the Public Service." *Addresses and Proceedings of the National Education Association* 54 (1916):351–355.

London, Stephen D. "Business and the Chicago Public School System, 1890–1966." Ph.D. dissertation, University of Chicago, 1968.

"Looking Forward." *Chicago's Schools* 14 (September 1947):2.

Lowry, Charles D. "Genesis of a School System." Paper read before the Chicago Literary Club, February 28, 1944. Newberry Library, Chicago.

McAndrew, William. "The Principal." *Chicago Schools Journal* 7 (November 1924):81–85.

———. "Speaking of This and That: Democracy, Appearances, Personalities, Professional Pride, Being Respectable." *Chicago Schools Journal* 8 (September 1925):1–5.

———. "Speaking of This and That." *Chicago Schools Journal* 8 (December 1925):121–124.

———. "What Public Schools are For." *Woman's City Club Bulletin* 15 (February 1926):197–200.

———. "Arithmetic Outside and Inside." *Chicago Schools Journal* 9 (October 1926):41–44.

"McAndrew's Regime Was What Sherman Called War." *Margaret Haley's Bulletin*, December 15, 1927, pp. 82–83.

McCarthy, Michael Patrick. "Businessmen and Professionals in Municipal Reform: The Chicago Experience." Ph.D. dissertation, Northwestern University, 1970.

McCoy, William T. "Giving the Junior High a Chance." Transcript of radio talk, in *Joint Bulletin of Chicago Federation of Men Teachers, Federation of Women High School Teachers, Elementary Teachers Union*, October 14, 1928, pp. 14–15.

———. "'Smoke.'" *American Teacher* 17 (February 1933):13–14.

McManis, John T. *Ella Flagg Young and a Half-Century of the Chicago Public Schools*. Chicago: McClurg, 1916.

March, Herbert. Interview conducted by Elizabeth Balanoff, Chicago, November 16, 1970. Transcript in Roosevelt University Oral History Project, Roosevelt University Library, Chicago.

"Mayor Harrison's Attitude toward the Educational Commission Bill." *Chicago's Schools* 1 (February 1899):107–108.

Mead, George Herbert. "The Educational Situation in the Chicago Public Schools." *City Club Bulletin* 1 (May 8, 1907):130–138.

———. "Gives Plan for Trade Schools; Prof. G. H. Mead Compares City Club Scheme with the Cooley Measure." *Chicago Tribune*, December 16, 1912, p. 4.

Merchants' Club of Chicago. "Commercial High Schools." In *Season of 1900–1901*, pp. 99–130 (meeting of February 9, 1901). Chicago: Merchants' Club.

———. *Public Schools and Their Administration*. Addresses delivered at meeting of December 8, 1906. Chicago: Merchants' Club, 1906.

Merriam, Charles E. "Home Rule Features of the New City Charter." *City Club Bulletin* 1 (June 19, 1907):148–152.

———. "The Charter Situation. What Next?" *City Club Bulletin* 1 (October 23, 1907):212–215.

———. *Chicago: A More Intimate View of Urban Politics*. New York: Macmillan, 1929.

Michels, Nicholas. "The Charter Situation. What Next?" *City Club Bulletin* 1 (October 23, 1907):215–217.

Miles, H. E. "How Shall the Obligation to Provide Industrial Education Be Met: The Obligation of the Employer." National Society for the Promotion of Industrial Education, bulletin no. 15. *Proceedings, Fifth Annual Meeting*, pp. 29–37, 1911.

———. "What I Am Trying to Do." *World's Work* 26 (October 1913): 667–673.

Miliband, Ralph. "The Capitalist State—Reply to Nicos Poulantzas." *New Left Review*, no. 59 (January–February 1970), pp. 53–60.

———. "Poulantzas and the Capitalist State." *New Left Review*, no. 82 (November–December 1973), pp. 83–92.

Moore, Ella Adams. "Trade Training Need Emphasized." *Chicago Tribune*, December 25, 1912, p. 8.

Mortenson, Peter A. "Report of the Superintendent of Schools." *Chicago Schools Journal* 5 (October 1922):61–70.

"Mrs. Young's Resignation." *Chicago Teacher and School Board Journal* 1 (June 1899):305–306.

Mullenbach, James. "Councils Furnished Intelligent Contact between Teachers and Administration." (Text of radio address.) *Margaret Haley's Bulletin*, April 15, 1927, pp. 227–228.

Municipal Voters' League. *Twenty-Seventh Annual Preliminary Report*. Chicago, 1923.

Murray, Elizabeth. "The Chicago Board of Education." Chapter 3 in Robert J. Havighurst, Robert L. McCaul, Elizabeth L. Murray et al., "Education and Society in Metropolitan Chicago: Studies in the Sociology and History of Urban Education." Manuscript, n.d. In possession of Robert J. Havighurst, University of Chicago.

"The Net Savings of the 'Economy' Program in Chicago's Schools." *Chicago's Schools* 1 (October 1934):1, 4.

"A New Attempt at the Political Control of Public School Teachers." *Chicago's Schools* 1 (December 1934):2.

Newell, Barbara Warne. *Chicago and the Labor Movement: Metropolitan Unionism in the 1930's.* Urbana, Ill.: University of Illinois Press, 1961.

Noble, David F. *America by Design: Science, Technology and the Rise of Corporate Capitalism.* New York: Knopf, 1977.

Norton, John K. "Financing the Schools." In George D. Strayer et al., *Report of the Survey of the Schools of Chicago, Illinois.* Vol. 1. New York: Teachers College Press, 1932.

Nottenburg, Robert. "The Relationship of Organized Labor to Public School Legislation in Illinois, 1880–1948." Ph.D dissertation, University of Chicago, 1950.

Olander, Victor A. Letter to Secretaries, Local Unions and Central Bodies, State of Illinois. Reprinted in *Margaret A. Haley's Bulletin*, October 21, 1915, p. 9.

———. "'Work' in Work-Study-Play Plan is Discussed at Convention; Victor Olander in Address before A. F. of L. Seeks Platoonists' Meaning." *Margaret Haley's Bulletin*, November 16, 1925, pp. 83, 92.

———. "Victor Olander Discusses Two Educational Questions; Platoon and Junior High Schools Considered in Second Installment of Address." *Margaret Haley's Bulletin*, November 30, 1925. pp. 103, 118.

———. "Intelligence Tests Akin to Hindu Caste System, Says Olander; Chicago Speaker Tells Labor Convention of Dangers." *Margaret Haley's Bulletin*, December 16, 1925, p. 123.

———. Victor Olander Papers, Special Collections, University of Illinois Library at the Chicago Circle Campus.

"Organized Labor Assails Mayor's Nominees; John Fitzpatrick Tells Schools' Committee of Labor's Treatment by Mrs. Hefferan." *Margaret Haley's Bulletin*, February 15, 1927, p. 165.

"Otis Law Has Never Had a Fair Trial, Says Shannon." *City Club Bulletin* 21 (February 27, 1928):1.

Patterson, George. Interview conducted by Ed Sadlowski, Chicago, December 1970. Transcript in Roosevelt University Oral History Project, Roosevelt University Library, Chicago.

Pawa, Jay M. "Workingmen and Free Schools in the Nineteenth Century: A Comment on the Labor-Education Thesis." *History of Education Quarterly* 11 (Fall 1971):287–302.

Pessen, Edward. "The Working Men's Parties of the 1820's and '30's." In *Labor and American Politics: A Book of Readings*, edited by Charles M. Rehmus and Doris B. McLaughlin, pp. 42–56. Ann Arbor: University of Michigan Press, 1967.

Peterson, Paul E. *School Politics, Chicago Style.* Chicago: University of Chicago Press, 1976.

Pfeil, Walter F. "Workers' Education in Chicago." M.A. thesis, University of Chicago, 1935.

Pierce, Bessie Louise. *A History of Chicago.* Vol. 2: *From Town to City, 1848–1871.* New York: Knopf, 1940.

Post, Louis F. "Comments on New Educational Bill." *Chicago Teachers' Federation Bulletin* 2 (February 6, 1903):1–2.

Potofsky, Jacob. Interview conducted by Elizabeth Balanoff, Chicago, August 4, 1970. Transcript in Roosevelt University Oral History Project, Roosevelt University Library, Chicago.

Poulantzas, Nicos. "The Problem of the Capitalist State." *New Left Review*, no. 58 (November–December 1969), pp. 67–78.

———. "The Capitalist State: A Reply to Miliband and Laclau." *New Left Review*, no. 95 (January–February 1976), pp. 63–83.

"The Principals Are Back." *Chicago's Schools* 1 (October 1934):2.

Public Administration Service. *The Public School System of Gary, Indiana.* Chicago: Public Administration Service, 1955.

Public Education Association of Chicago. *Bulletin No. 1* n.d.

———. *Bulletin No. 2*, March 3, 1917. (Bulletin incorrectly dated; should be March 3, 1916.)

———. *Bulletin No. 3.* March 9, 1916.

———. *Bulletin No. 4.* March 12, 1916.

Pullen, Paul Pike. "Population Movements in the Chicago Metropolitan Area from 1900 to the Present." M.A. thesis, Northwestern University, 1942.

Radosh, Ronald. *American Labor and United States Foreign Policy.* New York: Random House, 1969.

Rape, Arthur O. "What Mental Tests Mean to the Class-Room Teacher." *Chicago Schools Journal* 7 (September 1924):18–19.

Ravitch, Diane. *The Revisionists Revised: A Critique of the Radical Attack on the Schools.* New York: Basic Books, 1978.

"Reaping the Whirlwind." *Chicago's Schools* 3 (June 1937):1.

Reid, Robert Louis. "The Professionalization of Public School Teachers: The Chicago Experience, 1895–1920." Ph.D. dissertation, Northwestern University, 1968.

"Report of Commission on Superintendent." *Chicago Schools Journal* 1 (March 1919):21–23.

"Resolutions Adopted by Chicago Federation of Labor at Mass Meeting on School Situation, December 2, 1906." *Chicago Teachers' Federation Bulletin*, vol. 6 (December 7, 1906).

"Reviews Chicago School Record." *City Club Bulletin* (April 10, 1944):1.

Robins, Raymond. "The Charter Situation. What Next?" *City Club Bulletin* 1 (October 23, 1907):217–220.

Robinson, Theodore W. "Remarks of Theodore W. Robinson, Chairman, Public School Committee, before the Merchants' Club, on Saturday, December 8th, at the Auditorium." In Merchants' Club, *Public Schools and Their Administration*, pp. 3–12. Chicago: Merchants' Club of Chicago, 1906.

―――. *The Need of Industrial Education in Our Public Schools.* Pamphlet prepared for Commercial Club of Chicago of address delivered before the National Education Association, Boston, July 6, 1910. Chicago Historical Society.

―――. "The Need of Vocational Education." Report of address delivered at American Steel Institute meeting, Chicago, October 24, 1913. Victor Olander Papers, Chicago Historical Society.

Rose, Caroline Baer. "Workers' Education, the Labor Movement and the Intellectuals in the United States: 1920–1940." Ph.D. dissertation, University of Chicago, 1943.

Rosenblum, Frank. Interview conducted by Elizabeth Balanoff, Chicago, August 14, 1970. Transcript in Roosevelt University Oral History Project, Roosevelt University Library, Chicago.

Sanders, James W. "The Education of Chicago Catholics: A Social History." Ph.D. dissertation, University of Chicago, 1970.

Sargent, Fred W. "The Taxpayer Takes Charge." *Saturday Evening Post*, January 14, 1933, p. 21.

Schlesinger, Arthur M., Sr. *New Viewpoints in American History.* New York: Macmillan, 1922.

"School Board Department: Superintendent Andrews on the Proposed Changes in School Board Organization." *Chicago Teacher and School Board Journal* 1 (May 1899):244–245.

Sell, Harry Bird. "The American Federation of Labor and the Labor Party Movement of 1918–1920." M.A. thesis, University of Chicago, 1922.

Shedd, John G. "Remarks on 'Commercial High Schools.'" In Merchants' Club of Chicago, "Commercial High Schools" (addresses delivered at meeting of February 9, 1901) in *Season of 1900–1901*, pp. 125–130. Chicago: Merchants' Club of Chicago, 1901.

Simon, Brian. *Studies in the History of Education.* London: Lawrence and Wishart, 1960.

Simpson, Mabel P. (Executive Secretary), "Program and Accomplishments for 1935: Annual Report of the Citizen Citizens School Committee. *Chicago's Schools* 2 (January 1936):3–4.

Smedstad, Grace. Interview conducted by Isobel Grossner, Chicago, December 8, 1970. Transcript in Roosevelt University Oral History Project, Roosevelt University Library, Chicago.

Smith, Joan K. *Ella Flagg Young: Portrait of a Leader*. Ames, Iowa: Educational Studies Press and the Iowa State University Research Foundation, 1979.

Snedden, David. "Vocational Education." *New Republic* 2 (May 15, 1915):40–42.

"S.O.S. Plan and Platform for Ward Organization." *Chicago's Schools* 1 (August 1934):3.

"Spasmodic Diary of a Chicago School-Teacher." *Atlantic Monthly* 152 (November 1933):513–526.

"Speaking of Laps." *American Teacher* 17 (February 1933):19.

Spring, Joel H. *Education and the Rise of the Corporate State*. Boston: Beacon Press, 1972.

———. *The Sorting Machine: National Educational Policy Since 1945*. New York: David McKay, 1976.

Staley, Eugene. *History of the Illinois State Federation of Labor*. Chicago: University of Chicago Press, 1930.

Stillman, Charles B. "Chicago, a Key Situation." *American Teacher* 17 (October 1932):19–21.

———. "Financial Fascism." *American Teacher* 17 (April 1933):10–11.

Storrow, James J. "Remarks of Mr. James J. Storrow, of Boston, Mass., before the Merchants' Club of Chicago, Saturday, December 8th, at the Auditorium." In Merchants' Club, *Public Schools and Their Administration*, pp. 25–38. Chicago: Merchants' Club of Chicago, 1906.

Strayer, George D., and Bachman, Frank P. *The Gary Public Schools: Organization and Administration*. New York: General Education Board, 1918.

Strayer, George D.; Engelhardt, Fred; Norton, John K.; Dix, Lester; and Hegel, Newton H. *Report of the Survey of the Schools of Chicago, Illinois*. Vol. 1. New York: Teachers College Press, 1932.

Stuart, William H. *The Twenty Incredible Years*. Chicago: M. A. Donohue, 1935.

Sutherland, Douglas. *Fifty Years on the Civic Front*. Chicago: Civic Federation of Chicago, 1943.

"Teachers and Labor Unions." *Chicago Teachers' Federation Bulletin* 2 (January 30, 1903):4.

Thompson, Edward P. *The Making of the English Working Class*. New York: Vintage Press, 1963.

"Three Majors—or Four?" *Chicago's Schools* 5 (October 1938):3.

"Tribute to Mrs. Young." *Chicago Schools Journal* 4 (December 1921): 121.

Tyack, David B. *The One Best System: A History of American Urban Education*. Cambridge: Harvard University Press, 1974.

U.S. Department of Commerce. Bureau of the Census. *1970 Census of the Population.* Vol. 1, part 15 (Illinois):15–20. Washington, D.C.: U.S. Government Printing Office, 1973.

U.S. Department of the Interior. Census Office. *Report on the Population of the United States at the Eleventh Census: 1890.* Washington, D.C.: U.S. Government Printing Office, 1895.

Violas, Paul C. "Jane Addams and the New Liberalism." In *Roots of Crisis: American Education in the Twentieth Century,* Clarence J. Karier, Paul C. Violas, and Joel H. Spring, pp. 66–83. Chicago: Rand-McNally, 1973.

Walker, John. "President's Report; Cooley Measure." *Thirty-Third Annual Proceedings of the Illinois State Federation of Labor* (1915): 72–73.

Walker, Louise D. "The Chicago Association of Commerce, Its History and Policies." Ph.D. dissertation, University of Chicago, 1941.

Wattenberg, William W. *On the Educational Front: The Reactions of Teachers' Associations in New York and Chicago.* New York: Columbia University Press, 1936.

Weinstein, James. *The Decline of Socialism in America, 1912–1925.* New York: Vintage Press, 1967.

————. *The Corporate Ideal in the Liberal State, 1900–1918.* Boston: Beacon Press, 1968.

Wendt, Lloyd, and Kogan, Herman. *Big Bill of Chicago.* Indianapolis: Bobbs-Merrill, 1953.

Wexler, Philip. *The Sociology of Education: Beyond Equality.* Indianapolis: Bobbs-Merrill, 1976.

"Who Are Your Friends? Two Programs—Choose." *American Teacher* 17 (April 1933):16.

Wilson, James Q. *The Amateur Democrat: Club Politics in Three Cities.* Chicago: University of Chicago Press, 1962.

"Worth While Opinions on Teachers in Labor Unions; Jane Addams on Teachers Affiliating with Federation of Labor, November 8, 1902." *Margaret A. Haley's Bulletin,* October 21, 1915, p. 10.

Young, Ella Flagg. *Isolation in the School.* Contributions to Education, no. 1. Chicago: University of Chicago Press, 1900.

————. "The Educational Progress of Two Years." *Addresses and Proceedings of the National Education Association* 45 (1907):383–405.

————. "A Reply [to Jacob Loeb]." *Addresses and Proceedings of the National Education Association* 54 (1916):356–359.

INDEX